Cyberspace Solarium Comm
Report
March 2020

Since 1960, pockets of scientists, military officers, academics, technology innovators, and government officials have all wrestled with a dilemma: as connectivity expands, it creates both increasing opportunities and greater vulnerabilities. Every new device connected, and line of code added, presents adversaries with new attack surfaces they can use to undermine American security and prosperity. ese devices and applications, as well as the communications infrastructure on which they rely, are overwhelmingly controlled by the private sector. To defend cyberspace thus requires significant coordination across the public and private sectors.

This report explores the findings of the Cyberspace Solarium Commission.

It is published as a convenience to those who may wish to have a quality professionally printed copy of the manual.

Should you have suggestions or feedback on ways to improve this book

Edited 2021 Ocotillo Press
ISBN 978-1-954285-79-8

Ocotillo Press
Houston, TX 77017
Books@OcotilloPress.com

Disclaimer: The user of this book is responsible for following safe and lawful practices at all times. The publisher assumes no responsibility for the use of the content of this book. The publisher has made an effort to ensure that the text is complete and properly typeset, however omissions, errors, and other issues may exist that the publisher is unaware of.

A WARNING FROM TOMORROW

By Peter Singer and August Cole

You spend your whole career on Capitol Hill hoping for an office with a window.

Then when you finally get it, all you want to do is look away.

They set up our emergency offsite for essential Senate staff in vacant offices once belonging to one of the contractors that lobbied us before they went belly-up last year. The offices are in a high-rise in Rosslyn, with a literal million-dollar view; looking across the Potomac River, you can see past the National Mall and the monuments all the way into downtown DC.

And it just breaks your heart.

The rainbow of colors in the window paints how everything went so wrong, so fast. The water in the Potomac still has that red tint from when the treatment plants upstream were hacked, their automated systems tricked into flushing out the wrong mix of chemicals. By comparison, the water in the Lincoln Memorial Reflecting Pool has a purple glint to it. They've pumped out the floodwaters that covered Washington's low-lying areas after the region's reservoirs were hit in a cascade of sensor hacks. But the surge left behind an oily sludge that will linger for who knows how long. That's what you get from deciding in the 18th century to put your capital city in low-lying swampland and then in the 21st century wiring up all its infrastructure to an insecure network. All around the Mall you can see the black smudges of the delivery drones and air taxis that were remotely hijacked to crash into crowds of innocents like fiery meteors. And in the open spaces and parks beyond, tiny dots of bright colors smear together like some kind of tragic pointillist painting. These are the camping tents and makeshift shelters of the refugees who fled the toxic railroad accident caused by the control system failure in Baltimore. FEMA says it's safe to go back, now that the chemical cloud has dissipated. But with all the churn and disinfo on social media, no one knows who or what to trust. Last night, the orange of their campfires was like a vigil of the obstinate, waiting for everything to just return to the way it was.

But it won't.

A knock on the door shakes me out of it. It's the legislative director, checking back in. She's anxious because the boss promised that we'd get a draft of the bill out tonight to all the other committees that touch on cybersecurity. No cars are online and nobody wants to risk the Metro after what happened on the Blue Line, though, so it'll mean hours of walking from office to office. At least the irony of backpacking around paper printouts of new cybersecurity laws will be lost on no one.

I tell her that I'll get it done and turn back to wordsmithing the preamble. I mostly mined the language from old legislation that someone just like me wrote after the 9/11 attacks. I know some online troll or talking head on the news will end up calling it lazy, but it's the closest anyone can think of as a parallel. Of course, with the servers down, our poor intern had to run down a paper copy from the Library of Congress.

Whereas, for as long as the United States has been the nation that invented and then became dependent on the Internet, it has faced online threats; and

Whereas, as these threats grew in scale and frequency, we grew too accustomed to digital interference in our society, economy, and even elections; and

Whereas, AI and automation changed these networks from use not just for communications but to connect and operate the "things" that run our physical world; and

Whereas, a new type of vulnerability thus emerged, where software could be not just a means of theft, but a weapon of disruption and even physical destruction; and

Whereas, our government and industry failed to keep pace with this change of technology and threat, being ill-organized and ill-prepared; and

Whereas, these vulnerabilities have just been exploited in extraordinary acts of treacherous violence that caused massive loss of life and effectively held the nation hostage; and

Whereas, such acts continue to pose a threat to the national security and very way of life of the United States;

Now, therefore, be it Resolved by the Senate and House of Representatives of the United States of America in Congress assembled, that the government of the United States must...[1]

"Must" what?

What can we really do? No matter what legislation we pass now, after everything that's happened, we're too late.

CONTENTS

CHAIRMEN'S LETTER

Our country is at risk, not only from a catastrophic cyberattack but from millions of daily intrusions disrupting everything from financial transactions to the inner workings of our electoral system. Capturing the complexity of this challenge is hard. Even the man credited with inventing the term "cyberspace," the science fiction author William Gibson, would later criticize it as an "evocative and essentially meaningless" buzzword.[2]

In studying this issue, it is easy to descend into a morass of classification, acronyms, jargon, and obscure government organization charts. To avoid that, we tried something different: an unclassified report that we hope will be found readable by the very people who are affected by cyber insecurity—*everyone*. This report is also aimed squarely at **action**; it has numerous recommendations addressing organizational, policy, and technical issues, and we included an appendix with draft bills that Congress can rapidly act upon to put these ideas into practice and make America more secure.

The reality is that we are dangerously insecure in cyber. Your entire life—your paycheck, your health care, your electricity—increasingly relies on networks of digital devices that store, process, and analyze data. These networks are vulnerable, if not already compromised. Our country has lost hundreds of billions of dollars to nation-state-sponsored intellectual property theft using cyber espionage. A major cyberattack on the nation's critical infrastructure and economic system would create chaos and lasting damage exceeding that wreaked by fires in California, floods in the Midwest, and hurricanes in the Southeast.

To prevent this from happening, our report outlines a new cyber strategy and provides more than 75 recommendations for action across the public and private sectors. Here are some big ideas to get the conversation started.

First, **deterrence is possible in cyberspace**. Today most cyber actors feel undeterred, if not emboldened, to target our personal data and public infrastructure. In other words, through our inability or unwillingness to identify and punish our cyber adversaries, we are signaling that interfering in American elections or stealing billions in U.S. intellectual property is acceptable. The federal government and the private sector must defend themselves and strike back with **speed and agility**. This is difficult because the government is not optimized to be quick or agile, but we simply must be faster than our adversaries in order to prevent them from destroying our networks and, by extension, our way of life. Our strategy of *layered cyber deterrence* is designed with this goal in mind. It combines enhanced resilience with enhanced attribution capabilities and a clearer signaling strategy with collective action by our partners and allies. It is a simple framework laying out how we evolve into a hard target, a good ally, and a bad enemy.

Second, **deterrence relies on a resilient economy**. During the Cold War, our best minds were tasked with developing Continuity of Government plans to ensure that the government could survive and the nation recover after a nuclear strike. We need similar planning today to ensure that we can reconstitute in the aftermath of a national-level cyberattack. We also need to ensure that our economy continues to run. We recommend that the government institute a Continuity of the Economy plan to ensure that we can rapidly restore critical functions across corporations and industry sectors, and get the economy back up and running after a catastrophic cyberattack. Such a plan is a fundamental pillar of deterrence—a way to tell our adversaries that we, as a society, will survive to defeat them with **speed and agility** if they launch a major cyberattack against us.

Third, **deterrence requires government reform.** We need to elevate and empower existing cyber agencies, particularly the Cybersecurity and Infrastructure Security Agency (CISA), and create new focal points for coordinating cybersecurity in the executive branch and Congress. To that end, we recommend the creation of a National Cyber Director with oversight from new congressional Cybersecurity Committees, but our goal is not to create more bureaucracy with new and duplicative roles and organizations. Rather, we propose giving existing organizations the tools they need to act with **speed and agility** to defend our networks and impose costs on our adversaries. The key is CISA, which we have tried to empower as the lead agency for federal cybersecurity and the private sector's preferred partner. We want working at CISA to become so appealing to young professionals interested in national service that it competes with the NSA, the FBI, Google, and Facebook for top-level talent (and wins).

Fourth, **deterrence will require private-sector entities to step up and strengthen their security posture.** Most of our critical infrastructure is owned by the private sector. That is why we make certain recommendations, such as establishing a cloud security certification or modernizing corporate accountability reporting requirements. We do not want to saddle the private sector with onerous and counterproductive regulations, nor do we want to force companies to hand over their data to the federal government. We are not the Chinese Communist Party, and indeed our best path to beating our adversaries is to stay free and innovative. But we need C-suite executives to take cyber seriously since they are on the front lines. With support from the federal government, private-sector entities must be able to act with **speed and agility** to stop cyberattackers from breaking out in their networks and the larger array of networks on which the nation relies.

Fifth, **election security must become a priority.** The American people still do not have the assurance that our election systems are secure from foreign manipulation. If we don't get election security right, deterrence will fail and future generations will look back with longing and regret on the once powerful American Republic and wonder how we screwed the whole thing up. We believe we need to continue appropriations to fund election infrastructure modernization at the state and local levels. At the same time, states and localities need to pay their fair share to secure elections, and they can draw on useful resources—such as nonprofits that can act with greater **speed and agility** across all 50 states—to secure elections from the bottom up rather than waiting for top-down direction and funding. We also need to ensure that regardless of the method of casting a vote, paper or electronic, a paper audit trail exists (and yes, we recognize the irony of a cyber commission recommending a paper trail).

We didn't solve everything in this report. We didn't even agree on everything. There are areas, such as balancing maximum encryption versus mandatory lawful access to devices, where the best we could do was provide a common statement of principles. Yet every single Commissioner was willing to make compromises in the course of our work because we were all united by the recognition that the status quo is not getting the job done. The status quo is inviting attacks on America every second of every day. The status quo is a slow surrender of American power and responsibility. We all want that to stop. So please do us, and your fellow Americans, a favor. Read this report and then demand that your government and the private sector act with **speed and agility** to secure our cyber future.

Senator Angus King (I-Maine)
Co-Chairman
Cyberspace Solarium Commission

Representative Mike Gallagher (R-Wisconsin)
Co-Chairman
Cyberspace Solarium Commission

EXECUTIVE SUMMARY

AN URGENT CALL TO ACTION

For over 20 years, nation-states and non-state actors have used cyberspace to subvert American power, American security, and the American way of life. Despite numerous criminal indictments, economic sanctions, and the development of robust cyber and non-cyber military capabilities, the attacks against the United States have continued. The perpetrators saw that their onslaught damaged the United States without triggering a significant retaliation. Chinese cyber operators stole hundreds of billions of dollars in intellectual property to accelerate China's military and economic rise and undermine U.S. military dominance.[3] Russian operators and their proxies damaged public trust in the integrity of American elections and democratic institutions.[4] China, Russia, Iran, and North Korea all probed U.S. critical infrastructure with impunity. Criminals leveraged globally connected networks to steal assets from individuals, companies, and governments. Extremist groups used these networks to raise funds and recruit followers, increasing transnational threats and insecurity. American restraint was met with unchecked predation.[5]

The digital connectivity that has brought economic growth, technological dominance, and an improved quality of life to nearly every American has also created a strategic dilemma. The more digital connections people make and data they exchange, the more opportunities adversaries have to destroy private lives, disrupt critical infrastructure, and damage our economic and democratic institutions. The United States now operates in a cyber landscape that requires a level of data security, resilience, and trustworthiness that neither the U.S. government nor the private sector alone is currently equipped to provide. Moreover, shortfalls in agility, technical expertise, and unity of effort, both within the U.S. government and between the public and private sectors, are growing.

The 2019 National Defense Authorization Act chartered the U.S. Cyberspace Solarium Commission to address this challenge. The President and Congress tasked the Commission to answer two fundamental questions: What strategic approach will defend the United States against cyberattacks of significant consequences? And what policies and legislation are required to implement that strategy?

THE STRATEGY

After conducting an extensive study including over 300 interviews, a competitive strategy event modeled after the original Project Solarium in the Eisenhower administration, and stress tests by external red teams, the Commission advocates a new strategic approach to cybersecurity: **layered cyber deterrence**. The desired end state of layered cyber deterrence is a reduced probability and impact of cyberattacks of significant consequence. The strategy outlines three ways to achieve this end state:

1. *Shape behavior.* The United States must work with allies and partners to promote responsible behavior in cyberspace.
2. *Deny benefits.* The United States must deny benefits to adversaries who have long exploited cyberspace to their advantage, to American disadvantage, and at little cost to themselves. This new approach requires securing critical networks in collaboration with the private sector to promote national resilience and increase the security of the cyber ecosystem.
3. *Impose costs.* The United States must maintain the capability, capacity, and credibility needed to retaliate against actors who target America in and through cyberspace.

Each of the three ways described above involves a deterrent layer that increases American public- and private-sector security by altering how adversaries perceive the costs and benefits of using cyberspace to attack American interests. These three deterrent layers are supported by six policy pillars that organize more than 75 recommendations. These pillars represent the means to implement layered cyber deterrence.

While deterrence is an enduring American strategy, there are two factors that make layered cyber deterrence bold and distinct. First, the approach prioritizes deterrence by denial, specifically by increasing the defense and security of cyberspace through resilience and public- and private-sector collaboration. Reducing the vulnerabilities adversaries can target denies them opportunities to attack American interests through cyberspace. Second, the strategy incorporates the concept of "defend forward" to reduce the frequency and severity of attacks in cyberspace that do not rise to a level that would warrant the full spectrum of retaliatory responses, including military responses. Though the concept originated in the Department of Defense, the Commission integrates defend forward into a national strategy for securing cyberspace using all the instruments of power. Defend forward posits that to disrupt and defeat ongoing adversary campaigns, the United States must proactively observe, pursue, and counter adversaries' operations and impose costs short of armed conflict. This posture signals to adversaries that the U.S. government will respond to cyberattacks, even those below the level of armed conflict that do not cause physical destruction or death, with all the tools at its disposal and consistent with international law.

THE IMPLEMENTATION

Foundation: Government Reform

The three layers of cyber deterrence rest on a common foundation: the need to reform how the U.S. government is organized to secure cyberspace and respond to attacks. The U.S. government is currently not designed to act with the speed and agility necessary to defend the country in cyberspace. We must get faster and smarter, improving the government's ability to organize concurrent, continuous, and collaborative efforts to build resilience, respond to cyber threats, and preserve military options that signal a capability and willingness to impose costs on adversaries. Reformed government oversight and organization that is properly resourced and staffed, in alignment with a strategy of layered cyber deterrence, will enable the United States to reduce the probability, magnitude, and effects of significant attacks on its networks.

Pillar: *Reform the U.S. Government's Structure and Organization for Cyberspace.* While cyberspace has transformed the American economy and society, the government has not kept up. Existing government structures and jurisdictional boundaries fracture cyber policymaking processes, limit opportunities for government action, and impede cyber operations. Rapid, comprehensive improvements at all levels of government are necessary to change these dynamics and ensure that the U.S. government can protect the American people, their way of life, and America's status as a global leader. Major recommendations in this pillar are:

- The executive branch should **issue an updated National Cyber Strategy (1.1)** that reflects the strategic approach of layered cyber deterrence and emphasizes resilience, public-private collaboration, and defend forward as key elements.

- Congress should **establish House Permanent Select and Senate Select Committees on Cybersecurity (1.2)** to provide integrated oversight of the cybersecurity efforts dispersed across the federal government.

- Congress should **establish a Senate-confirmed National Cyber Director (NCD) (1.3)**, supported by an Office of the NCD, within the Executive Office of the President. The NCD will be the President's principal advisor for cybersecurity-related issues, as well as lead national-level coordination of cybersecurity strategy and policy, both within government and with the private sector.

- Congress should **strengthen the Cybersecurity and Infrastructure Security Agency (CISA) (1.4)** in its mission to ensure the national resilience of critical infrastructure, promote a more secure cyber ecosystem, and serve as the central coordinating element to support and integrate federal, state and local, and private-sector cybersecurity efforts. Congress must invest significant resources in CISA and provide it with clear authorities to realize its full potential.

- Congress and the executive branch should pass legislation and **implement policies designed to better recruit, develop, and retain cyber talent (1.5)** while acting to deepen the pool of candidates for cyber work in the federal government.

Layer 1: Shape Behavior

In the first layer, the strategy calls for shaping responsible behavior and encouraging restraint in cyberspace by strengthening norms and non-military instruments. Effective norms will not emerge without American leadership. For this reason, the United States needs to build a coalition of partners and allies to secure its shared interests and values in cyberspace.

Pillar: *Strengthen Norms and Non-military Tools.* A system of norms, built through international engagement and cooperation, promotes responsible behavior and, over time, dissuades adversaries from using cyber operations to undermine any nation's interests. The United States and others have agreed to norms of responsible behavior for cyberspace, but they go largely unenforced today. The United States can strengthen the current system of cyber norms by using non-military tools, including law enforcement actions, sanctions, diplomacy, and information sharing, to more effectively persuade states to conform to these norms and punish those who violate them. Such punishment requires developing the ability to quickly and accurately attribute cyberattacks. Building a coalition of like-minded allies and partners willing to collectively use these instruments to support a rules-based international order in cyberspace will better hold malign actors accountable. The major recommendations in this pillar are:

- Congress should **create an Assistant Secretary of State (2.1)** in the Department of State, with a new Bureau of Cyberspace Security and Emerging Technologies, who will lead the U.S. government effort to develop and reinforce international norms in cyberspace. This will help promote international norms that support and reflect U.S. interests and values while creating benefits for responsible state behavior through engagement with allies and partners.

- The executive branch should **engage actively and effectively in forums setting international information and communications technology standards (2.1.2).** Specifically, the National Institute of Standards and Technology should facilitate robust and integrated participation by the federal government, academia, professional societies, and industry.

- Congress should take steps to **improve international tools for law enforcement activities in cyberspace (2.1.4)**, including streamlining the Mutual Legal Assistance Treaty and Mutual Legal Assistance Agreement process and increasing the number of FBI Cyber Assistant Legal Attachés.

Layer 2: Deny Benefits

In the second layer, the strategy calls for denying benefits to adversaries by promoting national resilience, reshaping the cyber ecosystem, and advancing the government's relationship with the private sector to establish an enhanced level of common situational awareness and joint collaboration. The United States needs a whole-of-nation approach to secure its interests and institutions in cyberspace.

Pillar: *Promote National Resilience.* Resilience—the capacity to withstand and quickly recover from attacks that could cause harm or coerce, deter, restrain, or otherwise shape U.S. behavior—is key to denying adversaries the benefits of their operations and reducing confidence in their ability to achieve their strategic ends. National resilience efforts rely on the ability of the United States, in both the public and private sectors, to accurately identify, assess, and mitigate risk across all elements of critical infrastructure. The nation must be sufficiently prepared to respond to and recover from an attack, sustain critical functions even under degraded conditions, and, in some cases, restart critical functionality after disruption. Major recommendations in this pillar are:

- Congress should **codify responsibilities and ensure sufficient resources (3.1)** for the Cybersecurity and Infrastructure Security Agency and sector-specific agencies **in the identification, assessment, and management of national and sector-specific risk**.

- Congress should direct the U.S. government to **develop and maintain Continuity of the Economy planning (3.2)** in consultation with the private sector to ensure continuous operation of critical functions of the economy in the event of a significant cyber disruption.

- Congress should **codify a Cyber State of Distress** tied to a **Cyber Response and Recovery Fund (3.3)** to ensure sufficient resources and capacity to respond rapidly to significant cyber incidents.

- Congress should **improve the structure and sustain the funding of the Election Assistance Commission (3.4)**, enabling it to increase its operational capacity to support states and localities in defense of the digital election infrastructure that underpins federal elections and to ensure the widest use of voter-verifiable, auditable, and paper-based voting systems.

- The U.S. government should **promote digital literacy, civics education, and public awareness (3.5)** to build societal resilience to foreign, malign cyber-enabled information operations.

Pillar: *Reshape the Cyber Ecosystem toward Greater Security.* Raising the baseline level of security across the cyber ecosystem—the people, processes, data, and technology that constitute and depend on cyberspace—will constrain and limit adversaries' activities. Over time, this will reduce the frequency, scope, and scale of their cyber operations. Because the vast majority of this ecosystem is owned and operated by the private sector, scaling up security means partnering with the private sector and adjusting incentives to produce positive outcomes. In some cases, that requires aligning market forces. In other cases, where those forces either are not present or do not adequately address risk, the U.S. government must explore legislation, regulation, executive action, and public- as well as private-sector investments. Major recommendations in this pillar are:

- Congress should **establish and fund a National Cybersecurity Certification and Labeling Authority (4.1)** empowered to **establish and manage a program on security certifications and labeling** of information and communications technology products.

- Congress should **pass a law establishing that final goods assemblers of software, hardware, and firmware are liable for damages from incidents that exploit known and unpatched vulnerabilities (4.2)** for as long as they support a product or service.

- Congress should **establish a Bureau of Cyber Statistics (4.3)** charged with **collecting and providing statistical data on cybersecurity** and the cyber ecosystem to inform policymaking and government programs.

- Congress should resource and direct the Department of Homeland Security to **fund a federally funded research and development center (4.4)** to work with state-level regulators to **develop certifications for cybersecurity insurance products**.

- The National Cybersecurity Certification and Labeling Authority should **develop a cloud security certification (4.5)**, in consultation with the National Institute of Standards and Technology, the Office of Management and Budget, and the Department of Homeland Security.

- Congress should direct the U.S. government to **develop and implement an industrial base strategy for information and communications technology to ensure trusted supply chains (4.6)** and the availability of critical information and communications technologies.

- Congress should **pass a national data security and privacy protection law (4.7)** establishing and standardizing requirements for the collection, retention, and sharing of user data.

Pillar: *Operationalize Cybersecurity Collaboration with the Private Sector.* Unlike in other physical domains, in cyberspace the government is often not the primary actor. Instead, it must support and enable the private sector. The government must build and communicate a better understanding of threats, with the specific aim of informing private-sector security operations, directing government operational efforts to counter malicious cyber activities, and ensuring better common situational awareness for collaborative action with the private sector. Further, while recognizing that private-sector entities have primary responsibility for the defense and security of their networks, the U.S. government must bring to bear its unique authorities, resources, and intelligence capabilities to support these actors in their defensive efforts. Major recommendations in this pillar are:

- Congress should **codify the concept of "systemically important critical infrastructure" (5.1)**, whereby entities responsible for systems and assets that underpin national critical functions are ensured the full support of the U.S. government and shoulder additional security requirements befitting their unique status and importance.

- Congress should **establish and fund a Joint Collaborative Environment (5.2)**, a common and interoperable environment for **sharing and fusing threat information, insights, and other relevant data** across the federal government and between the public and private sectors.

- Congress should direct the executive branch to **strengthen a public-private, integrated cyber center in CISA (5.3)** to support its critical infrastructure security and resilience mission and to **conduct a one-year, comprehensive systems analysis review of federal cyber and cybersecurity centers**.

- The executive branch should establish a **Joint Cyber Planning Cell (5.4)** under CISA to coordinate cybersecurity planning and readiness across the federal government and between the public and private sectors.

Layer 3: Impose Costs

In the final layer, the strategy outlines how to impose costs to deter future malicious behavior and reduce ongoing adversary activities short of armed conflict through the employment of all instruments of power in the defense of cyberspace, including systemically important critical infrastructure. A key, but not the only, element of cost imposition is the military instrument of power. Therefore, the United States must maintain the capacity, resilience, and readiness to employ cyber and non-cyber capabilities across the spectrum of engagement from competition to crisis and conflict. The United States needs ready and resilient capabilities to thwart and respond to adversary action.

Pillar: *Preserve and Employ the Military Instrument of Power—and All Other Options to Deter Cyberattacks at Any Level.* Cyberspace is already an arena of strategic competition, where states project power, protect their interests, and punish their adversaries. Future contingencies and conflicts will almost certainly contain a cyber component. In this environment, the United States must defend forward to limit malicious adversary behavior below the level of armed attack, deter conflict, and, if necessary, prevail by employing the full spectrum of its capabilities, using all the instruments of national power. Examples of adversary actions below armed attack include cyber-enabled attacks on the U.S. election systems or cyber-enabled intellectual property theft. To achieve these ends, the U.S. government must demonstrate its ability to impose costs, while establishing a clear declaratory policy that signals to rival states the costs and risks associated with attacking the United States in cyberspace. Furthermore, conventional weapons and nuclear capabilities require cybersecurity and resilience to ensure that the United States preserves credible deterrence and the full range of military response options. The United States must be confident that its military capabilities will work as intended. Finally, across the spectrum of engagement from competition to crisis and conflict, the United States must ensure that it has sufficient cyber forces to accomplish strategic objectives in and through cyberspace. This demands sufficient capacity, capabilities, and streamlined decision-making processes to enable rapid and effective cyber response options to impose costs against adversaries. Major recommendations in this pillar include:

- Congress should direct the Department of Defense to **conduct a force structure assessment of the Cyber Mission Force (6.1)** to ensure that the United States has the appropriate force structure and capabilities in light of growing mission requirements and increasing expectations, in both scope and scale. This should include an assessment of the resource implications for the National Security Agency in its combat support agency role.

- Congress should direct the Department of Defense to **conduct a cybersecurity vulnerability assessment of all segments of the nuclear control systems and continually assess weapon systems' cyber vulnerabilities (6.2)**.

- Congress should require **Defense Industrial Base (DIB) participation in threat intelligence sharing programs (6.2.1) and threat hunting on DIB networks (6.2.2)**.

THE WAY FORWARD

The status quo in cyberspace is unacceptable. The current state of affairs invites aggression and establishes a dangerous pattern of actors attacking the United States without fear of reprisal. Adversaries are increasing their cyber capabilities while U.S. vulnerabilities continue to grow. There is much that the U.S. government can do to improve its defenses and reduce the risk of a significant attack, but it is clear that government action alone is not enough. Most of the critical infrastructure that drives the American economy, spurs technological innovation, and supports the U.S. military resides in the private sector. If the U.S. government cannot find a way to seamlessly collaborate with the private sector to build a resilient cyber ecosystem, the nation will never be secure. And, eventually, a massive cyberattack could lead to large-scale physical destruction, sparking a response of haphazard government overreach that stifles innovation in the digital economy and further erodes American strength.

To avoid these outcomes, the U.S. government must move to adopt the new strategy detailed in this report—layered cyber deterrence—and the more than 75 recommendations designed to make this approach a reality. The executive branch and Congress should give these recommendations and the associated legislative proposals close consideration. Congress should also consider ways to monitor, assess, and report on the implementation of this report's recommendations over the next two years.

Layered Cyber Deterrence

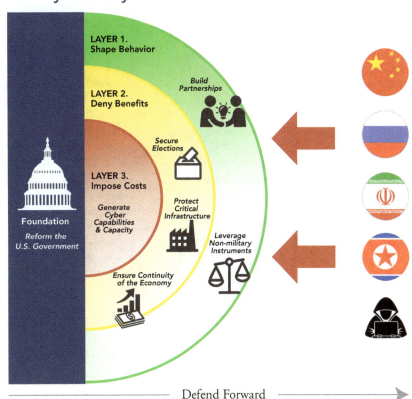

Desired End State

Reduce the frequency and severity of cyber attacks of significant consequence.

Limit the ability of great powers, rogue states, extremists, and criminals to undermine American power and influence.

LAYER 1. Shape Behavior
LAYER 2. Deny Benefits
LAYER 3. Impose Costs

Build Partnerships
Secure Elections
Generate Cyber Capabilities & Capacity
Protect Critical Infrastructure
Leverage Non-military Instruments
Ensure Continuity of the Economy

Foundation
Reform the U.S. Government

Defend Forward
concurrent, continuous, collaborative

THE CHALLENGE

THE THREAT

The NotPetya attack illustrates the changing character of cyber threats. The chaos started in battle-torn Ukraine.[6] In June 2017 Russian cyber operators launched destructive malware adapted from a series of widespread vulnerabilities common to unpatched Windows operating systems. Because it exploited operating system vulnerabilities in wide use across innumerable private- and public-sector applications, the NotPetya attack quickly spread from targeted Ukrainian banks, payment systems, and federal agencies to power plants, hospitals, and other life-critical systems worldwide. The attack even affected the Windows-based radiation-monitoring systems in the Chernobyl nuclear power plant.[7] Global companies from Maersk—a shipping and logistics firm—and FedEx's European subsidiary to pharmaceutical companies found their systems offline, with losses estimated as high as $10 billion. In an ironic twist of fate, the reckless nature of the malware allowed the infection to spread to Russia, where it hit Rosneft, the leading Kremlin-linked oil and gas producer.[8] NotPetya affected tens of thousands of individuals, organizations, and businesses around the world. Yet most Americans were completely unaware of the damage.

NotPetya, while far from the first cyberattack, exemplifies the potential chaos that major cyberattacks can cause. Like an infection in the bloodstream, the malware spread along global supply chains.

From China, Russia, Iran, and North Korea to extremist groups and criminals, a broad array of threat actors are exploiting global connectivity to achieve their objectives. These objectives range from undermining American economic and military power to suppressing political rivals to stealing money and seeking illicit gain. Even if the United States is not the intended target, the interconnected nature of cyberspace may still render the nation a victim. Without

---

Major U.S. Public-Sector Cyber Threats

- Attacks on election processes and other democratic institutions designed to damage American legitimacy and weaken the nation.
- Espionage efforts intended to undermine both U.S. military capability and the Defense Industrial Base.
- Targeting of civilian agencies for intelligence collection and to obtain other advantages over the United States.
- Loss of leadership in research and development of key technologies.

Absent significant reform, adversaries will continue to target U.S. elections and erode U.S. military advantages through cyber operations designed to steal sensitive data, while U.S. technical leadership in research and development will continue to decline.

---

a new strategy to secure cyberspace, a more connected world will be a more vulnerable world.

Cyber operations offer adversaries—including non-state actors—instruments of coercion, sabotage, espionage, and extortion optimized for the 21st century.[9] These new tools take advantage of the terrain, exploiting the inherent vulnerability of the digital networks on which the United States and other countries rely.[10] As more people and devices connect to each other, the power and reach of cyber operations grow. Great powers can pressure rivals without committing military forces and declaring their intent—for example, by holding their critical infrastructure at risk with threats of blackouts and disruption.[11] Regional powers target critical commercial networks, from the financial system to the global energy supply chain, to raise the costs and risks associated with U.S. military operations. Extremist groups rely on social networks for recruitment

> ### *Major U.S. Private-Sector Cyber Threats*
> - Cybercrime and ransomware that exploit people, processes, and systems for individual financial gain or to fund criminal enterprises.
> - Intellectual property (IP) theft that hinders long-term growth and prosperity and jeopardizes U.S. leadership in key technologies.
> - Holding private-sector critical infrastructure at risk to influence the decision making of American leaders at times of conflict or heightened tension.
>
> *Absent significant reform, adversaries will continue stealing hundreds of billions of dollars from businesses and individuals, conducting widespread theft of U.S. technologies, and accessing the electrical grid, water treatment facilities, financial institutions, and other critical infrastructure.*

and radicalization. Criminals plunder individuals, companies, and even states by exploiting network vulnerabilities. Unless there is a significant change in how the United States and other free nations approach cybersecurity, these trends will only get worse and jeopardize the connectivity on which the world depends.

Our modern way of life depends on the integrity, confidentiality, and availability of data. From medical records, financial information, and our most personal communications to modern military operations, the individual and the state rely on data. But as we increase our reliance on data, our adversaries have developed new tools that hold data and essential information systems at risk. The entire system through which data flows into products, devices, and services is vulnerable.

This threat is compounded by new technologies that enable more sophisticated cyberattacks at greater scale for lower cost, and by a host of capable adversaries who have demonstrated a willingness and ability to adapt to U.S. prevention and response measures. These adversaries have moved beyond simple denial-of-service and website defacement campaigns to conducting intelligence collection, ransomware attacks, and destructive operations, as well as disruptive attacks on critical infrastructure. Increasingly these attacks revolve around compromising the technological systems used to collect, process, and analyze data.

State Cyber Threats

Every state with a modern military possesses cyber capability. Great powers like China and Russia use cyber operations to enable their warfighting capabilities, advance their interests short of armed conflict, and undermine American economic strength, political will, and military might.[12]

China uses cyberspace to accelerate its economic rise, undermine U.S. comparative strength, and suppress political opponents at home and abroad.[13] Chinese advanced persistent threat (APT) groups steal intellectual property and sensitive national security information. Beijing wages cyber-enabled economic warfare to fuel its rise while simultaneously undercutting U.S. economic and military superiority. Chinese cyber campaigns have enabled the theft of trillions of dollars in intellectual property.[14] At the same time, Chinese APTs' aggressive cyber-enabled intelligence collection operations provide Chinese officials with improved intelligence information to use against the United States and its allies. Chinese operators constantly scan U.S. government and private-sector networks to identify vulnerabilities they can later exploit in a crisis. Targeting America's weapons and Defense Industrial Base enables Beijing to undermine opponents from within: for example, by threatening the U.S. Defense Industrial Base or driving a wedge between America and its allies.[15] Taken to the extreme, China has the ability to launch cyberattacks in the United States that could cause localized, temporary disruptive effects on critical infrastructure—such as disruption of a natural gas pipeline—for days to weeks.[16]

Moreover, the Chinese Communist Party routinely harasses foreign and domestic dissidents in cyberspace while state-linked firms build a global mass-surveillance capability connecting information and communications equipment, surveillance cameras, facial recognition software, and massive data sets of private citizens. China is exporting these intrusive practices and technologies abroad, fueling a trend toward digital authoritarianism that threatens democracy at a global scale.[17] Chinese national companies like Huawei are part of an integrated strategy to use predatory pricing to dominate and eventually monopolize key information and communications technology supply chains. The goal is to drive non-Chinese alternatives out of business, leaving the Chinese Communist Party and its business allies with a stranglehold on the global supply chain. As China exports this equipment, it becomes the central hub of a new network of authoritarian states that use mass surveillance and technologies of control, such as social credit, to suppress fundamental human rights. Unchecked, Chinese economic warfare, espionage, and repression of civil liberties are likely to continue.

Without a new whole-of-nation strategy and significant changes to how the United States defends its networks in cyberspace, Chinese operations will continue to threaten long-term American economic prosperity and national security. Revelations of high-profile security failures of information will undermine confidence in the U.S. government's ability to protect its citizens and businesses. Along with the loss in national power, trust in American institutions will wither. In the minds of regional allies, perceptions of unchallenged Chinese operations will reduce the credibility of American security guarantees. Exfiltration of private-sector intellectual property could compel investors to question the viability of the U.S. economy as a hub of technological innovation. Breaches could also yield intelligence coups that threaten the United States' clandestine personnel and advance Beijing's diplomatic and economic goals. Stolen U.S. military technology will enable the production of capable facsimiles and support the design of People's Liberation Army weapon systems that exploit newly identified vulnerabilities in U.S. counterparts. Compromised supply chains could undermine American military operations in future wars.[18] China is seeking to monopolize how people around the world interact, pay

> ### Major Cyber Operations Publicly Attributed to China: 2006–2019
>
> - 2006–18: APT10 conducts a systematic cyber espionage campaign stealing intellectual property and compromising computer systems containing personally identifiable information on over 100,000 U.S. Navy personnel.[19]
> - 2008: Operators exfiltrate terabytes of data and schematics from the F-35 and F-22 stealth fighter jet programs.[20]
> - 2012: China compromises computers in a new African Union headquarters it helped build in Ethiopia with malware that exports massive amounts of data nightly to servers in Shanghai.[21]
> - 2012: Chinese groups target oil and natural gas pipelines in the United States.[22]
> - 2013: *IP Commission Report* highlights Chinese efforts at intellectual property theft efforts linked to an estimated $300 billion in business losses a year.[23]
> - 2014: Cloud Hopper campaign attacks managed service providers to access their client networks, including those of leading international technology companies, and steal their clients' intellectual property.[24]
> - 2014–15: The Office of Personnel Management is breached, exposing sensitive information used for security background checks on 21 million federal employees.[25]
> - 2017: Chinese military hackers breach the networks of Equifax, an American credit reporting agency, stealing the personal information of over 145 million Americans.[26]
> - 2018: Hackers breach servers of Marriott International, extracting information on 500 million guests.[27]
> - 2019: Operators compromise iPhones in a domestic spying campaign targeting Uighurs, a Muslim minority in China.[28]

for goods, and relate to their governments. As Chinese-built networks and applications mediate interactions, Beijing gains unprecedented power to surveil and control the lives of individuals worldwide. Civil liberties and open markets will struggle to survive in this new era of cyber repression. China presents a persistent cyber espionage threat and a growing attack threat to our core military and critical infrastructure systems. China remains the most active strategic competitor responsible for cyber espionage against the U.S. government, corporations, and allies. It is improving its cyberattack capabilities and altering information online, shaping Chinese views and potentially the views of U.S. citizens.[29]

Russia, a revanchist power, turns to cyber operations to undermine U.S. and allied interests. A mix of spies and criminal networks often masks Moscow's role. Across multiple operations, from elections to public referendums, the Kremlin has combined cyber intrusions and propaganda to distort democratic processes, weaken trust in institutions, and sow chaos in liberal democratic societies. Leading into the 2016 and 2018 elections, Russian online trolls whipped into a digital frenzy the factions the *Federalist Papers* cautioned against more than 230 years ago. The resulting breakdown in political will and social cohesion limits the ability of Western nations to check Russia's advances in states that formerly belonged to the Soviet Union.[30]

During recent armed conflicts, Russia used cyber capabilities both to enhance military operations and to conduct information operations campaigns designed to isolate their opponents.[31] In peacetime competition, Russian operators signal the risk of escalation by probing critical infrastructure across NATO member states.[32] The openness, connectivity, and commitment to shared international norms of liberal democracies are a threat to Russia's interests.[33] By subverting these ideas, exploiting cracks in international alliance networks, and subtly encouraging domestic instability, the Kremlin hopes to achieve its strategic objectives without risking all-out war.

> ### *Major Cyber Operations Publicly Attributed to Russia: 2007–2019*
>
> - 2007: Using distributed denial-of-service attacks, Russian hackers target the websites of Estonian government entities, banks, and media properties in one of the first sophisticated and wide-scale cyberattacks in support of strategic objectives.[34]
> - 2008: During the Russo-Georgian War, a series of cyberattacks disable and deface the websites of Georgian government and private-sector entities.[35]
> - 2015: As war rages in eastern Ukraine, Russian hackers cripple three Ukrainian energy companies, disrupting power for millions of customers.[36]
> - 2016: During the 2016 U.S. presidential campaign, Russian operatives use cyber operations to collect on political parties and candidates and conduct influence operations using social media.[37]
> - 2017: NotPetya attack spills out of Ukraine, affecting businesses globally.[38]
> - 2017: Russia-linked groups target nuclear power plants in the United States, gaining access to business and administrative networks.[39]
> - 2017–18: Russia-linked groups target critical infrastructure ranging from electricity to health care systems, and compromise router traffic globally.[40]

Left unchecked, Russian cyber operations will continue to increase in sophistication and frequency. Moscow will target democratic institutions, military assets, and critical infrastructure in the United States and its liberal democratic allies, as well as the smaller neighbors Russia views as modern-day tributary states (its near abroad). Russian interference in U.S. elections in 2016 and 2018, as well as in elections in Europe, was part of a longer, larger campaign to undermine democracy and its institutions. It was also an indicator of future operations that will target voting systems and the broader information environment in new and dangerous ways.[41] A key priority of Russian cyber operations will be to degrade the strategic cohesion of Western alliance and security cooperation networks, especially NATO.[42] And if these structures decline, Russia's neighbors will be increasingly vulnerable to sophisticated cyber and influence operations, resulting in a network of central and eastern European states subservient to Moscow. Unencumbered by international norms and empowered by new technologies, the Kremlin will further refine its use of cyber operations to advance its strategic objectives at the expense of the United States and its allies and partners.

Regional powers increasingly exploit cyberspace to advance revisionist interests. These cyber-enabled rogue states are often more willing to accept risk and more brazen than China and Russia, launching large-scale cyberattacks against commercial firms and suppressing dissidents. Lacking conventional tools sufficient to achieve their political and economic objectives, these states exploit their newfound cyber capabilities to steal funds for illicit purposes, disrupt international commerce, and threaten their adversaries.

Iran uses cyber operations to undermine the U.S. deterrent posture and network of alliances in the Middle East. In place of a nuclear deterrent, Tehran relies on the threat of cyber intrusions, proxy groups, terrorists, and ballistic missiles to hold other states at risk.[43] Iranian cyber operations focus on the commercial networks of energy and finance entities of particular importance to the global economy. They leverage the inherent difficulties of coordinating cyber defenses between public and private partnerships and sovereign states. Unless it faces a more robust deterrent, Iran will continue to view cyber operations as a low-cost means of ensuring regime survival and achieving regional goals.

Like other autocratic states, Iran is becoming a digital authoritarian. Groups linked to the Iranian regime turn

> ### Major Cyber Operations Publicly Attributed to Iran: 2011–2019
>
> - 2011–13: Iran targets 46 U.S. financial institutions and companies and a dam in Rye, New York, with distributed denial-of-service attacks.[44]
> - 2012: Iran conducts destructive attacks against the Saudi Arabian state-owned oil firm, Saudi Aramco, with the Shamoon malware, which result in 30,000 computers being taken offline and rendered unusable.[45]
> - 2013: Through computer intrusions Iranian-based Mabna Institute actors commit wire fraud, unauthorized access of a computer, and aggravated identity theft, stealing more than 30 terabytes of academic data and intellectual property valued at $3.4 billion.[46]
> - 2014: Iranian hackers attack the Sands Casino, infecting multiple systems and wiping hard drives.[47]
> - 2017: Iran launches Shamoon 2, affecting 15 government agencies and organizations in Saudi Arabia.[48]
> - 2018: Shamoon 2 hits an Italian oil services company, taking hundreds of servers and computers offline.[49]
> - 2019: APT39, an Iranian-linked group, is implicated in a widespread cyber espionage campaign targeting the personal information of citizens in the United States and Middle East and striving to establish a foothold, escalate privileges, and conduct reconnaissance in support of future operations.[50]

to cyberspace to suppress dissidents and undermine democratic institutions around the world. These operations harass activists at home and abroad.[51] Like Russia, Iran even extends its cyber-enabled political warfare campaign to the free media and electoral institutions. Iranian groups have been caught using fake social media accounts to spread disinformation[52] and attempting to hack the 2020 U.S. presidential campaigns.[53]

North Korea views cyber operations as a tool of coercion and source of illicit financing via cyber criminal activities. North Korean front companies operating abroad provide opportunities for North Korea to expand the scope and reach of its operations, despite the limited connectivity at home.[54] From these safe havens, North Korean cyber operators probe the networks of the United States and its allies, seeking to steal military plans, technology, and weapon system information while identifying vulnerabilities in critical infrastructure for Pyongyang to exploit in a future crisis.[55] When dissidents or foreign companies oppose the regime, North Korean operators retaliate online.[56]

> ### *Major Cyber Operations Publicly Attributed to North Korea: 2014–2019*
>
> - 2014: North Korea conducts destructive attack against U.S.-based Sony Pictures Entertainment.[57]
> - 2015: North Korean–linked groups use 5,986 phishing emails containing malicious code to gain access to noncritical systems at a South Korean nuclear power plant.[58]
> - 2016: North Korean groups are linked to an estimated $81 million cyber heist of Bangladesh's central bank account at the Federal Reserve Bank of New York.[59]
> - 2017: North Korea launches the WannaCry ransomware attack that infects over 300,000 computers in 150 countries; its effects include temporarily knocking some U.K. hospitals offline.[60]
> - 2019: A UN report concludes that North Korea used cyberattacks against financial institutions and cryptocurrency exchanges to steal an estimated $2 billion it used to fund its weapons of mass destruction program.[61]

The regime extracts illicit gains from the modern global economy by conducting attacks against systems critical to financial institutions' wire transfers.[62] These operations give North Korean leadership a funding lifeline in the face of otherwise crippling economic sanctions.[63] Left unchallenged, North Korea will only grow bolder, complicating diplomatic efforts to check its nuclear ambitions.

Without a new U.S. strategic approach, revisionist regional powers will seek new opportunities to use increasingly powerful yet inexpensive cyber operations to undermine U.S. economic, diplomatic, and military power. They will challenge the U.S.-led system of alliances designed to limit major wars and use the resulting chaos to ensure the safety of corrupt elites.

Non-state Cyber Threats

Though we are in an era of great power competition, one need not be a great power to have a great impact in the cyber domain. Cyber capabilities, unlike nuclear capabilities, can be built or obtained without access to national resources and power. From extremist groups to criminals and illicit businesses, new threat actors take advantage of modern connectivity to undermine the integrity of open societies. Sophisticated criminal enterprise and cybercrime groups now target some of the world's largest businesses and municipalities, stealing money and encrypting critical data for ransom.[64] Internet-enabled social connectivity provides extremist groups new ways of conducting targeted recruitment unimaginable just a generation ago. The so-called Islamic State is an omen of 21st-century terror movements. The group has demonstrated a sophisticated understanding of how mobile applications, web content, and online forums can be used to support operations.[65]

The growing demand for cyber capabilities to spy on and coerce rivals has created entirely new types of businesses and marketplaces for state and non-state actors.[66] Former cyber operators from multiple countries can sell their skills to the highest bidder.[67] Left unchecked, these actors could turn the connectivity our world relies on into a chaotic, fragmented space where states, businesses, and individuals lose trust and confidence in formal institutions.

Major Cyber Operations Publicly Attributed to Non-state Actors: 2011–2019

- 2011–present: Cybercrime group Evil Corp uses Dridex malware to infect computers and harvest credentials from banks and financial institutions in over 40 countries, causing more than $100 million in theft.[68]
- 2011: The GameOver Zeus malware, created by the Russian cybercriminal Evgeniy Mikhailovich Bogachev, infects more than 1 million devices worldwide and causes damages in excess of $100 million.[69]
- 2013: Cryptolocker ransomware infects more than 234,000 computers and actors obtain more than $27 million in ransom payments.[70]
- 2014: Four hackers breach the servers of JPMorgan Chase, compromising the data of 76 million households and 7 million small businesses in one of the biggest data breaches in history.[71]
- 2015: Members of the Islamist hacker group the Cyber Caliphate gain control of U.S. Central Command's Twitter and YouTube accounts and post numerous propaganda videos.[72]
- 2015: GozNym malware is used by a transnational organized cybercrime network to steal an estimated $100 million from unsuspecting victims in the United States and around the world.[73]
- 2016: Self-declared affiliates of the groups Anonymous and New World Hackers disrupt internet service across North America using a botnet composed of numerous Internet of Things (IoT) devices.[74]
- 2018: After a sophisticated ransomware attack shut down several critical municipal websites, the city of Atlanta declines to pay a $52,000 ransom demanded by hackers, instead opting to spend $2.6 million to rebuild its systems.[75]
- 2019: More than 20 Texas towns and the city of Baltimore are hit with ransomware attacks, disrupting critical municipal services.[76]

Increasingly, cybercriminals are migrating toward the "crime-as-a-service" model in which threat groups purchase and exchange malicious code on the dark web.[77] Businesses across the globe could lose $5.2 trillion to these criminal enterprises by 2024.[78] In addition, criminals can use cyber operations to target state and local government through ransomware attacks. Many of these thefts are masked through techniques that make attribution and prosecution difficult.

Criminal groups are expanding their cyber operations. Ransomware attacks are on the rise and increasing in sophistication. In 2019, ransomware incidents grew over 300 percent compared to 2018.[79] The onslaught was so severe that the Federal Bureau of Investigation released a public service announcement warning of the risks of targeted attacks against "health care organizations, industrial companies, and the transportation sector."[80] These attacks target not just businesses and individuals, but increasingly American cities. In 2019 ransomware attacks hit more than 40 municipalities across the United States.[81]

WHERE ARE WE NOW?

The United States is struggling to address the changing character of cyber threats. The government still lacks clear, coordinated response mechanisms that build security into the cyber ecosystem and deter attacks of significant consequence. The public and private sectors struggle to coordinate cyber defenses, leaving gaps that decrease national resilience and create systemic risk. New technology continues to emerge that further compounds these challenges.

Unclear Strategy

The United States lacks a clear, comprehensive, publicly declared doctrine that incorporates all of the instruments of power to address less-than-catastrophic attacks on public and private networks in cyberspace. Despite U.S. progress in shifting to a more aggressive posture in cyberspace, adversarial states and non-state actors find cyber operations ideal low-cost, high-payoff methods for eroding U.S. power that do not risk direct counterattacks. To date, the United States has not sufficiently changed the cost-benefit calculus made by adversaries

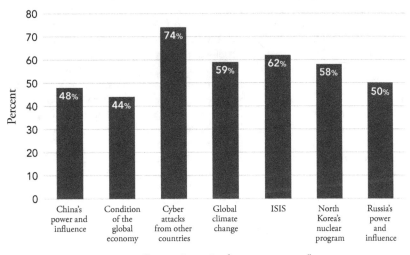

Issues Americans Perceive as a Major Threat

China's power and influence: 48%
Condition of the global economy: 44%
Cyber attacks from other countries: 74%
Global climate change: 59%
ISIS: 62%
North Korea's nuclear program: 58%
Russia's power and influence: 50%

"_____ is a major threat to our country"

Source: Pew Research Center, Spring 2018 Global Attitudes Survey

when determining whether or not to attack in cyberspace below the level of armed conflict.

Just as cost-benefit analysis highlights the ease of cyber operations, the balance of risk is similarly skewed. Adversaries suspect that the U.S. government would retaliate for turning off the power in a major city but doubt American resolve to respond to intellectual property theft, the implanting of malware in critical infrastructure, and election interference. They know they can achieve their objectives on the cheap. Both state and non-state actors know that in the current environment, new vulnerabilities that they can exploit emerge every day across the private sector while government and private-sector responses will be uncoordinated and sporadic at best.

Poorly Positioned to Lead

The U.S. government is currently poorly positioned to act with the speed and agility required to secure its interests in cyberspace. The nation that brought the digital era into being is weighed down by an industrial-era

bureaucracy and a labyrinth of outdated rules, laws, and regulations that limit America's ability to defend cyberspace. While the U.S. government has taken a more proactive role over the past four years and started to use multiple instruments of power to respond to threats, these responses still fall short. Technological change is outpacing the U.S. government's ability to adapt. Innumerable barriers to private- and public-sector collaboration compound the problem. With each new innovation, the legacy structures and approaches amended by the federal government to govern cyberspace become less and less relevant to the growing range of activities that take place there.

This growing irrelevance is partly a result of the character of innovation and of cyberspace technologies. In previous eras, the federal government was a significant driver of technological advancement—including the development of the internet—through its national laboratories, funding of scientific research, and defense-driven research initiatives.[82] Over time, as technological innovation began to overtake manufacturing and resource extraction as the primary means of generating corporate advantage, the private sector began to outspend the government in cutting-edge research.

As the U.S. government sought to manage how technology shaped society, it developed a wide range of programs. From congressional oversight bodies to new departments, the government expanded. Many of these new efforts have had significant impact (e.g., U.S.

Cyber Command, the National Cyber Investigative Joint Task Force, the Cybersecurity and Infrastructure Security Agency), but the overall federal effort has failed to comprehensively address the inherent vulnerabilities associated with increased connectivity. There is still not a clear unity of effort or theory of victory driving the federal government's approach to protecting and securing cyberspace.

To make matters worse, the U.S. government lacks the number of cyber professionals needed to secure its own networks, much less support private-sector partners or treaty allies, who also operate cyber systems that the U.S. government relies on. There are over 33,000 unfilled cybersecurity positions in the U.S. government and 500,000 unfilled positions throughout the United States.[83] Moreover, a 2015 survey of information technology executives from the United States, United Kingdom, Israel, Germany, France, Japan, Australia, and Mexico found that 76 percent of respondents believed that their governments are not investing enough money in cybersecurity talent.[84] The military services are adapting to recruit and train their own cyber warriors, but they anticipate difficulties recruiting and retaining sufficient top-flight talent.[85]

Uncoordinated Public and Private Sectors

Because the majority of the critical infrastructure, hardware, and software that powers the information age resides in the private sector, there is a unique requirement to build a public-private partnership to protect the nation. However, businesses are often reluctant to let governments onto private, commercial networks without a clear understanding of their shared interests and responsibilities. Afraid of creating moral hazard, the federal government invests little in protecting the cybersecurity of commercial infrastructure or key systems controlled by states and local municipalities.

This lack of accountability for managing risk leads to blind spots. Who is responsible for setting priorities (and providing funding) when it is necessary to "turn the lights back on" following a major cyberattack? Who coordinates continuity of the economy during a series of large-scale attacks on American financial institutions and transportation infrastructure? How do local hospitals, water

How Can Artificial intelligence and Machine Learning Affect Cybersecurity?

Advances in artificial intelligence and machine learning (AI/ML) are creating both opportunities and challenges in cyberspace. On the one hand, these technologies can increase cybersecurity. For example, the Defense Advanced Research Projects Agency (DARPA) tested AI/ML capabilities during its 2016 Cyber Grand Challenge pitting teams of supercomputers hunting vulnerabilities against one another.[86] Competitors relied on supercomputers to write self-healing code to rapidly search for flaws and write corrections in real time. Each supercomputer sought to protect itself while searching for and exploiting gaps in the other competitors. The competition illustrated that an AI/ML-enabled cyber defense was able to detect, and even repair, vulnerabilities significantly more quickly than humans alone ever could.

On the other hand, AI/ML risks creating a new arms race. China is aggressively investing in AI/ML applications with military, domestic surveillance, and economic implications.[87] Other countries, such as Russia, and even violent extremist organizations are exploring how to adapt free and widely available AI/ML algorithms to attack U.S. interests.[88]

As a result, the United States must ensure that its research and development investments in AI/ML and other possible breakthrough technologies match those technologies' potential consequences for national security. The National Security Commission on Artificial Intelligence is doing critical research to inform this competition, but this much is already clear: in the future cyberspace environment, the advantage will not necessarily go to the most powerful among nations, but to the actors that field the best algorithms or technologies.

treatment facilities, and municipal offices ask the federal government for assistance during a sustained ransomware campaign? Who is responsible for establishing the minimum-security standards, providing vulnerability assessments, and proactively managing the funding processes required to prepare for and prevent major cyber incidents? How can the public and private sectors collaborate to create a joined picture of the threat landscape?

As a result, everyone is left to independently balance risk, make investments, and take ad hoc responsibility for increasingly vulnerable networks, thereby producing dangerous security gaps. Public- and private-sector responses are left uncoordinated and the nation's critical infrastructure is left unprotected and vulnerable to adversaries who can, and will, exploit this opportunity.

WHERE ARE WE HEADED?

Two trends are fundamentally reshaping cyberspace: (1) increasing connectivity and (2) new technology that helps users make sense of—and derive value from—vast quantities of data. These trends can be harnessed with equal ease by state and non-state actors.

The speed and accessibility of digital connectivity only continue to improve. When the first smartphone was released, mobile internet speeds barely supported the transmission of images. Today, high-definition video streaming, real-time GPS tracking, and wirelessly accessible cloud computing have launched new economic sectors. Fifth-generation (5G) mobile networking is poised to further advance this trend toward faster and more reliable telecommunications. Satellite-based mesh communications networks—with nodes connected directly to each other rather than through a hierarchy—will bring the internet to every point on the globe.

Together, these advancements will enable the massive deployment of smart sensors—an Internet of Things—that autonomously gather, analyze, and act on data underpinning almost every facet of human life. Advanced approaches to connectivity promise global internet coverage free of constraints imposed by traditional geography, infrastructure, or even governments.

Driven by miniaturization and 5G networks, the so-called Internet of Things will create new networks of communication, data collection, and autonomous action connecting medical devices, streetlights, cars, sensors, and even common household appliances. These devices will allow the internet of our future access to new sources of vast amounts of information, from the personal (e.g., our sleeping habits, dietary patterns, or exercise routines) to the logistic (e.g., micropatterns in traffic or granular weather information). As the private lives of citizens become further enmeshed within networks, new vulnerabilities will be created.

Authoritarian states will take advantage of preferred relationships with technology firms to build in backdoors for government access that allow them to surveil the private lives of citizens and political opponents at home and abroad. In addition to advertising, propaganda will be micro-targeted and tailored to an individual based on personal data and search history. As networks connect individuals to transportation and electrical grids, public works, telecommunications, and the financial system, new vulnerabilities will become available for adversaries to exploit. Botnets could hijack billions of devices to disrupt entire regions, creating new national security challenges.

A connected world is also prone to cyber weapons spilling into the wild. Such spillage, associated with both great power competition and a black market for malware, creates new risk vectors. As states spy on each other, they release malware into the wild that can be repurposed to attack commercial interests, support authoritarian domestic spying campaigns, and compromise individual privacy. Research and development by non-state cyber weapon developers accelerate this trend, adding new vulnerabilities. While it might be difficult to buy sophisticated kinetic weapons on the black market, for both states and criminal groups it is easy to buy malware to support

Are We Losing the International Standards Race?

At its inception, advocates proclaimed that cyberspace was a force for good, inherently promoting freedom and democracy. They heralded the growing presence in China of the internet—a free and open medium invented and dominated by American entities—as proof that political and economic liberalization would be just around the corner.[89] Today, technical and international initiatives by countries like China and Russia have made it clear that digital connectivity—and the power it affords to selectively target, amplify, or isolate audiences ranging in size from one to billions—is a tool, like any other, that can be wielded for good or bad.

Because the networks that connect us all in cyberspace eclipse nation-state geographical boundaries and sovereignty, they create unique challenges for governance. No single nation-state can standardize cyberspace. As a result, standards are developed by decentralized international bodies primarily driven by academia and the private sector. Even when such bodies include nation-state representation, like the International Telecommunications Union (ITU), the United States tends to encourage a bottom-up, private-sector-driven process, while China and Russia send full diplomatic delegations and take a more active role in these bodies.[90]

This dynamic is at play in the rollout of 5G networks. In 2013, the Chinese government committed resources and attention across three ministries to actively coordinate with industry on early 5G development standards.[91] This effort was combined with state support of companies like Huawei to speed research and development toward early patents, which can often inform the foundations of subsequent technical standards. As a result, by early 2019, Huawei led the world with 1,529 of these "standards-essential patents" for 5G technology.[92] In addition, China has invested in international standards-making bodies, frequently sending large delegations to working meetings and paying bonuses to their representatives who secure leadership positions.[93]

As Chinese technologies increasingly inform international technical standards, so do the values and policies accompanying Beijing's vision for the use of those technologies. China is exporting these technologies around the world, particularly to Africa and Southeast Asia, where too often invasive surveillance regimes and repressive censorship laws soon follow.[94] As China helps design and deploy the foundational infrastructure over which the world's data flows, it is ensuring that the same level of authoritarian control is available to those governments that wish to purchase it. While the United States and its partners champion a nascent framework for "secure-by-design" standards, including mandatory cybersecurity measures and open, auditable, and interoperable telecommunications equipment, China is writing a digital future of proprietary technologies in which "surveillance by design" can too easily become the default.

The global standards governing the connectivity of cyberspace and its enabling technologies are too important to be left to authoritarian nation-states that do not value open, free expression or democratic institutions. For the internet to fulfill its original promise, the United States and its network of democratic allies must engage with standards-making bodies and have well-researched agendas informed by a clear-eyed understanding of both technological and geopolitical trends. While the original vision for the internet and digital connectivity is an attractive one, the U.S. government is now only one of many actors defining the rules for cyberspace. The United States must collaborate with its partners—both government and private-sector entities—to ensure that our most critical technologies are designed using standards that align with American values.

brazen cyberattacks. Because cyber weapons are not in the exclusive control of nation-states, traditional arms control methods are difficult to coordinate, much less enforce.

AN INFLECTION POINT

The United States thus stands at a strategic inflection point. While America looks forward to the potential of cyberspace and associated technologies to improve the quality of human life, threats continue to grow at an accelerating pace. America is facing adversary nation-states, extremists, and criminals that are leveraging emerging technologies to an unprecedented degree. Authoritarian states seek to control every aspect of life in their societies and export this style of government, in which surveillance trumps liberty, to the rest of the world. There is no public square, only black boxes proliferating propaganda and organizing economic activity to benefit the few at the expense of the many. Rogue states, extremists, and criminals thrive on the dark web, taking advantage of insecure network connections and a market for malware to prey on victims.

In a world where the United States fails to check the spread of surveillance technologies beloved by dictators and fails to champion a new strategy to secure the connectivity on which societies around the world rely, democracy withers. Chinese technology exports could help Beijing censor topics that it, or despot clients, deems taboo, and the free world would have no way of knowing the facts. The security of global networks would be corrupted from the inside out, handing the Chinese Communist Party compromising personal information on people around the world. At the same time, China, Russia, Iran, and North Korea will use cyber operations to interfere with elections in free countries, bringing the legitimacy of the democratic process into question. These nations, along with extremist groups, will further weaponize social media, distorting public discourse and deepening polarization in societies around the world. The world is on the brink of a second information revolution.

If democracies do not devise a new strategy to provide confidentiality, integrity, and availability of information in cyberspace, they are unlikely to be the leading beneficiaries or guarantors of this new, connected world.

Technological trends are creating markets and practices that challenge the U.S. government's ability to provide the stability required for freedom and prosperity to flourish. Today, the private sector is the hub for technological innovation, with the government at times struggling to import that innovation back into its own systems and processes.[95] This shift is further magnified by private-sector ownership of most of the physical and logical layers of cyberspace.[96] The result is an unprecedented reversal of dependencies: while the U.S. government has traditionally provided for the collective defense, it now requires enhanced cooperation and partnership with the private sector.

Across American history, the Republic has weathered large-scale change and strategic inflections by forging new strategies and partnerships. Democracies adapt, powered by open debate and an ability to build bridges between the public and private sectors that take advantage of new opportunities and mitigate emergent risks. The opportunities and vulnerabilities associated with growing connectivity and the reach of cyberspace into all of our lives is no different. The United States needs a new strategic posture to defend its interest in cyberspace. Because the domain relies disproportionately on private-sector networks, this strategy must incentivize public- and private-sector collaboration and deny adversaries the ability to hold America hostage in cyberspace. This strategy must combine non-military instruments of power with defensive mechanisms to secure critical infrastructure—backed by a credible capability and capacity to impose costs through cyber and non-cyber military operations at time and place of the nation's choosing—both to shape competition beneath the level of armed conflict and to win in armed conflict.

HISTORICAL LEGACY AND METHODOLOGY

HISTORICAL LEGACY

The Cyberspace Solarium Commission draws its inspiration from President Dwight D. Eisenhower's 1953 Project Solarium.[97] With the Soviet Union looming as an existential threat, Eisenhower tasked his national security team with designing a long-term competitive strategy that would outlast his presidency.[98] Project Solarium pitted three teams, each developing a different strategic framework, against each other over the course of six weeks working at the National War College and a day-long debate at the White House. Their work eventually culminated in NSC 162/2—Eisenhower's "New Look" grand strategy—a sustainable variant of containment that laid the foundation for success against the Soviet Union.[99] This whole-of-nation strategy called upon the talents of citizens, corporations, academia, and government alike.[100] The United States' extended competition with the Soviet Union would yield, among other things, arguably the most consequential technological innovation of the postwar period: the internet.[101]

Similar to the original Solarium effort, the world is now living through a period of strategic adjustment. The United States is struggling to defend its interests in cyberspace and leverage its comparative advantages: technological prowess, an innovative workforce, an open society, and a free market. For the past 25 years, each presidential administration has reached out to academics, business leaders, and innovators to develop new ideas to solve this problem but has consistently fallen short. There are enduring challenges at the heart of securing American interests in cyberspace. In the early 1960s, computer scientists and national security experts began to identify the inherent vulnerabilities and threats associated with the increasing connectivity afforded by computers. At the RAND Corporation, Willis Ware began to conceptualize a gathering threat unique to emerging computer networks.[102] While his colleague Paul Baran argued that the decentralization of computer systems would reduce the risk of destruction or disruption, Ware worried that decentralization would also increase the risk of error and intrusion.[103] Recognizing that the advance of computer networking—particularly in service of national security—was unstoppable, Ware set about creating a theory of security in the cyber domain. In 1970, working at the behest of the Defense Science Board, Ware published "Security Controls for Computer Systems," later known as the "Ware Report." This analysis took a holistic view of network security, arguing that information must be secured through a comprehensive set of "hardware, software, communication, physical, personnel, and administrative-procedural safeguards."[104] Many of the vulnerabilities foreseen by the Ware Report—including user and administrator errors, insider subversion, weak authentication, and persistent threats—remain fundamental concerns in cybersecurity 50 years later.

The concept of cybersecurity (if not yet the word itself) entered American pop culture in 1983 with the release of the film *WarGames*, a production on which Ware consulted.[105] The buzz surrounding the film, which features a teenager hacking into national defense systems and nearly causing a nuclear exchange with the Soviet Union, caught the attention of the Reagan administration. After a private viewing of the film at Camp David, President Ronald Reagan tasked his national security team with determining the real-world plausibility of such an incident.[106] In 1984, President Reagan signed National Security Decision Directive 145, "National Policy on Telecommunications and Automated Information Systems Security."[107] NSDD-145 would be the first in a long line of presidential directives, congressional bills, commissions, and national strategies all aimed at protecting the United States from the hazards of its revolutionary creation.

There have been some successes in organizing the nation for resilience. Since 1997, the U.S. government has established numerous cybersecurity and critical infrastructure commissions that have each released noteworthy plans for improvement,[108] and the federal government has also stood up new organizations to coordinate policies and operations in cyberspace such as the National Cyber Investigative Joint Task Force in 2008, U.S. Cyber Command in 2009, the Cybersecurity and Infrastructure Security Agency in 2018, and the National Security Agency's new Cybersecurity Directorate, created in 2019.[109] Cyberspace commissions, reports, and directives have helped shape laws such as the 1986 Computer Fraud and Abuse Act, the 1999 Financial Services Modernization Act, the 2002 Federal Information Security Management Act, and the 2015 Cybersecurity Information Sharing Act.[110]

Yet despite these efforts, new threats and vulnerabilities appear daily for many of the same reasons highlighted by the Ware Report. This phenomenon has not been lost on previous reports and commissions. In 1996, the Defense Science Board's Information Warfare-Defense report noted with apparent frustration that it was "the third consecutive year a DSB Summer Study or Task Force [had] made similar recommendations." The 2009 Cyberspace Policy Review echoed many of the same recommendations offered by similar strategic reviews in the 1990s and in 2003.[111] There are many more examples of such efforts from the past 50 years that produced overwhelming expert consensus but limited policy action. This effort seeks to avoid this fate by developing both a coherent strategy for securing cyberspace and concrete policy recommendations the executive branch and Congress can act on without delay.

METHODOLOGY

The Cyberspace Solarium Commission used a multimethod approach combining interviews with subject matter experts, red teaming, stress tests, and quantitative analysis to develop a strategy for defending American interests. Like the original

Solarium event—which used strategic concepts such as containment, rollback, and massive retaliation to calibrate a strategic approach to competing with the Soviet Union—the Cyberspace Solarium Commission adapted strategic approaches optimized for the complex connectivity of cyberspace and assigned them to its three Task Forces. Each Task Force used one of these approaches—active disruption and cost imposition, denial and defense, and entanglement through norms-based regimes that encourage responsible behavior in cyberspace[112]—to articulate key lines of effort, or pillars, paired with key recommendations.

First, each Task Force conducted independent research. This research focused on interviewing subject matter experts from government, academia, and industry in more than 300 sessions over five months, as well as conducting a literature review. These sessions enabled the Task Forces to build a collaborative research network to test emerging ideas and existing approaches to securing cyberspace. Attendees at these meetings included full-time staff, part-time subject matter experts, and Commissioners themselves.

> ### *Task Force Engagements*
> - 200+ meetings with industry experts
> - 25+ meetings with academics
> - 50+ meetings with federal, state, and local officials
> - 10+ seminars/roundtables hosted by think tanks
> - 20+ meetings with officials from international organizations/foreign countries

The research phase produced independent task force reports outlining alternative strategies and policy approaches for securing America's vital networks in cyberspace. Each Task Force had a different theory of victory, independently describing the core challenge to securing cyberspace and how best to apply instruments of national power to defend American interests.

Second, the Task Forces turned to a series of red teams to assess their strategies. As external, independent groups, the red teams challenged the theories of victory and key recommendations, providing both verbal and written feedback to each Task Force. This feedback was then used by the teams to fine-tune each approach and supporting recommendations.

Third, the Commission stress-tested each Task Force strategic approach. As was done during the original Eisenhower Solarium project, an event was held at Fort McNair in partnership with the National Defense University.[113] Unlike the original Solarium event, the 2019 forum adapted key concepts from stress tests and red team techniques to help the Commissioners evaluate the inherent strengths and weaknesses of each approach. The stress tests used complex scenarios involving the widespread use of cyber operations against a hypothetical country and its allies.[114] These attacks targeted a complex mix of political institutions, military forces, the Defense Industrial Base, and economic targets ranging from financial institutions to critical infrastructure. During the Solarium event, each Task Force responded to questions from Commissioners and red team members on how their strategy would address the crises outlined in the scenarios.

(U.S. Cyberspace Solarium Commission)

Senator Angus King asks a question at the Commission's Solarium event, hosted by the National Defense University on October 25, 2019, while fellow Commissioners Representative Mike Gallagher and FBI Director Christopher Wray look on.

Fourth, following the Solarium event, the Commissioners assessed each strategy and its supporting policy recommendations, providing formal feedback. The staff tabulated this feedback and used the insights and guidance gained to further refine the recommendations.

Unlike the original Solarium, this was not a top-secret process driven by the President. Instead, it was an open process created by Congress in collaboration with the executive branch. This process enabled the Commission to evaluate competing perspectives and recommend a strategy that defines the core objectives and priorities required to secure American interests in cyberspace.

STRATEGIC APPROACH: LAYERED CYBER DETERRENCE

Since 1960, pockets of scientists, military officers, academics, technology innovators, and government officials have all wrestled with a dilemma: as connectivity expands, it creates both increasing opportunities and greater vulnerabilities. Every new device connected, and line of code added, presents adversaries with new attack surfaces they can use to undermine American security and prosperity. These devices and applications, as well as the communications infrastructure on which they rely, are overwhelmingly controlled by the private sector.[115] To defend cyberspace thus requires significant coordination across the public and private sectors.

In this dilemma reside the seeds of a new strategy: *layered cyber deterrence*. Layered cyber deterrence combines a number of traditional deterrence mechanisms and extends them beyond the government to develop a whole-of-nation approach. Since America relies on critical infrastructure that is primarily owned and operated by the private sector, the government cannot defend the nation alone. The public and private sectors, along with key international partners, must collaborate to build national resilience and reshape the cyber ecosystem in a manner that increases its security, while imposing costs against malicious actors and preventing attacks of significant consequence.

First, the approach combines traditional methods of altering the cost-benefit calculus of adversaries (e.g., denial and cost imposition) with forms of influence optimized for a connected era, such as promoting norms that encourage restraint and incentivize responsible behavior in cyberspace. Strategic discussions all too often prioritize narrow definitions of deterrence that fail to consider how technology is changing society. In a connected world, those states that harness the power of cooperative, networked relationships gain a position of advantage and inherent leverage.[116] The more connected a state is to

others and the more resilient its infrastructure, the more powerful it becomes. This power requires secure connections and stable expectations between leading states about what is and is not acceptable behavior in cyberspace. It requires shaping adversary behavior not just by threatening costs but also by changing the ecosystem in which competition occurs. It requires international engagement and collaborating with the private sector.

Second, layered cyber deterrence emphasizes working with the private sector to efficiently coordinate how the nation responds with speed and agility to emerging threats. The federal government alone cannot fund or solve the challenge of adversaries attacking the networks on which America and its allies and partners rely. It requires collaboration with state and local authorities, leading business sectors, and international partners, all within the rule of law established by the Constitution that protects the rights of individuals. This strategy also contemplates the planning needed to ensure the continuity of the economy and the ability of the United States to

Whole-of-Nation Framework

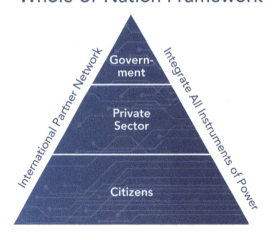

rebound in the aftermath of a major, nationwide cyber-attack of significant consequence. Such planning adds depth to deterrence by assuring the American people, allies, and even our adversaries that the United States will have both the will and capability to respond to an attack on its interests, no matter how devastating.

Third, the strategy builds on the defend forward concept, originally articulated in the Department of Defense (DoD) Cyber Strategy, to include all of the instruments of national power. It integrates defend forward into a whole-of-nation approach for securing American interests in cyberspace. Defend forward is a proactive, rather than reactive, approach to adversary cyber threats. Specifically, it addresses the fact that the United States has not created credible and sufficient costs against malicious adversary behavior below the level of armed attack—even as the United States has prevented cyberattacks of significant consequences.[117] Therefore, defend forward posits that the United States must shift from responding to malicious behavior after it has already occurred to proactively observing, pursuing, and countering adversary operations and imposing costs to change adversary behavior. By shaping the strategic environment and creating meaningful costs for malicious behavior, defend forward aims to disrupt and defeat ongoing malicious adversary cyber campaigns, deter future campaigns, and reinforce favorable international norms of behavior. This posture implies persistent engagement[118] with adversaries as part of an overall integrated effort to apply every authority, access, and capability possible (e.g., laws, financial regulation, diplomacy, education) to the defense of cyberspace in a manner consistent with international law.

Layered cyber deterrence combines different ways to shape adversaries' decision making. The central idea is simple: **increase the costs and decrease the benefits that adversaries anticipate when planning cyberattacks against American interests**. This can be achieved by employing multiple deterrent mechanisms concurrently, continuously, and collaboratively across the public and private sectors. If deterrence fails, the United States retains a multitude of options that comply with international law.

In the first layer, the United States together with our partners and allies collectively develops and implements cyber norms based on our shared interests and values. These norms have the potential to shape behavior, largely by encouraging restraint and incentivizing responsible behavior. Actions in this layer include, but are not limited to, diplomacy, law enforcement cooperation, and intelligence sharing on emerging and persistent threat vectors and vulnerabilities. Over time, growing coalitions of like-minded partners and allies can limit the number of targets that adversaries can attack through capacity building and can increase the costs of malign behavior through collective action. This approach will not eliminate state-sponsored cyber operations or cybercrime, but consistently enforced consequences and rewards can begin to erode the incentives for bad behavior.

In the second layer, the U.S. government collaborates with the private sector to reduce vulnerabilities and deny benefits to adversaries. The strategy for this layer of deterrence is to force adversaries to make difficult choices regarding resources, access, and capabilities. When U.S. vulnerabilities are reduced and adversaries are forced to expend more resources, burn sensitive accesses, or utilize unique and expensive cyber weapons to achieve their desired results, cyberattacks will be reduced. Actions in this layer include, but are not limited to, expanding operational collaboration between government and private sector, prioritizing support to systemically important critical infrastructure, exercising local authorities and the private sector's ability to respond to significant cyberattacks through such mechanisms as Continuity of the Economy (COTE) planning, pooling public and private data on cyber intrusions, incentivizing companies and individuals to reduce systemic vulnerabilities, and ensuring that the intelligence resources of the U.S. government are effectively brought to bear in supporting the private sector's own cybersecurity efforts.[119] Over time, these activities make it harder for adversaries to find easy attack vectors and hold at risk American networks in cyberspace. The U.S. government must find ways to collaborate with private-sector vendors and state as well as local governments to use red teams to anticipate possible cyberattacks against critical infrastructure. In the worst-case scenario of a major, nationwide cyberattack, properly exercised COTE plans will help ensure the reconstitution of the country's critical economic drivers.

In the third layer, the United States is prepared to impose costs to deter conflict, limit malicious adversary behavior below the level of armed conflict, and, if necessary, prevail in war by employing the full spectrum of its capabilities. Deterrence must extend to limiting attacks on the U.S. election system and preventing large-scale intellectual property theft. To that end, the U.S. government must demonstrate its ability to impose costs using all instruments of power, while establishing a clear

declaratory policy that signals to rival states the costs and risks associated with attacking America in cyberspace. Defend forward is an important part of the cost imposition layer. The original defend forward concept put forth by DoD focuses on the military instrument of power to impose costs to "disrupt or halt malicious cyber activity at its source, including activity that falls below the level of armed conflict."[120] Reimagined as a key element of layered cyber deterrence, defend forward in this context comprises the proactive and integrated employment of all of the instruments of power. Defend forward requires the United States to have the capability and capacity for sustained engagement in cyberspace to impose costs on adversaries for engaging in malicious cyber activity. The cost imposition layer also demands that the U.S. government protect its ability to respond with military force at a time and place of its choosing. A key aspect of this ability is ensuring the security and

Layered Cyber Deterrence

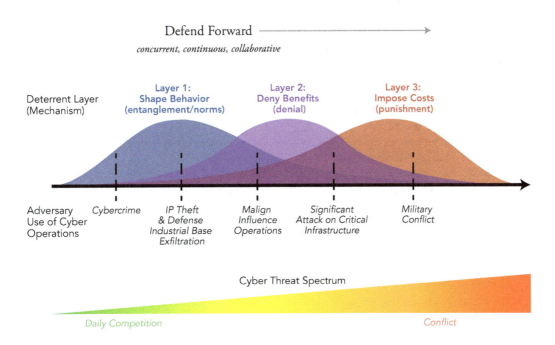

resilience of critical weapons systems and functions in cyberspace.

THE STRATEGIC LOGIC OF DETERRENCE

Layered cyber deterrence adapts an enduring strategy to defend American interests in cyberspace.[121] Over the past seven decades, deterrence has been the foundation of U.S. strategy.[122] As a strategic concept for managing great power competition, deterrence played a pivotal role in U.S. foreign policy during the Cold War.[123]

Scholars define deterrence as "dissuading someone from doing something by making them believe the costs to them will exceed their expected benefit."[124]The deterrence literature distinguishes between a number of different deterrence strategies, including denial, punishment, entanglement, and normative taboos. These strategies take on unique attributes in cyberspace.

Deterrence by punishment, which gained prominence during the nuclear age, rests on the credible threat to harm a target's civilian population or economy, thereby making the perceived costs of an action unacceptably high ("countervalue" targeting).[125] In cyberspace, deterrence by punishment entails the threat of latent violence against the non-military assets that a target holds dear. America's commitment to international law appropriately places constraints on its willingness to implement deterrence by punishment in cyberspace. In addition, scholars of cyber strategy debate the extent to which cyber capabilities offer a feasible punishment mechanism, or whether punishment requires lethal capabilities.[126] Therefore, in cyberspace the preferred punishment strategy for democratic nations is to impose costs on adversaries through targeting key—often government or illicit, as opposed to commercial and civilian—networks and infrastructure used to conduct cyber campaigns.

Deterrence by denial entails threatening to physically impede, reduce the impact of, or increase the costs of an adversary's ability to successfully attack American interests.[127] Traditionally, this form of deterrence works by targeting the adversary's military capabilities ("counterforce" targeting) and/or by shoring up one's own defenses to such an extent that offensive operations by the attacking state are perceived to be inordinately costly.[128] In cyberspace, deterrence by denial works by increasing the costs to the attacker—beyond just financial costs—of breaching the deterring state's defenses. When the government and private sector collaborate to build security into connected systems, they reduce the number of vulnerabilities adversaries can exploit. This form of denial is especially important for deterring non-state actors, such as extremists and criminals.

In addition to punishment and denial, deterrence can be achieved through entanglement and normative taboos.[129] Entanglement can deter under conditions of mutual interdependence, when an attack would create meaningful costs for the attacker as well as the defender.[130] Entanglement implies shared risk. For example, two states may be interconnected through mutually beneficial economic relationships.[131] In cyberspace, we all rely on the same networks and underlying infrastructure that supports global connectivity. Cyber operations threaten this connectivity and create shared risks. Norms can also contribute to deterrence by "imposing reputational costs that can damage an actor's soft power beyond the value gained from a given attack."[132] In cyberspace, these reputational costs can amplify the threat of punishment and denial-based activities that deter extreme attacks by states, helping to discourage espionage and subterfuge beneath the threshold of armed conflict.

The success of deterrence typically rests on four factors. First, the deterring state must clearly communicate the terms of a threat so that the target understands the behavior expected of it and the potential consequences of ignoring the threat. Second, the deterrer should ensure that the threatened costs inflicted on the adversary outweigh the latter's perceived benefits from conducting the undesired action. Third, deterrent threats must be credible: the deterrer must possess both the capability to carry out the terms of a threat and the resolve or political will to do so. Importantly, and related to the first point, the target of deterrence must perceive that costs will actually be imposed, which means that a deterring state has to develop mechanisms for signaling credibility to the target. Finally, deterrent threats should be coupled with some form of reassurance to the target that if it complies and does not act, the deterrer will refrain from carrying out the threatened response.

These criteria illustrate some of the fundamental challenges associated with successfully implementing deterrence in cyberspace. Rather than clearly communicating an ultimatum to a target, which may tie their hands and create politically infeasible "red lines," states may prefer to retain strategic ambiguity and flexibility. Communication and signaling could also be complicated by the potential for misperception. These dynamics are compounded in cyberspace, where states initially conceal their attacks and often seek to obscure the source through misattribution, false flags, and proxies. For example, challenges in establishing timely and accurate attribution can weaken cyber deterrence by generating doubt about the identity of the perpetrator of a cyberattack and undermining the credibility of response options.[133]

In addition, credibility is a central challenge of deterrence, which is why in his seminal work on the topic, *Arms and Influence*, Thomas Schelling devotes considerable energy to this problem and the various means by which states could enhance the credibility of their threats (e.g., what he calls hand-tying, brinkmanship, or the art of commitment).[134] In the domain of cyberspace, states must signal credible commitments not just by making threats but by taking actions that demonstrate their willingness and ability to respond to cyber threats. Signaling, which includes statements or actions that are meant to communicate information to a target,[135] is especially difficult in cyberspace. The target may simply not perceive the threatened cyber costs to be high enough to affect its calculus, or the target may be willing to gamble—knowing that cyber operations and effects are often unpredictable and fleeting—that a threatened

action may not produce the effect intended by the deterring state.[136] Furthermore, cyber signaling about capability may be ineffective, misinterpreted, or misperceived.[137] Conversely, a deterring state may be loath to reveal certain cyber capabilities that would enhance the credibility of deterrence because the act of revealing them may render them ineffective.[138]

Finally, measuring the success of deterrence can be a trying enterprise, because a positive outcome is something that does not happen and effects are often uncertain. Uncertainty surrounding the effects of cyber capabilities—both anticipating their likely impact in advance and measuring the actual harm they cause—can muddle the battle damage assessments that are essential for any deterrence calculus.[139] In the absence of unique intelligence collection against adversary decision making, it can be difficult to determine whether a target chose not to act mainly because the deterrent threat worked or for unrelated reasons. In cyberspace, this dynamic implies a need to support operations designed to deter an adversary with extensive, all-source intelligence about adversary decision making that can be used to calibrate the response. Deterrence is more likely to succeed when situated within the strategic context and refined to focus on specific types of behavior or specific adversaries, rather than on cyber activities in general.[140]

Deterrence is an enduring American strategy, but it must be adapted to address how adversaries leverage new technology and connectivity to attack the United States. Cyber operations have become a weapon of choice for adversaries seeking to hold the U.S. economy and national security at risk.[141] Therefore, the concept of deterrence must evolve to address this new strategic landscape. Following nearly two decades in which the U.S. government prioritized counterterrorism and counterinsurgency, great power competition has resurfaced as America's central strategic challenge.[142] The United States now faces emerging peer competitors, particularly as China and Russia reassert their influence regionally and globally, often through cyber and influence operations that undermine American power below the level of armed conflict.[143] Reducing the scope and severity of these adversary cyber operations and campaigns requires adopting the strategy of layered cyber deterrence.

DEFEND FORWARD AND LAYERED CYBER DETERRENCE

Layered cyber deterrence places the U.S. Department of Defense's concept of defend forward in a larger, whole-of-nation framework that uses multiple instruments of power to secure American networks in cyberspace.[144] Since the end of World War II, the United States has used forward-deployed military forces to advance American interests. This strategic posture was an integral component of the grand strategy of containment for the United States and NATO. Cold War forward defense involved both projecting power by positioning U.S. and allied forces on the front lines of the potential battlefields of the next world war, and leveraging multiple instruments of power. These forward-deployed forces served several purposes: deterrence and signaling U.S. resolve and capabilities to the Soviet Union; enabling rapid response from a more advantageous position if conflict should break out; a source of intelligence and early warning; and a form of credible commitment to allies.

The connectivity and global reach of cyberspace make forward defense even more essential today. During the Cold War, the United States could anticipate where the front lines would likely be. In cyberspace, it is difficult to anticipate the battlefield or identify clear front lines. As NotPetya illustrates, cyberattacks often spill beyond their

Why Is Cyberspace an Odd Domain?

Cyberspace is a fundamentally new, novel, and odd domain for human activity. Unlike the traditional (and more tangible) domains of land, sea, air, and space, cyberspace is entirely human-made and has existed for only a few decades. Application of the laws, norms, and expectations of the traditional domains—the fundamental "physics" that has governed the course of human relations—is challenged by and in cyberspace.

In the four traditional domains, strategic competition is shaped by governments; cyberspace is shaped primarily by market forces. Cyberspace exists almost entirely on privately owned and operated information and communications technology (ICT) infrastructure, making it at least as much a good or service as a domain. As a domain of conflict, cyberspace is a "gray zone" where malicious actors get away with acts of theft, disruption, and even war that would not be permissible in a traditional domain.[145]

Outside of cyberspace, hundreds of years of legal tradition and iterative jurisprudence have produced commonly accepted principles—principles that slowly formed the foundations on which states built their domestic laws and guided their relations with other nations. Many existing laws still apply in cyberspace, but as technology continues to evolve, there can be uncertainty about how those laws pertain to this changing landscape, which is altering the relationship between governments and their citizens.[146] As an emerging legal frontier, cyberspace imposes new and different expectations on the public and private sectors to engage with one another in the defense of the nation.

Since the creation of cyberspace, the U.S. government, the private sector, and individual Americans have collectively struggled to secure it. Its existence defies millennia of human precedents and traditions. Cyberspace is an odd domain.

initial targets and infect other networks. This complication creates an imperative to defend forward and counter adversaries' use of cyber operations.[147]

Layered cyber deterrence builds on the original DoD defend forward concept. First, like the DoD concept, it operates as a general strategic principle during day-to-day competition, in which the U.S. government "will defend forward to disrupt or halt malicious cyber activity at its source, including activity that falls below the level of armed conflict."[148] This posture includes operating in "gray" and "red" space in a manner consistent with international law.[149] Second, it plays a role in ensuring that the U.S. government retains the ability to apply all instruments of power to respond to crisis or conflict. Applied to military power, this includes ensuring "the cybersecurity and resilience of DoD, DCI [Defense Critical Infrastructure], and DIB [Defense Industrial Base] networks and systems."[150] Finally, cyber layered deterrence, like defend forward, secures critical infrastructure and safeguards American networks by finding ways "to stop threats before they reach their targets."[151]

Changes to law in the FY2019 National Defense Authorization Act (NDAA)[152] and the issuance of National Security Presidential Memorandum (NSPM) 13[153] enable the U.S. government to adopt a defend forward posture. This posture was an integral part of the overall U.S. effort to counter Russian election interference in the 2018 midterm elections.[154] As the Commander of U.S. Cyber Command, General Paul Nakasone, testified in February 2019, "Working together under my command, U.S. Cyber Command and the National Security Agency (NSA) undertook an initiative known as the Russia Small Group to protect the elections from foreign interference and influence. By enabling our fellow combatant commands and other partners, U.S. Cyber Command assisted the collective intelligence and defense effort that demonstrated persistent engagement in practice."[155] These initiatives are continuing as part of the interagency effort to defend the 2020 presidential elections.[156]

However, additional improvements to existing law and policy would further support defend forward and address some of the challenges that have emerged in the early phases of its implementation. Most importantly, defend forward should be integrated at the national level as part of a U.S. national cyber strategy that incorporates all of the instruments of power. Including defend forward as a key element of layered cyber deterrence to counter malicious campaigns below the level of armed conflict addresses this issue and articulates how these activities support efforts to shape adversary behavior, deny benefits, and reinforce norms of responsible behavior.

THE IMPLEMENTATION OF LAYERED CYBER DETERRENCE

Layered cyber deterrence calls for reconceptualizing how the U.S. government coordinates cyber policy and the organizations and authorities aligned to defend American interests. To date, the U.S. government has built and operated a number of organizations specifically to support this mission set (e.g., the Cybersecurity and Infrastructure Security Agency, the National Cyber Investigative Joint Task Force, the Cyber Threat Intelligence Integration Center, U.S. Cyber Command, and the National Security Agency's Cybersecurity Directorate). Yet the creation of more organizations, congressional committees, and study groups makes it difficult to achieve the unity of effort required to conduct layered cyber deterrence and build the type of systemic resilience that changes the cost-benefit calculus in cyberspace. As a result, the United States finds it difficult to collaborate with the private sector and conduct cyber operations as part of whole-of-nation campaigns. Despite the new authorities outlined in the 2019 NDAA and NSPM-13 designed to improve government cyber campaign planning and to conduct offensive cyber operations, as well as multiple executive orders on securing critical infrastructure and promoting information sharing, the U.S. government is still struggling to secure its interests in cyberspace.

Layered cyber deterrence is the blueprint that the government and American public need to build bridges across government agencies, international partners, and most importantly the private sector in order to secure American networks in cyberspace. It is the best way for the government to implement new authorities and take appropriate proportional action that builds national resilience as well as disrupts, defeats, and deters active cyber campaigns, including those targeting critical economic and political institutions like election systems.[157]

To translate layered deterrence into action requires three lines of effort organized into six pillars and more than 75 supporting recommendations that enhance the ability of the U.S. government to shape adversary behavior, deny benefits, and impose costs. Defend forward spans all three lines of effort to identify, isolate, and counter threats consistent with existing authorities and legal frameworks.

Layered Cyber Deterrence

CURRENT STATE	APPROACH	PILLARS		DESIRED END STATES
Adversaries are conducting cyber campaigns that target U.S. networks in cyberspace and threaten American safety and security, economic interests, political institutions, and ability to project military power. The U.S. government has the authorities but lacks the optimal structure and relationships with the private sector and other partners to achieve a unity of effort at the scale required to defend forward.	Shape Behavior	*Foundation: Reform the U.S. Government Structure and Organization for Cyberspace*	*Strengthen Norms and Non-military Tools*	A digital environment that is safe and stable, promotes continued innovation and economic growth, protects personal privacy, ensures national security, and does so by building: • An international community that observes and enforces norms of responsible state behavior • Critical elements of national power and infrastructure that are secure, resilient, and supported by a defensible digital ecosystem • Public-private partnerships based on a shared situational awareness, combined action, and full support of the U.S. government in defense of the private sector • An agile, proactive U.S. government organized to rapidly and concurrently employ every instrument of national power in defense of cyberspace and to generate deterrent options tailored to each adversary • A cyber force equipped with the resources, capabilities, and processes to maneuver and rapidly engage adversaries in and through cyberspace
	Deny Benefits		*Promote National Resilience*	
			Reshape the Cyber Ecosystem toward Greater Security	
			Operationalize Cybersecurity Collaboration with the Private Sector	
	Impose Costs		*Preserve and Employ the Military Instrument of Power*	

REFORM THE U.S. GOVERNMENT'S STRUCTURE AND ORGANIZATION FOR CYBERSPACE

In democratic governance, structure is policy. To achieve the outcomes the United States requires to be more secure and prosperous in cyberspace—the outcomes this report seeks to realize—the U.S. government must be structured properly to realize them. Because cyberspace increasingly pervades every aspect of our government, economy, and society, however, this is a uniquely challenging problem. An effective government for the digital era means a government that has the right authorities, a coherent strategy, the critical partnerships, and the best talent. To realize this modern vision of policy requires a modern structure of government.

The U.S. government has taken necessary and significant steps to deter and disrupt threats from cyberspace, but they nonetheless remain insufficient to the scale of the problem. Governmental action has too often been piecemeal and independent of private-sector insights and interests, too much information remains over-classified or narrowly distributed, and a lack of strategic coherence continues to hinder attempts at improving systemic national cybersecurity.

The legislative and executive branches must each better align their authorities and capabilities to produce the speed and agility of action required to defend America in cyberspace. There needs to be greater collaboration between the public and private sectors in the defense of critical infrastructure and better integration in the planning, resourcing, and employment of government cyber resources. The recommendations in this pillar are intended to provide the U.S. government with the strategic continuity and unity of effort necessary to support the other pillars and recommendations of this report in achieving layered cyber deterrence and defending U.S.

critical infrastructure against cyberattacks of significant consequence.

First, the executive branch should issue a new national cyber strategy bringing coherence to the federal government's efforts. That strategy should be based on this Commission's framework of layered cyber deterrence, emphasize resilience and public-private collaboration, build on the Department of Defense's (DoD) concept of defend forward as a government-wide effort, and prioritize a bias for action.

Second, Congress must improve its oversight of cybersecurity by reorganizing and centralizing its committee structure and jurisdiction. Responsibility for cybersecurity is currently dispersed throughout numerous committees and subcommittees, hamstringing legislative authority, muddling oversight, and impeding Congress's ability to act with the speed and vision necessary for a domain so critical to national security and the modern economy.

Third, the executive branch must be organized to achieve the agility and coherence necessary to effectively plan, support, and employ government cyber resources. There

(*The Domino Effect | Khanh Tran, The Cybersecurity Visuals Challenge*)

is no single voice charged and empowered with harmonizing the executive branch's policies, budgets, and responsibilities in cyberspace; instead, many departments and agencies, with different responsibilities for and interests in cybersecurity, compete for resources and authority.

Fourth, the federal government must reform how it recruits, trains, and educates its workforce to ensure that

it has the necessary cybersecurity talent. Shortages in such talent are widespread in both the public and private sectors, and the federal government has a role to play (in partnership with academia and industry) to "grow the pie" of qualified cybersecurity workers, make certain that existing sources of talent are not overlooked, and build the pipelines and career paths that put the right people in the right places for confronting threats from cyberspace.

STRATEGIC OBJECTIVE #1:
ALIGN U.S. GOVERNMENT STRATEGY WITH LAYERED CYBER DETERRENCE

The executive branch should develop and issue a new national cyber strategy reflecting the strategic approach of layered cyber deterrence, emphasizing resilience and public-private collaboration, and including the concept of defend forward, to raise the costs and lower the benefits for malicious cyber activity. Today various departments and agencies constitute critical but separate components of an effective national cyber strategy that should be better integrated into a coherent national strategy. This approach will enable the U.S. government to achieve speed and agility, a bias for action, and effectiveness in cyberspace.

Key Recommendation

1.1 The executive branch should issue an updated National Cyber Strategy.

The executive branch should issue an updated National Cyber Strategy that embraces the concept of layered cyber deterrence, with an emphasis on resilience, public- and private-sector collaboration, and defend forward as key elements.

Any effective strategy for cyberspace will require a coordinated effort across the multiple stakeholders within the federal government, state and local governments, and the private sector that are all responsible for securing and defending the United States in this domain. Therefore, the strategy must explicitly align and synchronize stakeholder strategic objectives, identify lines of effort to put the strategy into operation, clarify what priority should be given to various efforts, and articulate common principles of risk.

Importantly, the National Cyber Strategy should include key concepts of layered cyber deterrence. The first is deterrence, which has been a long-standing strategic posture of the United States. Deterrence seeks to prevent an adversary from taking an undesired action by making a credible threat to impose costs, deny gains, or shape behavior. Second, it should prioritize deterrence by denial, which, in cyberspace, must include increasing the defense and security of cyberspace through resilience and public- and private-sector collaboration. As more and more of our critical systems—including those that underpin our national security, economy, public health and safety, and elections—come to rely on technology, ensuring the resilience of these technological systems becomes synonymous with ensuring the resilience of the nation as a whole. A resilient nation deters adversaries by denying them the gains they seek from attacking the United States. Furthermore, as the majority of U.S. systems and assets are owned and operated by the private sector, ensuring resilience and defense should be a responsibility shared between government and industry. Working together with the private sector to reduce the vulnerabilities adversaries can target, and mitigating the consequences even if vulnerabilities are successfully exploited, the United States can deny them opportunities to attack American interests through cyberspace.

Third, defend forward, which currently anchors the DoD's 2018 Cyber Strategy, should be integrated into the broader framework of how the government employs authorities that bear on cyber defense in support of overall layered cyber deterrence goals. Defend forward posits that to disrupt and defeat adversaries' ongoing malicious cyber campaigns, deter future campaigns, and reinforce favorable international norms of behavior, the United States must proactively observe, pursue, and counter adversary operations and impose costs in day-to-day competition. The strategy should clearly express that defend forward is an integral part of a comprehensive approach that encompasses all of the instruments of national power beyond the employment of strictly military capabilities; these include trade and economic efforts, law enforcement activities, and diplomatic tools.

In describing its defend forward component, the National Cyber Strategy must clarify a number of points:

- Defend forward is an inherently defensive strategy that seeks to defend the United States in cyberspace. However, there are offensive components at the tactical and operational levels. This is because to achieve defensive strategic objectives in cyberspace, forces and capabilities must be forward-positioned, both geographically and virtually. Such positioning is consistent with defensive strategic objectives of analogous historical strategies of forward defense.
- Defend forward is consistent with norms of acceptable behavior defined by the United States and

like-minded nations with a shared global interest in a stable cyberspace. At the same time, the National Cyber Strategy should acknowledge that norms of acceptable behavior will not emerge unless the United States is willing to act, in concert with allies whenever possible, to impose meaningful costs on bad actors in cyberspace to change their behavior.
- To induce adversaries to change their behavior, the United States must create costs below the threshold at which the full spectrum of credible retaliatory response options may be triggered. In doing so, the United States must ensure that effective policies and processes are in place to guide such actions consistent with the rule of law and adequate risk assessments.

Finally, the National Cyber Strategy should articulate a framework for how the U.S. government should put the approach into operation that is organized around six pillars: reform the U.S. government's structure and organization for cyberspace, strengthen norms and non-military tools, promote national resilience, reshape the cyber ecosystem toward greater security, operationalize cybersecurity collaboration with the private sector, and preserve and employ the military instrument of power.

Enabling Recommendations

1.1.1 Develop a Multitiered Signaling Strategy

A key objective of defend forward, as a component of layered cyber deterrence, is to create costs for adversaries in order to change their behavior, while minimizing the risks of escalation. However, the logic of defend forward (as detailed in the 2018 DoD Cyber Strategy) is missing an explicit discussion of signaling. To change adversaries' behavior, it is not sufficient to simply counter their campaigns and impose costs. Rather, the United States must signal capability and resolve, as well as communicate how it seeks to change adversary behavior and shape the strategic environment. Signaling is also essential for escalation management so that actions taken in support of defend forward are not unintentionally perceived as escalatory. Cyber operations and campaigns that are not combined with deliberate signaling, so that adversaries understand what the United States seeks to achieve, will not always be sufficient to change adversary behavior. Signaling should entail coordinated employment of various instruments of power.

Therefore, the U.S. government should develop a multitiered signaling strategy aimed at altering adversaries' decision calculus and addressing risks of escalation. This signaling strategy should also effectively communicate to allies and partners U.S. goals and intent.

- The strategic level of signaling should involve overt, public diplomatic signaling through traditional mechanisms that have already been established for other domains, as well as private diplomatic communications through mechanisms such as hotlines and other nonpublic channels (including third-party channels in instances in which the United States may lack robust diplomatic relationships).

- The operational and tactical levels should involve clandestine, protected, and covert signaling (including through non-cyber means) that is deliberately coupled with cyber operations. An example of this type of signaling is tailored messaging preceding or running concurrently with defend forward cyber operations.

A signaling strategy should also include a framework to guide when and under what conditions the U.S. government will voluntarily self-attribute cyber operations and campaigns for the purposes of signaling capability and intent to various audiences.

1.1.2 Promulgate a New Declaratory Policy

When buttressed with clear and consistent action, a declaratory policy is essential for deterrence because it can credibly convey resolve. The United States' declaratory policy regarding cyberspace now is organized around a use-of-force threshold—which is deliberately politically and legally ambiguous—and reserves the right for the United States to respond to a cyberattack in a time, place, and manner of its choosing. There are two notable challenges with the current stance.

- First, the existing declaratory policy does not sufficiently communicate resolve or articulate a compelling logic of consequences. Therefore, the U.S. government should promulgate a new declaratory policy around a use-of-force threshold. Specifically, the U.S. government should publicly convey that it will respond using swift, costly, and, where possible, transparent consequences against cyber activities that constitute what the United States defines as a use of force. This would reinforce deterrence of strategic cyberattacks.

- Second, our adversaries are clearly exploiting the current threshold to conduct a range of malicious activities that do not rise to a level warranting a major retaliatory response. Examples include cyber-enabled large-scale theft of intellectual property and cyber-enabled influence operations. Therefore, the U.S. government should announce a second declaratory policy. This policy should clearly state that the United States will respond using cyber and non-cyber capabilities to counter and impose costs against adversary cyber campaigns below a use-of-force threshold. These responses would create sufficient costs to alter the adversary's calculus, but they would be different from responses to adversary actions above the use-of-force threshold in their means (e.g., conventional vs. unconventional military capabilities) and their magnitude, consistent with international law. Essentially, the U.S. government should publicly declare that it will defend forward, and couple its declaration with decisive and consistent action across all elements of national power.

STRATEGIC OBJECTIVE #2:
STREAMLINE CONGRESSIONAL OVERSIGHT AND AUTHORITY OVER CYBERSECURITY ISSUES

Congress should establish clear oversight responsibility and authority over cyberspace within the legislative branch of the U.S. government. Responsibility for cyberspace is currently dispersed throughout Congress, and the large number of committees and subcommittees claiming some form of jurisdiction impedes action and clarity of oversight. By centralizing responsibility in the new House Permanent Select and Senate Select Committees on Cybersecurity, Congress will be empowered to provide coherent oversight to government strategy and activity in cyberspace.

Key Recommendation

1.2 Congress should create House Permanent Select and Senate Select Committees on Cybersecurity to consolidate budgetary and legislative jurisdiction over cybersecurity issues, as well as traditional oversight authority.

Currently, and in both chambers of Congress, legislative and budgetary jurisdiction and oversight for cybersecurity are dispersed across numerous committees and subcommittees. This congressional structure on cybersecurity prevents Congress from effectively providing strategic oversight of the executive branch's cybersecurity efforts or exerting its traditional oversight authority for executive action and policy in cyberspace.

Congress has previously faced a comparable challenge. When the 94th Congress (1975–77) investigated allegations of abuses of authority, illegal activity, and improprieties by members of what we now refer to as the intelligence community, Congress substantiated many of the claims and found them to have been enabled by poor congressional oversight. Congress addressed this problem by establishing the House Permanent Select and Senate Select Committees on Intelligence.[158]

To consolidate oversight and ensure the implementation of effective cybersecurity strategy and policy, the Commission recommends establishing a Permanent Select Committee on Cybersecurity in the House and a Select Committee on Cybersecurity in the Senate. These committees would have legislative jurisdiction over the broad integration of systemic cybersecurity strategy and policy both within government and between the government and the private sector. They would also have oversight responsibilities for executive branch responses to domestic and foreign cybersecurity threats, government organization or reorganization to deal with cybersecurity threats, the protection of federal networks, the confirmation of relevant Senate-confirmed cybersecurity officials, and the consolidation of federal reporting requirements for cyber initiatives and relevant data.

Membership and Structure: Like the Select Committees on Intelligence, these committees should be structured in a bipartisan manner while prioritizing expertise. Committee membership, including chair and ranking member roles, should be determined by congressional leadership as conventional committee assignments, while the chairs and ranking members of other cyber-relevant committees (as determined by congressional leadership) should also serve as ex-officio members of this committee. Also, like the Select Committees on Intelligence, these committees should have a membership structure designed to encourage cross-committee collaboration and the sharing of best practices. The final committee composition should be proportionate to each party's composition of the House, and one more seat given to the majority party in the Senate; to promote institutional knowledge, committee members should be exempt from any term limits.

Jurisdiction and Authorities: The House Permanent Select and Senate Select Committees on Cybersecurity would consider legislation, hold hearings, subpoena witnesses, and consider nominations relevant to improving the United States' public and private systemic cybersecurity against domestic and foreign risks (including state-sponsored threats); they would oversee development and implementation of national cybersecurity strategies and policies, oversight of the compliance of components of federal agencies charged with cybersecurity policy and defensive operations, the organization or reorganization of agencies related to cybersecurity threats or incidents, and authorizations for appropriations relating to protecting against cybersecurity threats and relevant incidents or actions. These committees would also receive recurring briefings on national-level risk management assessments, national-level tabletop exercises, and other federal reporting requirements for cyber initiatives and relevant data.

This jurisdiction is designed to emphasize advancing national systemic cybersecurity, strengthening the digital ecosystem, and improving whole-of-nation cybersecurity

resilience. It is not intended to include activities already overseen by the House and Senate Armed Services Committees or the two chambers' committees on intelligence (such as Title 10 or Title 50 activities, or counterintelligence activities carried out under Title 18), or to be excessively duplicative of existing executive branch oversight channels.

Enabling Recommendation

1.2.1 Reestablish the Office of Technology Assessment

Congress should reestablish and fund the Office of Technology Assessment (OTA), or another similar agency, to advise both chambers on cyber and technology policy issues. Before it was dissolved in 1995, OTA produced over 750 reports in nearly a quarter century of operations for both congressional and public consumption, ensuring that the legislative branch was fully informed on technology-related legislative issues that fell within its purview.[159] Other congressional efforts to build capacity in this area, such as charging the Government Accountability Office with responsibility for technical assessment, have not been able to satisfactorily fill the gap left by the loss of OTA. The scientific and technology challenges facing policymakers are only becoming more complex, and Congress would benefit from the agility, depth, breadth, and objectivity of insight and analysis provided by an office focused on technology.

STRATEGIC OBJECTIVE #3:

REFORM THE EXECUTIVE BRANCH TO BE MORE AGILE AND EFFECTIVE IN CYBERSPACE

The executive branch should be restructured and streamlined in order that clear responsibilities and authorities over cyberspace can be established while it is empowered to proactively develop, implement, and execute its strategy for cyberspace. Many departments and agencies, with different responsibilities for and interests in securing cyberspace, compete for resources and power, resulting in conflicting efforts sometimes carried out at cross-purposes. More consolidated accountability for harmonizing the executive branch's policies, budgets, and responsibilities in cyberspace while it implements strategic guidance from the President and Congress is needed to achieve coherence in the planning, resourcing, and employing of government cyber resources.

Key Recommendation

1.3 Congress should establish a National Cyber Director (NCD), within the Executive Office of the President, who is Senate-confirmed and supported by the Office of the National Cyber Director. The NCD would serve as the President's principal advisor for cybersecurity and associated emerging technology issues; the lead for national-level coordination for cyber strategy, policy, and defensive cyber operations; and the chief U.S. representative and spokesperson on cybersecurity issues.

The NCD would be appointed by and report directly to the President, be Senate-confirmed, and be supported by a concurrently established Office of the National Cyber Director inside the Executive Office of the President (EOP). (It thus would be positioned similarly to the Office of the U.S. Trade Representative.) The NCD nomination to the Senate would be considered by both the Armed Services and Homeland Security and Governmental Affairs Committees, until and unless a Select Committee on Cybersecurity (recommendation 1.2) is established, at which time the latter committee should assume primary jurisdiction over the NCD nomination and office.

Numerous commissions, initiatives, and studies have recommended a more robust and institutionalized national-level mechanism for coordinating cybersecurity and associated emerging technology issues, and for overseeing the executive branch's development and implementation of an integrated national cybersecurity strategy. As emerging technology- and cyberspace-related issues become more complex, and consequently a greater threat to U.S. national security, the President's need for sound advice and timely options will be increasingly critical.

The NCD would not direct or manage day-to-day cybersecurity policy or the operations of any one federal agency, but instead will be responsible for the integration of cybersecurity policy and operations across the executive branch. Specifically, the NCD would (1) be the President's principal advisor on cybersecurity and associated emerging technology issues and the lead national-level coordinator for cyber strategy and policy; (2) oversee and coordinate federal government activities to defend against adversary cyber operations inside the United States; (3) with concurrence from the National Security Advisor or the National Economic Advisor, would convene Cabinet-level or National Security

Council (NSC) Principals Committee–level meetings and associated preparatory meetings; and (4) would provide budgetary review of designated agency cybersecurity budgets.

Structure and Responsibilities: The NCD, supported by the Office of the National Cyber Director within the White House's EOP, would report directly to the President. The NCD would serve on the NSC for relevant (cybersecurity and associated emerging technology) issues. The NCD would lead the development and coordination of national-level cyber strategy, cyber policy, and defensive cyber operations, including working through the NSC process to set national-level priorities and produce the National Cyber Strategy of the United States. The NCD would also lead White House efforts to support and develop the private-public collaboration needed to defend our national critical infrastructure and provide coordination on emerging cross-cutting technology and security challenges, such as intellectual property theft, 5G infrastructure policy, and internet governance.

Authorities: The NCD would be added to the statutory list of National Security Council regular attendees. With concurrence from the National Security Advisor or the National Economic Advisor, the NCD would have the capability to convene Cabinet or NSC Principals Committee meetings and the numerous associated preparatory meetings to address cybersecurity and emerging technology issues. Further, the NCD would oversee the compliance of executive departments and agencies with national-level guidance on cybersecurity priorities, strategies, policies, and resource allocations. The NCD will coordinate interagency efforts to defend against adversary cyber operations against domestic U.S. interests; this will not impinge on DoD responsibility for Title 10 activities, Office of the Director of National Intelligence (ODNI) responsibility for Title 50 activities, or the U.S. Department of Justice (DOJ) and Federal Bureau of Investigation (FBI) responsibility for counterintelligence activities, but the NCD would be kept fully apprised of those activities.

The NCD would have budgetary oversight over the cybersecurity community, which is defined as including those areas within the executive branch whose work is critical to the success of the National Cyber Strategy. In the executive branch, each program manager, agency head, and department head with responsibilities under the National Cyber Strategy shall transmit the cyber budget request of the program, agency, or department to the NCD prior to sending it to the Office of Management and Budget (OMB). If the NCD determines that the budget proposed is not in alignment with the National Cyber Strategy, then he or she will recommend appropriate revisions. The NCD's passback revisions must be addressed in the proposed budget and submitted to OMB along with a statement describing the impact of the required budgetary changes on the ability of that program, agency, or department to perform its mission, or, if they cannot be implemented under reasonable circumstances or timelines, what obstacles must be overcome in order to do so. Any significant changes by OMB to the cybersecurity budget of any agency or department would require the concurrence of the NCD.

Resources: The Office of the National Cyber Director would be staffed at a size similar to that of comparable EOP institutions (approximately 50 persons).[160]

Key Recommendation

1.4 Congress should strengthen the Cybersecurity and Infrastructure Security Agency (CISA) in its mission to ensure national resilience of critical infrastructure, to promote a more secure cyber ecosystem, and to serve as the central civilian cybersecurity authority to support federal, state and local, and private-sector cybersecurity efforts.

Congress and successive administrations have worked diligently to establish CISA, creating a new agency that can leverage broad authorities to receive and share information, provide technical assistance to operators, and partner with stakeholders across the executive branch, state and local communities, and private sector. CISA has the mission of ensuring the security and resilience of critical infrastructure and is intended to be a keystone of national cybersecurity efforts. CISA, through partnering with the private sector and coordinating across government, is charged with securing the critical infrastructure and functions on which the American government and economy rely and ensuring a coordinated civilian response to cyber threats.

While CISA has worked aggressively to carry out these significant duties, it has not been adequately resourced or empowered to do so. The agency's convening power, though a critical tool in public-private collaboration, is not widely understood or consistently recognized. In addition, the agency lacks the analytic capacity to assess, plan for, and lead efforts to mitigate national systemic cyber risk; nor does it have the dedicated resources to extend its activities sufficiently beyond federal information technology (IT) practices to capture a nationwide perspective on cybersecurity risk and resilience. The establishment of CISA has not effectively centralized federal civilian responsibilities; rather, uncertainty and ambiguity about the roles of sector-specific agencies and other federal agencies continue. To realize policymakers' ambitions for CISA to improve the nation's cybersecurity, it must be strengthened and resourced appropriately for its growing role and status as an operational agency within DHS.

Strengthen the Director Position: Congress should give the Director of CISA a five-year term and elevate the position to level II of the Executive Schedule, or equivalent to a Deputy Secretary and to Military Service Secretaries. Congress should also consider making the posts of Assistant Director career positions to provide greater consistency and continuity.

Program and Support Resources: Congress should increase CISA's funding for administrative and programs support, so that it can enhance current operations and transition from being a headquarters element to an operational agency within DHS. Resources are particularly needed to underwrite personnel recruitment, development, and retention as well as analytic and big data processing to support current programs.

Expanded Budget: Congress should review CISA's budget and consider giving proportionally greater resources to projects and programs intended to support private-sector cybersecurity, to promote public-private integration, and to increase situational awareness of threat. Nearly 60 percent of CISA's budget is dedicated to federal cybersecurity, with only 15 percent committed to initiatives supporting the private sector. In addition, Congress should consider providing stable multiyear funding to ensure the flexibility necessary to build lasting analytical capability across multiple budget years.

Appropriate Facilities: In developing the resources and support model, the executive branch and Congress should examine current CISA facilities and assess their suitability to fully support current and projected mission requirements nationally and regionally. The General Services Administration should provide a report to Congress including recommendations for further

CISA Director Christopher Krebs and former DHS Secretary Kirstjen Nielsen hold a press conference on election security in the National Cybersecurity and Communications Integration Center (August 2018).

resources to procure or build a new facility or augment existing facilities to ensure sufficient size and accommodations for the integration of personnel from the private sector and other departments and agencies to meet the goals of this report.

Incident Management and Recovery: Congress and the U.S. government should strengthen CISA's ability to aid the public and private sectors in recovering from a significant cyber incident. The agency should be sufficiently funded and empowered to coordinate whole-of-government efforts in managing incidents that are not met with an "emergency declaration," and to seamlessly integrate with the Federal Emergency Management Agency when they are. CISA must be prepared to use new authorities and funds detailed in the "Promote National Resilience" pillar, such as the Cyber State of Distress and Cyber Response and Recovery Fund (recommendation 3.3), and ensure that they are integrated into updates of the National Cyber Incident Response Plan and a national cyber response doctrine. Further, additional resources are needed to conduct cross-agency and jurisdictional cybersecurity tabletop exercises and to support CISA's hunt and incident response team.

National Risk Management: Congress should recognize and provide sufficient resources to support CISA's emergent efforts to identify and mitigate risks to national critical functions and to serve as the primary federal entity responsible for organizing and coordinating whole-of-government, public-private activities to identify, assess, and manage national risk. As detailed in the "Promote National Resilience" pillar, Congress should codify CISA responsibilities and ensure sufficient resources for its national risk management programs, including its support to sector-specific agencies, its critical role in Continuity of the Economy planning (recommendation 3.2), and its identification of systemically important critical infrastructure (recommendation 5.1).

Cyber Defense and Security Collaboration: Congress and the U.S. government should strengthen CISA's operational capabilities by equipping it with the resources, tools, and authorities necessary to fully integrate the government's and the private sector's understanding of cyber threat into a cohesive, national picture and coordinated action. To support these efforts, further detailed below in the "Operationalize Cybersecurity Collaboration with the Private Sector" pillar, Congress should increase government support to systemically important critical infrastructure (recommendation 5.1), establish and fund a Joint Collaborative Environment (recommendation 5.2), increase integration among federal cyber centers and CISA (recommendation 5.3), and establish a Joint Cyber Planning Cell (recommendation 5.4).

Cybersecurity Advisory Committee: The Secretary of Homeland Security should establish a Cybersecurity Advisory Committee to advise, consult, and make recommendations to CISA on policies, programs, and rulemakings, among other items, to account for non-federal interests. The committee should be exempt from the requirements of the Federal Advisory Committee Act and be composed of state, local, and private-sector

representatives from across the 16 critical infrastructure sectors.[161]

Continuous Threat Hunting: Congress should strengthen CISA's ability to conduct continuous threat hunting across .gov networks, which will enhance CISA's ability to both protect federal civilian networks and provide useful threat intelligence to critical infrastructure. Continuous threat hunting on the .gov domain will enable CISA to quickly detect, identify, and mitigate threats to federal networks. Resulting information on malware, indicators of compromise, and adversary tactics, techniques, and procedures can be shared with public and private critical infrastructure, which may be similarly targeted by these actors, to bolster their defenses.

Enabling Recommendations

1.4.1 Codify and Strengthen the Cyber Threat Intelligence Integration Center

The Office of the Director of National Intelligence, through its Cyber Threat Intelligence Integration Center, plays a critical role in generating a whole-of-government understanding of significant cyber threats affecting the United States and could assist in providing analysis and coordination necessary for rapid and accurate attribution. In the 2015 Presidential Memorandum that establishes it, CTIIC is charged with acting as the primary federal integration point for all-source analysis, production, and dissemination of intelligence on significant malicious cyber activity—to inform both U.S. government and private-sector decision makers. However, CTIIC needs to be fully resourced to carry out the entire scope of its mission, including sufficient funding, manpower, and analytical resources to fully support federal departments and agencies in their operations and the intelligence products that these agencies provide to private-sector and international partners.

To ensure adequate resources, Congress should codify and establish CTIIC through legislation, using as a model the 2015 Presidential Memorandum that created the center, and strengthen CTIIC's ability to carry out its responsibilities, especially in enhancing the quality and speed of attribution.

- Congress should appropriate the resources necessary for CTIIC to carry out all mission areas enumerated in the 2015 Presidential Memorandum.
- Congress should appropriate all necessary funds to ensure that CTIIC can reliably provide reimbursement to departments and agencies for detailees.
- ODNI should continue existing efforts to improve and expand the office's cyber mission, including operational and organizational improvements to CTIIC.

1.4.2 Strengthen the FBI's Cyber Mission and the National Cyber Investigative Joint Task Force

The cyber threat presents a unique challenge—it typically involves foreign-based actors making use of domestic infrastructure to obscure their true origin before victimizing U.S. organizations and individuals. Therefore, understanding the cyber threat requires domestic intelligence gathering, evidence collection, technical and human operations, and the cooperation of victims and third-party providers to support investigative efforts.

The FBI has a unique dual responsibility: to prevent harm to national security as the nation's domestic intelligence agency and to enforce federal laws as the nation's primary federal law enforcement agency. Both roles are essential to investigating and countering the cyber threat, and are critical in supporting whole-of-government campaigns supporting layered cyber deterrence. FBI's cyber mission—synthesized through the multiagency National Cyber Investigative Joint Task Force (NCIJTF) and a nationwide network of field offices and Cyber Task Forces—has long participated in these coordinated cyber campaigns. Officially established in 2008 under National Security Presidential Directive (NSPD) 54, the NCIJTF is composed of over 20 partnering agencies

from across law enforcement, the intelligence community, and the Department of Defense to coordinate, integrate, and share information to support cyber threat investigations. Additional resources for FBI and NCIJTF, in combination with complementary recommendations to strengthen CISA and ODNI's CTIIC, will ensure that they each can support the other and carry out their respective missions.

Congress and the executive branch should take steps to ensure that the FBI is properly resourced to carry out its cyber mission, perform attribution, strengthen whole-of-government counter-threat campaigns, and enable other agencies' missions in support of national strategic objectives. Specifically:

- *Enhance investigative and analytical personnel* – FBI investigators, analysts, and computer scientists are located throughout the country to conduct the investigations and analysis necessary to attribute attacks to and impose consequences on malicious cyber actors.
- *Expand technical capability* – The FBI's responses to cyber incidents require sophisticated tools and platforms to collect and analyze essential evidence and enable investigative techniques. These technologies are used by cyber investigators throughout the field and by the FBI's elite Cyber Action Team, deployed worldwide as needed.
- *Empower interagency collaboration* – To ensure that all relevant agencies, such as U.S. Secret Service, are able to participate in the NCIJTF, additional resources are needed to adequately fund personnel-related expenses.
- *Support joint operational resources* – NCIJTF operates the 24/7 CyWatch and the CyNERGY platform for coordinating targeted entity (or victim) notifications. These capabilities must be scaled up to meet the requirements identified by CISA and other stakeholders, including sector-specific agencies.

STRATEGIC OBJECTIVE #4:

RECRUIT, DEVELOP, AND RETAIN A STRONGER FEDERAL CYBER WORKFORCE

The U.S. government should recruit, develop, and retain a cyber workforce capable of building a defensible digital ecosystem and enabling the agile, effective deployment of all tools of national power in cyberspace. Doing so will require designing innovative programs and partnerships to develop the workforce, supporting and expanding good programs where they are already in place, and connecting with a diverse pool of promising talent. Sometimes success in building a robust federal workforce depends on elements outside of the federal government. In those cases, the U.S. government can and should play a supporting role by providing its partners in workforce development the tools needed to accelerate the increase in cyber personnel.

Key Recommendation

1.5 Congress and the executive branch should pass legislation and implement policies designed to better recruit, develop, and retain cyber talent while acting to deepen and diversify the pool of candidates for cyber work in the federal government.

The challenge of achieving effective security and defense in cyberspace depends on people as much as it does on technology or policy. Today, the U.S. government suffers from a significant shortage in its cyber workforce. Across the public sector more broadly, one in three positions (more than 33,000) remains unfilled.[162] These shortages are driven by a need for personnel that have specific cybersecurity skills and experience, but they are complicated by government hiring, training, and development pathways that are not well-suited to recruit and retain those personnel.

Commit to Recruiting beyond Conventional Pathways into Government: The good news is that today's cybersecurity skills and experiences can be gained with unusual ease outside standard channels of education and training. That means, however, that the government must more effectively take advantage of those unconventional pathways, especially when they do not include typical college education or prior government experience. Overall government approaches to successfully deepen and diversify this candidate pool should include:

- Developing programs to bring in new employees via apprenticeships, promoting cooperative study, and expanding training programs so that existing workers can enhance their career trajectories.
- Researching and implementing measures of competency alongside more commonly used certifications.
- Streamlining processes and reducing institutional barriers to onboarding cyber talent quickly.
- Identifying opportunities and building hiring pathways for members of underrepresented communities, including the neurodiverse,[163] women, and people of color.

Provide Policy and Legislative Tools to Grow the Cyber Workforce: To achieve these objectives for recruiting today's cybersecurity talent into public service, the government should pursue the following:

- Congress should fund research into the current state of the cyber workforce, paths to entry, and demographics in coordination with the ongoing work at the Office of Personnel Management (OPM), DHS, the National Science Foundation (NSF), and the National Institute of Standards and Technology (NIST). This research should align with and/or build on NIST's National Initiative on Cybersecurity Education (NICE) Cybersecurity Workforce Framework, which outlines cybersecurity work roles and the knowledge, skills, abilities, and tasks involved in each role. New research should also build on emerging work from NICE and others on career paths and certifications.

- Congress should resource recruiting programs specifically designed to target cyber talent and expand current programs that have made demonstrated progress in innovating recruitment.

- Congress and the executive branch should reinforce and authorize the role of the NICE in coordinating U.S. government efforts to advance cybersecurity workforce development nationwide, and resource the office sufficiently for this role.

- Congress should require the Government Accountability Office (GAO) to issue a report within one year: (1) estimating how frequently candidates are deterred from pursuing government careers because of delays in issuing security clearances; (2) assessing the effectiveness of current clearance processes at striking a balance between the national security risk of insider threats, and the national security risk of leaving cyber jobs vacant; and (3) recommending a lead agency for developing and implementing a plan for addressing any shortcomings discovered.

Develop and Retain Cybersecurity Talent: Upon entering government, cybersecurity personnel should have rewarding career paths and the education and training opportunities necessary to keep their skills relevant and up-to-date in a rapidly changing field. To meet these objectives, Congress should:

- Fund DHS, NSF, and OPM to expand the existing CyberCorps: Scholarship for Service program. Since its inception in 2001, this proven program has graduated 3,600 students. The program should be

resourced to grow steadily and eventually reach as many as 2,000 students per year.

- Direct and fund CISA to design a process for one- to three-year exchange assignments of cyber experts from both CISA and the private sector. If successful, this model should be expanded to other agencies as well.

- Direct OPM, NICE, and DoD to design cybersecurity-specific upskilling and transition assistance programs for veterans and transitioning military service members to move into federal civilian cybersecurity jobs.

- Direct OPM to require departments and agencies to develop training for managers to cultivate practices that foster a more diverse cyber workforce and more inclusive work environment.

- Require federal cyber contractors to implement known best-practice workplace policies in order to improve employee retention on federal contracts.

- Direct OPM, in partnership with federal departments and agencies including NIST and DHS, to issue a report evaluating the potential for a new Civil Service Cyber: a system of established cyber career paths that allows movement between departments and agencies and into senior leadership positions. In order to facilitate movement between different departments and agencies, this plan should:

  o Establish greater standardization and demonstrated equivalences across the government.

  o Incorporate competence-based metrics, work-based learning programs, and—after rigorous assessment of their utility and impact—cyber aptitude tests.

  o Include standardization tools such as the NICE Cybersecurity Workforce Framework and the Cyber Talent Management System (CTMS). The new CTMS—to be launched at DHS starting in FY2020—will establish a new DHS cybersecurity service, composed of civilian employees hired using streamlined processes, new assessments, and market-sensitive compensation. If CTMS is successful at DHS, it should be considered for aggressive expansion federal government–wide.

Enabling Recommendation

1.5.1 Improve Cyber-Oriented Education

In almost every industry and discipline, future careers will require both a basic and ongoing education in cyber. It is increasingly vital that schools teach students to value cybersecurity in their own decisions and to start cultivating the skills needed for a career in the field. Accordingly, the federal government should provide resources, tools, and incentives to encourage and aid local decision makers in implementing improved cyber education in their school systems. The U.S. government should:

- Develop a secure online clearinghouse for K-12 classroom resources on cybersecurity.
- Develop work-based learning programs and apprenticeships to supplement classroom learning.

- Support cybersecurity clinics at colleges and universities to serve as educational hands-on training opportunities for students while serving as a valuable resource to their community.
- Expand the existing Centers of Academic Excellence program to encourage cyber coursework in fields such as business, law, and health care.
- Incorporate cybersecurity into safety curricula for career and technical education programs focused on operational technology users, maintainers, and installers, particularly in critical infrastructure fields.[164]
- Promote professional development programs for K-12 teachers that encourage them to model safe, secure, and privacy-aware internet practices in classrooms (outside of specific cybersecurity instruction).
- Further explore ways to expand programs such as the FBI Cyber STEM program and CISA's Cybersecurity Education Training Assistance Program on a national scale.

How Can Public-Private Partnerships Help Build the Nation's Cybersecurity Workforce?

With more than 470,000 U.S. cybersecurity job vacancies in the private sector alone,[165] simply expanding government recruitment efforts is not sufficient to provide the cybersecurity workforce needed to protect national security. Rather, the nation's cybersecurity workforce development ecosystem must grow as a whole. Currently, innovative programs are taking the first steps toward addressing this need by building partnerships between educators, government, and industry. For example:

The Cybersecurity Apprenticeship Program in North Carolina: The state of North Carolina is working with Innovative Systems Group, a local IT contracting firm, to train cybersecurity apprentices. The firm selects candidates—most of whom are veterans—and places them in an immersive training program. Afterward, the apprentices work alongside mentors at the North Carolina Department of Information Technology.[166]

Cyber Talent Initiative: The Cyber Talent Initiative, a public-private partnership between Mastercard, Microsoft, Workday, the nonprofit Partnership for Public Service, and the U.S. government, provides recent cybersecurity graduates with a job in the federal government for two years and a chance to work for the partnering private-sector companies thereafter. Those who take private-sector jobs receive $75,000 in student loan support.[167]

By drawing on different resources from across academia, industry, and government, these programs increase the pool of skilled workers available throughout the ecosystem while reducing or eliminating the cost of learning to individuals in the programs. The federal government cannot focus merely on cutting itself a bigger slice of the cybersecurity workforce pie. Rather, by using tools like these partnerships—and carefully evaluating progress—the government must support growing the whole pie of talent needed throughout the nation.

STRENGTHEN NORMS AND NON-MILITARY TOOLS

Layered cyber deterrence includes shaping the behavior of cyber actors through strengthened norms of responsible state behavior and strengthened non-military tools. Norms, which are "collective expectations for the proper behavior of actors with a given identity,"[168] already exist in cyberspace but can be bolstered by building on the United States' network of international allies and partners and their shared commitment to enforcing those expectations. Together, like-minded states with a common vision of an open, free, and stable cyberspace can better shape behavior through the attribution of malign actors and the application of the full range of government powers in a cooperative and consistent manner. Non-military tools of state power such as law enforcement, sanctions, diplomatic engagement, and capacity building are among the options for generating credible costs and benefits for norms enforcement, and they are more effective when applied in concert with international partners and allies.

While unilateral activity can provide the greatest short-term flexibility, norms-based multilateral engagement provides a more effective means to reduce the likelihood and effectiveness of cyberattacks for three reasons.

First, norms change an adversary's decision calculus. When malicious actors know that rule breaking will be confronted by a global community of allies and partners—rather than a small group of individual states—they anticipate that bad behavior is likely to be more severely punished.

Second, a system of norms enforced by multiple actors is a relatively cost-effective means of bringing greater stability to cyberspace because it reduces the burden on any one nation to reinforce the system of norms. The costs and effort associated with activities such as intelligence collection and analysis, attribution, and response actions can be shared and the activities more effectively carried out by the coalition.

Third, frameworks of norms are sticky—once a pattern of behavior is set, the framework becomes hard to dislodge. The United States and its allies would therefore benefit from being the first to establish the norms agenda.[169] These three arguments for effectiveness underscore not that a norms-based system is infallible, but rather that it is well-suited to serve as a first layer of deterrence, complemented by other layers. Accordingly, maximizing the effectiveness of norms and non-military tools of statecraft leads to a more stable and secure cyberspace.

The United States is confronted with a challenge in building a community of like-minded states. A small coalition of its closest allies offers agility and trust because the members share principles and goals. However, engagement with a large and diverse community of partners builds broader support for an open, free, and stable cyberspace. Such an inclusive approach is especially important currently because U.S. adversaries are engaging diplomatically with non-aligned states to erode this common vision for the internet.[170] The United States has begun to address the task of striking the right balance between agility and inclusivity both through the U.S. State Department's Cyber Deterrence Initiative, which is designed to bring together like-minded partners and allies to deter malicious behavior, and through other diplomatic outreach. Though this is an important start, to be truly effective the State Department's efforts in cyberspace diplomacy must be adequately supported and resourced.

Having a community of like-minded states can better strengthen norms and shape behavior through the collective imposition of non-military tools of state power, including sanctions, law enforcement, and intelligence sharing. These partners can, on a voluntary basis, add their voices to public statements and attributions, and participate in other consequences outside of the cyber domain. They may also engage in exercises to demonstrate joint capacity and preparedness to adversaries. Ultimately, a coalition can be effective in enforcing rules only if rules exist and align with the U.S. vision for an open, interoperable, reliable, and secure internet.

Preserving a secure and open internet is not just a diplomatic challenge; it is also a technical one. An internet that prioritizes the confidentiality, integrity, and availability of information for all users depends on shared implementation of secure protocols and standards. By participating in standards-setting bodies and building a reputation for making contributions to the global body of best practices, the U.S. technical community, particularly the National Institute of Standards and Technology (NIST)—together

with like-minded state and non-state contributors—can serve as a defense against adversaries who would steer the internet toward greater surveillance and fragmentation.

The recommendations supporting this pillar emphasize strengthening norms and non-military tools of state power. Creating within the U.S. Department of State the Bureau of Cyberspace Security and Emerging Technologies, led by an Assistant Secretary of State, will bring leadership and focus to this effort. Enhanced tools, including cyber capacity building, international cyber law enforcement, sanctions and trade enforcement, attribution capability, and confidence-building measures as part of the non-military component of defend forward, can be used by the United States, along with its partners and allies, to impose costs, encourage responsible state behavior, and promote a stable cyberspace.

STRATEGIC OBJECTIVE:
EXPAND EFFORTS THROUGH INTERNATIONAL ENGAGEMENT TO STRENGTHEN AND REINFORCE NORMS IN CYBERSPACE

The United States should create a broad like-minded community of allies and partners to maintain and reinforce norms that underpin a favorable cyber landscape. International norms are the framework upon which all measures for shaping behavior in cyberspace are built. Aligning this framework with U.S. interests and values is critical. Moreover, if the international community does not generally agree to or understand what the United States considers acceptable behavior, then efforts to punish bad behavior and reward responsible behavior may be ineffective or misinterpreted.

Key Recommendation

2.1 Congress should create and adequately resource, within the U.S. Department of State, the Bureau of Cyberspace Security and Emerging Technologies (CSET), led by an Assistant Secretary of State.

Expectations for behavior—norms—already exist in cyberspace, but some state and non-state actors defy them, eroding their effectiveness. The United States can reinforce these expectations by assembling a coalition

of allies and like-minded partners to collectively incentivize responsible state behavior in cyberspace and hold states accountable for bad behavior. Responses to malign behavior are more effective when carried out by multiple governments acting in concert. Building this coalition in the face of competing efforts from China and Russia takes leadership, resources, and personnel, however. To enable the U.S. State Department to form such a coalition, Congress should create the Bureau of Cyberspace Security and Emerging Technologies (CSET), led by an Assistant Secretary reporting to the Under Secretary for Political Affairs or someone of higher rank.

In addition to guiding the formation of a coalition of like-minded partners and allies, the bureau should be responsible for a range of mission sets required to implement layered cyber deterrence. These areas should include advocating for norms of responsible state behavior in cyberspace and confidence-building measures, responding diplomatically with the international community to cyber threats, advocating for internet freedom, ensuring a secure digital economy, building capacity in our partners and allies to combat cybercrime, and any other mission areas that the Secretary of State assigns to the bureau. Collectively, these elements work together as part of defending forward. CSET will not replace the overseas work of other agencies, but rather will ensure the coherence of U.S. efforts abroad and ensure the alignment of those efforts with U.S. national strategy. The head of this bureau should be Senate-confirmed and hold the rank and status of ambassador. He or she should coordinate international issues with the National Cyber Director, and both would testify before the newly formed Select Cybersecurity Committees.

Congress should provide additional funding to this new bureau for its personnel and programs needed to carry out its international cyber mission, especially the mission of building a robust coalition. The mandate for the new CSET bureau is particularly critical because like-minded partners and allies who support a rules-based international order in cyberspace expand the capacity for enforcing such rules while reducing the expense to any one government of holding bad actors accountable for violating them. The U.S. government has already begun work to build a coalition of like-minded partners and allies,[171] and these efforts should be resourced to expand

to the fullest scale possible. This coalition building is the primary focus of the Department of State's emerging Cyber Deterrence Initiative (CDI). The U.S. government should maximize the utility of this approach by strengthening existing bilateral and multilateral relationships, such as the Five Eyes (the intelligence alliance comprising Australia, Canada, New Zealand, the United Kingdom, and the United States) and NATO, and by bringing new nations into the coalition.

Partners and allies contribute to the coalition in a variety of ways. A highly capable and committed core of closely aligned allies is essential, but cultivating new partners even among less closely aligned or technically capable states remains valuable. These partners can, on a voluntary basis, add their voices to public statements and attributions, and participate in other consequences outside of the cyber domain (e.g., sanctions). They may also engage in exercises to demonstrate to adversaries the coalition's joint capacity and preparedness. Over time, the coalition could expand its focus from guaranteeing clear and credible consequences for bad behavior to preventing and constraining such behavior before it happens.

Commitments with aligned allies and partners should not preclude broader international engagement. Coordinating with the international community writ large to harmonize policies and practices is a crucial first step toward creating a rules-based order in cyberspace. Ultimately, long-term change in norms enforcement requires engagement from the larger international community—a process that starts with appropriate leadership, resources, and personnel within the Department of State.

Enabling Recommendations

2.1.1 Strengthen Norms of Responsible State Behavior in Cyberspace

The international community has agreed to cyber norms in several forums, including the United Nations. However, these norms have been unevenly implemented and enforced. Furthermore, our adversaries are using these bodies to advance alternative visions for the future of cyberspace. Smart engagement with the international community there will strengthen existing norms and ensure countries' continued alignment with the U.S. vision for a free and open future of the internet. Therefore, the U.S. government, led by CSET, should:

- *Take a sector-by-sector approach to norms implementation:* Prioritize norms against malicious cyber activity targeting elements of critical infrastructure that underpin shared global stability, such as the financial services sector, building on the existing norm against attacking critical infrastructure (CI).
- *Discuss norms at head-of-state levels:* Seek to address, where practical, cyberspace policy in venues in which heads of state participate, such as the G7 and G20.

- *Engage in both inclusive and exclusive forums:* Expand engagement in the United Nations Group of Governmental Experts on Developments in the Field of Information and Telecommunications in the Context of International Security (UN GGE) and the Open-Ended Working Group (OEWG), the Organization for Security and Co-operation in Europe (OSCE), and other forums. These organizations provide important venues in which to reinforce rules that support the U.S. vision for an open, interoperable, reliable, and secure internet.

Since 2009, the UN GGE has been a productive venue for the United States. Although the group was unable

Why Is International Engagement So Critical to Securing Cyberspace?

If the United States does not proactively advocate for an open, interoperable, reliable, and secure internet, then those with an alternative authoritarian vision will win the day in international forums, harming both U.S. national security and U.S. economic interests. Achieving layered cyber deterrence against this authoritarian vision will require a resourced and effective Department of State to coordinate diplomatic efforts and reinforce free and open cyber norms.

Unfortunately, efforts to expand authoritarian norms have already begun. The United Nations in 2018 adopted a Russian- and Chinese-supported resolution that would fundamentally change efforts against cybercrime. It could eventually lead to a fragmented internet, undermining international cybercrime investigations and allowing greater state control of cyberspace infrastructure to suppress dissent.[172] The Russian- and Chinese-supported resolution threatens to normalize actions by authoritarian governments to exert greater control over online speech, block websites critical of their rule, and coordinate with other governments to isolate, undermine, and oppress dissidents abroad.[173]

Our competitors understand what is at stake and are investing heavily in shaping the diplomatic environment for this authoritarian vision of cyberspace—all while the United States' investments in cyberspace diplomacy have lagged. After significant increases, China is now the second-largest contributor to the UN budget, and it is seeking to maximize its influence in that body.[174] Outside the UN, analysts estimate that Chinese spending on public diplomacy and propaganda outpaces the U.S. Department of State's spending by about 17 times.[175] For the first time in decades, the United States no longer leads the world in the number of diplomatic posts—China is now the most-networked great power.[176] As Russia and China work together to challenge the U.S. vision of cyberspace, China's increasing diplomatic presence puts weight behind the strategic aims of Russia's UN proposal.

Governance of cyberspace is complex, and the domain cannot be kept free and open without widespread support. Without well-resourced and persistent diplomatic efforts, the United States will be unable to effectively advocate for and defend its values in international forums, leaving our adversaries to use cyberspace diplomacy as a means to promote their authoritarian interests and cause permanent damage to cyberspace and the internet's fundamental principles.

to produce a consensus report after its 2016–17 meeting,[177] it continues to serve as a gathering point for states to establish shared understandings of acceptable behavior in cyberspace. U.S. foreign policy can draw on those understandings to build consensus around the imposition of costs—for example, by using sanctions, indictments, diplomatic signaling,[178] and other mechanisms to punish rule breaking. But while the United States has focused on like-minded states to preserve the effectiveness of the UN GGE in the face of Russian and Chinese efforts to derail progress, Russia has recently initiated the OEWG, a parallel multilateral process that engages a much broader set of actors.[179] This larger OEWG risks taking the norms conversation in a direction that may not benefit the United States in the long term. However, the OEWG simultaneously provides the United States with an opportunity to engage with states that could be persuaded to embrace a more like-minded viewpoint on norms in cyberspace. In order to bring more states into the fold, the United States should continue to enter all such forums to discuss responsible state behavior with a diverse group of nations.

In addition, the U.S. government should take a multi-stakeholder approach to strengthening norms. While the ultimate authority to establish rules for responsible state behavior should be left to states themselves, non-state actors ideally should be included in a consultative capacity whenever possible. Because entities in the private sector and other non-state actors own and operate much of the internet's infrastructure, their involvement adds potentially valuable information and technical capabilities (e.g., taking down malicious infrastructure) to strengthen norms of behavior in cyberspace.

2.1.2 Engage Actively and Effectively in Forums Setting International Information and Communications Technology Standards

The U.S. government should more actively and effectively participate in forums setting international information

Deputy Secretary of State John Sullivan hosts the Ministerial Meeting on Advancing Responsible State Behavior in Cyberspace, on the margins of the 73rd Session of the United Nations General Assembly, in New York City on September 28, 2018.

(State Department Photo/ Public Domain)

and communications technology (ICT) standards. U.S. values, interests, and security are strengthened when ICT standards are developed and set with active American participation. Yet compared to its adversaries, the United States is not participating as much or as effectively in these forums, putting it at a distinct disadvantage. U.S. adversaries are currently sending a wide range of experts who are drawing on their technical depth, negotiating capability, and commercial expertise to shape international ICT standards in their favor.

Congress should empower and sufficiently resource the National Institute of Standards and Technology (NIST)—in alignment with the complementary recommendation 4.1.2, Expand and Support the National Institute of Standards and Technology Security Work—to facilitate robust and integrated U.S. participation from the federal government, academia, professional societies, and industry in forums setting ICT standards. To participate more effectively, the U.S. government should send not only technical and standards experts but also diplomats.

Government and the private sector can work together to promote U.S. values in the face of standards that would otherwise advance authoritarian ideals. The proposed National Cyber Director (NCD) should serve as the central coordination point among U.S.-based actors contributing to standards bodies. To preserve the integrity of the standards process, each actor—public, private, academic, and so on—must represent only their own opinion, but the NCD can help align those opinions to advocate for standards that promote a free and open internet. The NCD should consider encouraging U.S. business leaders to participate and collaborate in ICT standards forums to ensure the unified promotion of the most technically secure standards in the private sector.

Contributions to standards forums can be effective and meaningful only when members trust that all are contributing technically sound proposals in good faith. The best demonstration of good faith that the United States can give is to implement at home the agreed-on international standards. Accordingly, executive branch departments and agencies should, as a matter of regular practice, seek out and whenever practicable implement internationally agreed-on standards rather than those developed domestically.

2.1.3 Improve Cyber Capacity Building and Consolidate the Funding of Cyber Foreign Assistance

The U.S. government should assist allied and partner countries and organizations to build their cyber capacities. U.S. national security is improved if the capacity of our allies and partners to prevent, manage, and recover from cyberattacks is improved. Moreover, U.S. adversaries are using U.S. partner countries as test beds for cyber operations that could be used against the United States in the future. Bolstering the capacity of these partners helps stymie adversaries seeking to test and refine cyber weapons. Capacity-building efforts should involve the Department of State as well as the United States Agency for International Development (USAID), Department of Justice (DOJ), Department of the Treasury, International Development Finance Corporation (DFC), Department of Homeland Security (DHS), and other relevant U.S. government entities.

Combating cybercrime, which is almost never an exclusively domestic issue, would particularly benefit from building cyber capacity. Cooperation between countries and agencies is critical to effectively combating the threat. The U.S. government should facilitate additional partnerships with foreign law enforcement agencies and better incorporate interagency investigative teams within the overall U.S. strategic approach. Partnerships, such as that between the U.S. Secret Service, the Dutch National High Tech Crime Unit, and the Federal Bureau of Investigation's (FBI) Five Eyes cyber task force, should be fully supported and provided with additional resources. In addition, the U.S. government should expand its training programs for foreign law enforcement partners, such as through the Department of State's International Law Enforcement Academy (ILEA). These types of training programs dramatically enhance the capabilities of indispensable partners and allow for the kind of joint investigations necessary to combat a fundamentally transnational adversary.

Congress should consolidate the Department of State's foreign assistance funding to facilitate these efforts. A new funding line in the State, Foreign Operations, and Related Programs (SFOPS) appropriations legislation should be created specifically dedicated to building cyber capacity. The creation of this line item would have no initial impact on the Department of State's budget, as funding would be reallocated from other accounts. However, Congress should also consider increasing the budget for building cyber capacity, especially to countries that are being targeted by our adversaries.

2.1.4 Improve International Tools for Law Enforcement Activities in Cyberspace

Law enforcement tools like criminal indictments and international extraditions contribute to layered cyber deterrence by signaling the difference between responsible and unacceptable behavior in cyberspace, thereby helping to reinforce norms. Law enforcement activities also provide fruitful ground on which to work with international partners and allies to hold adversaries accountable. Improving the United States' ability to support other governments' law enforcement efforts enhances the overall effectiveness of norms in cyberspace.

Improve the MLAT/MLAA Process: Mutual Legal Assistance Treaties (MLATs) and Mutual Legal Assistance Agreements (MLAAs) are tools that enable U.S. law enforcement to prosecute cybercriminals. Having a streamlined MLAT/MLAA process assists with tasks such as attribution and extradition. Stronger U.S. alliances in cyberspace and more efficient MLATs/MLAAs help reduce the number of safe havens from which malicious cyber actors can act with impunity. To make the MLAT/MLAA process more efficient, Congress should take several actions. It should provide DOJ's Office of International Affairs with administrative subpoena authority, which would expedite MLAT/MLAA processing by bypassing the need to execute hundreds of court orders to obtain basic subscriber information. In addition, Congress should provide funding to the FBI to help automate the execution of MLAT/MLAA-related search warrants. In fiscal year 2019, the FBI executed 461 communication service provider (CSP) search warrants. These warrant executions required reviewing and filtering 834 accounts and, in 95 cases, the translation of materials from a total of 28 different languages.[180]

Increase the Number of FBI Cyber ALATs: Congress should create and fund 12 additional FBI Cyber Assistant Legal Attachés (ALATs) to facilitate intelligence sharing and help coordinate joint cyber operations. There are currently 10 ALATs; increasing the total number to 22 will help meet the required demand. These technically trained agents can also assist foreign counterparts by demonstrating investigative best practices in cyber cases. ALATs' overseas position gives them unique insight into emerging threats and the tactics, techniques, and procedures of particular adversaries. Congress should also consider increasing funding for other federal law enforcement

agencies to coordinate with foreign law enforcement on cyber investigations.

2.1.5 Leverage Sanctions and Trade Enforcement Actions

The U.S. government can better punish cyber aggressors and signal U.S. intent toward potential attackers when it leverages its tools of economic statecraft as a component of a multipronged enforcement strategy. However, the efficacy of sanctions depends heavily on a number of factors, including their target and timeline, the degree of international coordination, and the path to lifting them. The European Union (EU) has already begun to bolster its commitment to using sanctions to deter and respond to cyberattacks through the 2019 EU cyber sanctions regime, which includes banning violators from traveling to the EU and freezing their assets.[181] With this framework in mind, the United States should join the international community in strengthening its dedication to using economic sanctions, when possible and appropriate, against those who conduct cyberattacks on the U.S. electoral process and infrastructure.

Congress should codify into law Executive Order 13848, "Executive Order on Imposing Certain Sanctions in the Event of Foreign Interference in a United States Election." Congress has already codified Executive Order 13694, "Blocking the Property of Certain Persons Engaging in Significant Malicious Cyber-Enabled Activities," as a part of the Countering America's Adversaries Through Sanctions Act (CAATSA).

Furthermore, in cases dealing with unfair trade practices carried out via cyber means, the Office of the United States Trade Representative should consider taking action under Section 301 of the Trade Act of 1974, and the Department of Commerce should consider using the Entity List—part of the Export Administration Regulations—to impose further requirements. Special care should be taken to ensure that designation under Section 301 is not used in response to cases unrelated to trade.

2.1.6 Improve Attribution Analysis and the Attribution-Decision Rubric

Accurate and timely attribution of a cyber incident enables U.S. leaders to make the most informed decisions to protect the country through consideration of appropriate response actions in order to enforce norms of accountability in cyberspace.

The Office of the Director of National Intelligence (ODNI), in partnership with the private sector through DHS and the FBI, should improve attribution analysis. This can be achieved by (1) standardizing ODNI's Attribution Guidelines and assessment timeline; (2) establishing an attribution analysis working group (not standing but designated), which should include key private-sector analysis and data to accelerate the federal government's response; and (3) advancing analytic capabilities by applying emerging technologies and diversifying data sources to overcome evolving technical challenges. Recommendation 1.4.1, "Codify and Strengthen the Cyber Threat Intelligence Integration Center," further supports this recommendation by strengthening the aggregation and deconfliction entity for assessing attribution.

In addition, the National Security Council and the NCD, in consultation with the ODNI, should develop an attribution-decision rubric. The purpose of the rubric is to clarify available responses that should be made based on attribution at some *minimally required* level of confidence. The NSC should appoint an entity to implement the rubric. Even when a cyber incident lacks high-confidence attribution, the rubric will enable the U.S. government to reduce vulnerabilities and take appropriate actions by matching attribution levels to deliverable non-military instruments of state power. When necessary, the U.S. government must be comfortable responding with appropriate actions (i.e., policy decisions) without requiring that a specific level of confidence be present.

2.1.7 Reinvigorate Efforts to Develop Cyber Confidence-Building Measures (CBMs)

The Department of State should reinvigorate the development and exercise of bilateral and multilateral cyber confidence-building measures (CBMs). Cyber CBMs are nonbinding, cooperative arrangements and actions that reassure allies, signal adversaries, and demonstrate intent, such as maintaining appropriate points of contact for incident response and emergency hotlines. Cyber CBMs can and should be implemented in concert with the updated National Cyber Strategy. In their current format, CBMs can be used to mitigate risks that relationships between cyber actors will become unstable, thereby helping to avoid crises. Over time, CBMs can also be used as a foundation for the future development of arms-control regimes. Moreover, CBMs can help bolster the development of norms. Recommendation 1.1.1, "Develop a Multitiered Signaling Strategy," is an example of how a CBM can be applied, by providing clarity to adversaries, partners, and allies on how the United States intends to act.

The Department of State should continue to develop and implement both regional and global cyber CBMs, together with non-state stakeholders such as private-sector entities.[182] Specifically, the Department of State should build on the CBMs enumerated in the 2015 Report of the UN GGE and Decision Document No. 1202 (2016) of the OSCE in the Field of Information and Telecommunications in the Context of International Security.[183] The U.S. government should actively implement CBMs, coordinated by the National Cyber Director, that account for the unique attributes and dynamics of the cyber domain. These CBMs can help actors share information, mitigate uncertainty, create lines of communication that can restrain unwanted escalation in emergencies and crises, and facilitate crisis management, thereby promoting stability between states.

PROMOTE NATIONAL RESILIENCE

Resilience—the capacity to withstand and quickly recover from attacks that could compel, deter, or otherwise shape U.S. behavior—is a foundational element of layered cyber deterrence, ensuring that critical functions and the full extent of U.S. power remain available in peacetime and are preserved in crisis. It denies adversaries benefits by reducing the chances that their attacks can achieve strategic objectives or have strategic consequences.[184] National security, economic security, public health and safety, and the integrity of our political system are all elements of national strength and stability that must be preserved. However, as the United States has become more technologically advanced, the systems and assets—or critical infrastructure—that support these elements of national power have come under increasing risk of cyberattack, placing their continued function in jeopardy.[185] To enhance the nation's overall resilience, this pillar focuses on three strategic objectives.

First, national resilience efforts fundamentally depend on the ability of the United States to accurately and comprehensively understand, assess, and manage risk across the critical infrastructure ecosystem.[186] To better understand risk at a national level, the United States should clarify and codify the roles played by sector-specific agencies and the Cybersecurity and Infrastructure Security Agency in working together and with the private sector to gather and assess risk information on an ongoing basis. However, addressing national risk cannot stop there. The U.S. government must also institutionalize and routinize a process to regularly build an understanding of how the risks of different sectors come together and to translate this understanding into a multiyear strategy, priorities, and a budget for U.S. government and private-sector efforts. By understanding, assessing, and managing

national risk, the United States will be in a better position to diminish both the incidences and the consequences of attempts by adversaries to erode the integrity of the elements of America's national strength.

Second, national resilience requires sufficient national capacity and preparedness to respond to and recover from attacks when they do happen, ensuring continuity of critical functions where possible and quickly restarting where not. The United States has well-established mechanisms and processes to respond to physical and natural disasters. The same rigor has not yet been applied to understanding and responding to cyber states of distress and disasters. Doing so requires planning and exercising to guarantee that the U.S. government and private sector are coordinated in response to significant and potentially catastrophic cyber incidents. It also means ensuring that the U.S. government is equipped with the requisite authorities, capabilities, and resources to meaningfully aid in response and recovery should the time come that they are required.

Third, Americans' trust in the political system, and in the democratic institutions that underpin it, remains a foundational element of national resilience. Our recent past has shown that our democratic institutions represent a soft and attractive target for malicious actors seeking to undermine the American peoples' trust in the integrity of our democracy. Building a truly resilient America in the face of growing cyber threats means ensuring that the cornerstones of our democracy are impervious to these threats. To do so, we must update the way we both approach the security of our election systems and campaigns and harden the American people against the malign influence of adversaries who wish to subvert them.

UNDERSTAND, ASSESS, AND MANAGE NATIONAL RISK

The U.S. government should build the necessary structures and processes to continuously understand, assess, and manage national-level cyber risk across the critical infrastructure ecosystem. Owners and operators of critical infrastructure are not always fully aware of the risk they inherit, the risk they own, the risk they pass on, and, more relevant to the federal government, the risk they bear for national security, economic security, and public health and safety. Creating an accurate picture of "national risk" has thus far eluded the U.S. government and the private sector working independently, and the United States should focus on strengthening the public-private mechanisms for both understanding and mitigating national risk in areas where such mitigation is most critical.

Key Recommendation

3.1 Congress should codify responsibilities and ensure sufficient resources for the Cybersecurity and Infrastructure Security Agency (CISA) and sector-specific agencies (SSAs) in the identification, assessment, and management of national and sector-specific risk.

Led by the Department of Homeland Security (DHS) and the Cybersecurity and Infrastructure Security Agency (CISA), critical infrastructure resilience and national risk management rely on a complex system of partnerships with the private sector and a number of agencies across the federal government. While empowering CISA is a critical step in building national resilience, the executive branch must also take steps to strengthen sector-specific agencies (SSAs). As defined in Presidential Policy Directive 21, SSAs manage much of the day-to-day engagement between the federal government and private-sector entities within a given critical infrastructure sector. National resilience requires that each of these agencies is able to identify, assess, and support the private sector in managing risks within the sector under its charge and to contribute to managing risks at the national level, where cross-sector risks—both physical and cyber—can be identified and controlled over time. However, there are significant imbalances and inconsistencies in both the capacity and the willingness of these agencies to manage sector-specific risks and participate in government-wide efforts. In addition, the lack of clarity and consistency concerning the responsibilities and

requirements for these agencies, both within their sectors and in their relations with CISA, continues to cause confusion, redundancy, and gaps in resilience efforts. It also confounds the efforts of Congress, or overseeing departments and agencies, to hold these agencies accountable. These features reveal significant limitations in the U.S. government's ability to comprehensively understand and mitigate national risk.

Congress should codify SSAs into law as "Sector Risk Management Agencies"; establish responsibilities and requirements for identifying, assessing, and assisting in managing risk for the critical infrastructure sectors under their purview; and appropriate the respective agency's funds necessary to carry out these responsibilities.[187] As a corresponding measure, Congress should recognize CISA's lead role in national risk management and the functions of the National Risk Management Center. This legislation should clarify roles and responsibilities between these agencies assisting in managing sector-specific risks and CISA. To alleviate the issue of inconsistent maturity, this codification should provide the resources necessary for both agencies assisting in managing sector-specific risks and CISA to implement their responsibilities for their sectors and act as mature, steadfast partners in overall national resilience efforts. The ability of the federal government to scale up its efforts and advance a deeper collaboration with the private sector on cybersecurity and resilience fundamentally depends on guiding SSAs to maturity, ensuring their consistency across sectors, and empowering them to represent their sectors and fully integrate with national risk management efforts led by CISA, with the supporting efforts of the U.S. intelligence community.

Designation of Sector Risk Management Agencies: As part of this codification, Congress should direct the U.S. government, in a process led by DHS, to review the current critical infrastructure model, propose revisions based on an updated understanding of risk, and revise the National Infrastructure Protection Plan in accordance with proposed changes. The updated model should form the basis for one or more presidential determinations that designate a primary Sector Risk Management Agency aligned with each sector. This presidential determination would act as the mechanism by which newly codified responsibilities and authorities are assigned or delegated to departments and agencies with commensurate funds to fulfill those duties.

Risk Identification and Assessment: In a process led by CISA and codified in a "National Risk Management Cycle" (recommendation 3.1.1), Sector Risk Management Agencies should have the responsibility and be empowered to identify and assess risk within their critical infrastructure sectors, both to inform their own programs and to participate in the more general work of CISA's cross-sector risk identification and assessment. Congress should ensure that the information necessary to inform this process, such as common interdependencies and vulnerabilities, is protected from public disclosure.

Intelligence Needs Identification and Assessment: In a process led by the Office of Director of National Intelligence and CISA, as suggested in recommendation 5.1.1, Sector Risk

Management Agencies should have the responsibility and be empowered to work with industry, including sector-coordinating councils, and information sharing and analysis centers to identify common intelligence gaps and areas of critical risk or vulnerability so that the intelligence community can provide actionable, focused intelligence.

Sector Risk Management Agency Audit and Scorecard: Congress should additionally direct the Office of Management and Budget, in coordination with CISA, to establish a process to evaluate the performance of each Sector Risk Management Agency in driving down the risk in its respective sector. This assessment will include, but not be limited to, how each agency implements the "Critical Infrastructure Resilience Strategy" (described in recommendation 3.1.1) and participates in activities prescribed by CISA in the National Risk Management Cycle. This assessment should include the perspective of the private sector and sector-coordinating councils, and be made available to Congress yearly. Each agency head will be responsible for providing a report on the adequacy and effectiveness of its programs and activities in fulfilling the strategy and priorities, as well as any other relevant information requested by the Directors of the Office of Management and Budget and CISA.

Cyber Incident Response, Management, and Coordination: Government agencies mounting incident response and technical assistance efforts, such as CISA, the Federal Bureau of Investigation (FBI), and, within its authority, the Department of Defense (DoD), should be required to notify Sector Risk Management Agencies when cyber incidents affect an entity within their sector, unless precluded from doing so by a legal constraint or by considerations of operational sensitivity. This process ensures that such efforts can benefit from the unique insight and expertise that Sector Risk Management Agencies provide, as well as ensure that each Sector Risk Management Agency maintains situational awareness of its sector. This requirement should be protected from public disclosure, with penalties associated with inappropriate disclosure to regulatory or non-federal entities.

Centralized Programmatic Support to Sector-Specific Agencies: Congress should, in coordination with the Office of Management and Budget and relevant departments and agencies, appropriate funds for shared-service programs to enable CISA to support Sector Risk Management Agencies. These would include shared services, common programs, and foundational tools used by Sector Risk Management Agencies and provided or managed by CISA. This approach will help enable these agencies in their mission, provide consistent private sector–focused programs and approaches across the federal government, reduce redundancy, and ensure that certain services, like information sharing, can benefit from economies of scale and best practices.

Enabling Recommendations

3.1.1 Establish a Five-Year National Risk Management Cycle Culminating in a Critical Infrastructure Resilience Strategy

Critical infrastructure resilience requires the United States to be able to develop a comprehensive understanding of national risk and to translate that understanding into resources to manage or minimize that risk over time. These activities should be cyclical, mutually supporting, and routinely exercised, so that the government gains an ever-evolving understanding of a shifting risk landscape and adjusts its programs and priorities to follow suit. While the U.S. government has made great strides at understanding national risk by concentrating on how national critical functions work and applying that understanding to its priorities and programs, significant limitations remain. The U.S. government still lacks rigorous, codified, and routinely exercised processes for identifying, assessing, and prioritizing critical infrastructure risks across the federal government and between the public and private sectors. In areas where critical infrastructure risks have been identified, risk management efforts have been further limited by annual funding of programs rather than the stable, multiyear funding necessary to fully minimize that risk over time.

To address this shortcoming, Congress should direct the executive branch to establish a five-year National Risk Management Cycle that culminates in a Critical Infrastructure Resilience Strategy. This strategy would then be implemented, and adjusted as necessary, in the following five-year cycle. Through this five-year risk management cycle, the federal government would identify and assess national risk, implement plans for managing or mitigating that risk, and update national critical functions. Specifically:

- Congress should direct the executive branch to conduct an initial two-year risk identification and assessment of critical infrastructure based on currently defined national critical functions. The results would inform the first Critical Infrastructure Resilience Strategy, to be delivered in the initial two years and every five years thereafter.

- Congress should also direct the executive branch to establish processes and procedures to establish a five-year National Risk Management Cycle, including defining procedures for identifying, assessing, and prioritizing risks and translating this understanding into strategy, budget, and programmatic priorities for relevant departments and agencies. These processes and procedures should be made in consultation with private industries, posted publicly and made available for public comment, and be adaptive and iterative to account for lessons learned from previous cycles.

- Risk identification and assessments formed in the cycle should directly inform and culminate in a Critical Infrastructure Resilience Strategy, which will set programmatic and budgetary priorities to be implemented in the following five-year National Risk Management Cycle.

- These activities should provide quantitative and qualitative data to inform the National Cybersecurity Assistance Fund (recommendation 3.1.2), Continuity of the Economy planning (recommendation 3.2), and the U.S. government's resilience and preparedness programs and should be informed, guided, and updated through regular exercises, such as the Biennial National Cyber Tabletop Exercise (recommendation 3.3.5).

3.1.2 Establish a National Cybersecurity Assistance Fund to Ensure Consistent and Timely Funding for Initiatives That Underpin National Resilience

While the Homeland Security Grant Program and resourcing for national preparedness under the Federal Emergency Management Agency (FEMA) are well-established,[188] the U.S. government has no equivalent for cybersecurity preparation or prevention. The lack of a consistent, resourced fund for investing in resilience in key areas inhibits the U.S. government from conveying its understanding of risk into strategy, planning, and action in furtherance of core objectives for the security and resilience of critical infrastructure.

To address this shortcoming, Congress should pass a law establishing a National Cybersecurity Assistance Fund for projects and programs aimed at systematically increasing the resilience of public and private entities, thereby increasing the overall resilience of the United States. Grant programs organized under this fund would be, depending on purpose, available to public or private entities.

- The fund should be used only for solutions, projects, and programs for which (1) there is a clearly defined, critical risk to be mitigated, (2) market forces do not provide sufficient private-sector incentives to mitigate the risk without government investment, and (3) there is clear federal need, role, and responsibility to mitigate the risk.
- The fund would be administered by FEMA and directed by CISA in coordination with Sector Risk Management Agencies, and would be authorized and appropriated for 10 years.
- DHS would be required to submit a yearly report updating Congress on new programs established under the fund and on the progress of existing programs.
- The fund should have sufficient flexibility to be used in instances in which timely resilience or security investment would neutralize or substantially mitigate an overriding, serious threat to national security, economic security, or public health and safety.
- Grants provided to state, local, tribal, and territorial (SLTT) entities under this fund should require 10 percent matching funds in the first year of its establishment, to be increased every subsequent year by 10 percent until 50 percent matching funds are required. Grants would require 50 percent matching funds every year thereafter to minimize moral hazard.

STRATEGIC OBJECTIVE #2:
ENSURE NATIONAL CAPACITY TO RESPOND TO AND RECOVER FROM A SIGNIFICANT CYBER INCIDENT

The United States should establish a national capacity to respond to and recover from a significant cyber event, and provide the government with the authorities necessary to ensure economic continuity and cyber resilience—in partnership with the owners and operators of public- and private-sector critical infrastructure. National resilience requires the nation to be sufficiently prepared to respond to and recover from attacks, sustain critical functions even under degraded conditions, and, in some cases, restart critical functionality after disruption—man-made or not. While the U.S. government maintains robust processes and mechanisms to respond to and recover from physical disasters or national emergencies through Continuity of Operations, Continuity of Government, and FEMA operations, there are gaps in other areas. The 2017 National Security Strategy identifies economic security as national security, but there are no comparably robust continuity mechanisms and planning efforts in place to ensure a rapid restart and recovery of the national economy in the event of a truly catastrophic disruption. In addition, the U.S. government faces both institutional and resource limitations in its ability to assist the private sector and SLTT governments in the prevention of, response to, and recovery from a significant cyber incident that falls below the level that would elicit an emergency declaration.

Key Recommendation

3.2 Congress should direct the executive branch to develop and maintain Continuity of the Economy planning in consultation with the private sector to ensure the continuous operation of critical functions of the economy in the event of a significant cyber disruption.

While Continuity of Operations and Continuity of Government have long been cornerstones of government contingency planning, no equivalent effort exists to ensure the rapid restart and recovery of the U.S. economy after a major disruption.[189] Such disruptions could include an attack on major stock exchanges, an electronic-magnetic pulse event, a regional disruption of power, or any other attack that compromises the national conveyance of goods or services. In developing and conducting Continuity of the Economy planning, the United States should focus its efforts on maintaining the continuity of national- or international-level distribution or exchange of goods and services, on which U.S. economic strength and public confidence are founded. While disruption of these regional or local mechanisms may have consequences of their own, existing resilience and recovery efforts can often account

for, respond to, and mitigate localized effects. However, disruption of upstream, national-level mechanisms in many sectors—including bulk power distribution, stock exchanges, wholesale payments, medicine, telecommunications, and trade or logistics—would have cascading effects downstream, creating further failures at regional and local levels and causing shortages that would hamper U.S. response, recovery, and mobilization efforts. Should a significant cyber event occur during wartime, military readiness and mobilization would be significantly hindered. Moreover, long-term disruptions to core economic functions would undermine the United States' international standing, credibility, and appeal in an increasingly competitive global marketplace. Creating and exercising a Continuity of the Economy plan will serve as a deterrent to adversaries by demonstrating that the United States has the wherewithal to respond and remain resilient to a significant cyberattack.

Congress should direct the executive branch to develop and maintain Continuity of the Economy planning to ensure continuous operation of critical functions of the economy in the event of a significant cyber disruption. The planning process should include the Department of Homeland Security, Department of Defense, Department of Commerce, Department of the Treasury, Department of Energy, and any other departments or agencies as determined by the President. The executive branch should report back to Congress on the status of its planning effort within one year and provide updates to Congress on a yearly basis thereafter. As part of the planning process, the executive branch should determine any additional authorities or resources that would be required to implement plans in the case of a disaster or for the establishment of programs that support and maintain department and agency planning capabilities for Continuity of the Economy efforts. In forming or updating Continuity of the Economy planning, the executive branch should draw on insights from the National Risk Management Cycle and planning should inform the Critical Infrastructure Resilience Strategy (recommendation 3.1.1).

Analyze National Critical Functions: A Continuity of the Economy plan should focus on the national-level distribution of goods and services necessary for the reliable economic functioning of the United States. Leveraging work on the national critical functions already in development, the plan should outline the key private-sector entities that constitute or are integral to these distribution mechanisms and bear primary responsibility in maintaining and operating them for sectors, regions, or the economy as a whole. These key mechanisms include, but are not limited to, the following:

- Bulk power and electric distribution systems.
- National or international financial exchanges, including wholesale payments, stocks, monetary exchanges, and payment clearing and settlement systems.
- National or international communications networks, data hosting, and cloud services.

- Interstate oil and natural gas pipelines.
- National-level trade and logistics, including maritime shipping, interstate railways, and airline cargo.

Prioritize Response and Recovery: The plan should establish a framework for rapidly restarting and recovering core functions in a crisis. Using a schema for setting priorities similar to those used for Continuity of Operations and Continuity of Government, the plan should give precedence to functions whose disruption could cause catastrophic economic loss, lead to runaway loss of public confidence, imperil human life on a national scale, or undermine response, recovery, or mobilization efforts in a crisis. The plan should also outline standard operating procedures for plan activation, execution, and implementation.

Identify Areas for Investments in Resilience: Continuity of the Economy planning should identify areas where risk of disruption is so catastrophic that establishment of secure, separate critical systems, including analog or retro systems, would be an effective use of resources. Continuity of the Economy planning should further review the feasibility of "disconnecting," or air gapping, critical services or specific industrial control networks if national security concerns overwhelm the need for internet connectivity. Finally, this work should emphasize the importance of developing plans to mitigate the consequences of successful cyberattacks.

Identify Areas for Preserving Data: Continuity of the Economy planning should identify critical segments of the economy where particular data, preserved in a protected, verified, and uncorrupted format, would be required to quickly restart the economy in the face of disruption or significant cyberattack. The United States should further explore options to store backup, protected data across borders with allies or partners, particularly in areas where economic disruption in either country could have cascading effects on the global economy.

Identify Key Materials, Goods, and Services: The executive branch should consider whether to include a list of raw materials, industrial goods, and key services whose absence would significantly undermine the ability of the United States to avoid or recover from an economic collapse and a recommendation as to whether the United States should maintain a strategic reserve of those materials, goods, and services.

Extend Credit: The executive branch should also consider mechanisms, when presented with a declaration of national emergency by the President, to ensure the extension of credit to key participants in the national economy when such credit would be necessary to avoid catastrophic economic collapse or would allow the recovery from such a collapse. Such mechanisms could include authorizing the Department of the Treasury or the Federal Open Market Committee to extend the credit of the United States to these entities for their rapid recovery.

Expand Education and Readiness of the General Public: By its very nature, Continuity of the Economy planning will prioritize the most essential functions of our country—and their locales—both to enable a rapid recovery from a devastating cyberattack and to preserve the strength and will to quickly punish the attacker. Many industries will not be included in this planning, and most citizens will not be able to rely on government assistance in the period following such an attack. But as is also true of natural disaster preparedness, the American people do not need to be helpless. DHS and other relevant agencies should expand citizen preparedness efforts and public awareness mechanisms to be ready for such an event.

Key Recommendation

3.3 Congress should codify a "Cyber State of Distress" tied to a "Cyber Response and Recovery Fund" to ensure sufficient resources and capacity to respond to significant cyber incidents.

Though FEMA mechanisms may be available to aid response to and recovery from a cyber incident that approaches the level of a natural disaster, few cyber incidents are likely to cross that threshold.[190] Current mechanisms for cyber incident response, outlined under Presidential Policy Directive 41 and detailed in the National Cyber Incident Response Plan, do not empower federal agencies with additional authority, funding, or resources to respond to or aid non-federal entities even when a "significant cyber incident" designation has been made. The absence of such empowerment remains a key check on the U.S. government's ability to ensure appropriate capacity, support, and organization in its response to cyber incidents.

To address this shortcoming, Congress should pass a law codifying a "Cyber State of Distress"—a federal declaration that would trigger the availability of additional resources through a "Cyber Response and Recovery Fund"—to assist SLTT governments and the private sector beyond what

is available through conventional technical assistance and cyber incident response programs. The declaration would be used exclusively for responding to, or preemptively preparing for, cyber incidents whose significance is above "routine" but below what would trigger an emergency declaration and for incidents that exceed or are expected to exceed the capacity of federal civilian authorities to effectively support critical infrastructure in response and recovery. The fund would be used to augment or scale up government technical assistance and incident response efforts in support of public and private critical infrastructure. A key provision is the inclusion of preemptive action and preparation, which accounts for instances when the federal government has a reasonable expectation that a significant cyber incident is likely to occur and preemptive action and preparation would reduce potential consequences of disruption or compromise.

Threshold for State of Distress Declaration: The declaration should be made in response to or in anticipation of a "significant cyber incident," or one that is (or group of related cyber incidents that together are) likely to result in demonstrable harm to the national security interests, foreign relations, or economy of the United States or to the public confidence, civil liberties, or public health and safety of the American people. Such cyber incidents could include a coordinated campaign of multiple, individual incidents occurring over time that are not significant on their own but collectively yield significant consequences. A major consideration for making this declaration should be when an incident or series of incidents exceeds the capacity of civil authorities to effectively aid the private sector and SLTT in preparation, response, or recovery.

Incident Response Coordination and Management: The declaration would invoke current authority that establishes

the Secretary of Homeland Security as principal federal official responsible for coordinating incident response, recovery, and management efforts on behalf of the entire federal government. In addition to covering response and recovery efforts, this coordination would need to account for, and protect, law enforcement interests, including the preservation of forensic data necessary to attribute the attack and enable subsequent investigations by law enforcement agencies. This coordination role should not supersede other existing department and agency authorities or direct law enforcement activity.

Disbursement of a Cyber Response and Recovery Fund: Congress should establish and appropriate funds to maintain a Cyber Response and Recovery Fund, administered by FEMA and directed by CISA. Disbursement would be

Is Our Water Supply (Cyber) Secure?

Every American, every day, depends on a supply of clean water. Yet most Americans would be surprised to learn that even though water is critical in our daily lives, and even though our water supply is known to be a target for malign actors, water utilities remain largely ill-prepared to defend their networks from cyber-enabled disruption.[191]

The U.S. water supply is operated by nearly 70,000 utilities[192] that are turning to digital networks to manage real-world physical processes critical to water treatment and distribution—but these utilities are approaching this transition with dramatic variations in capacity and sophistication. Like our electoral system, this distributed network can provide a measure of resilience. Also like our electoral system, it can limit the effectiveness of federal action and slow the deployment of best practices or the responsible incorporation of secure technologies. Gaps in utilities' network configurations, insecure remote access systems, and outdated training regimes are just a few of the vectors through which Americans' water infrastructure is vulnerable to cyber-enabled exploitation.[193] Malign actors have already attempted to breach water infrastructure systems, and they could eventually exploit these vulnerabilities to disrupt or contaminate the American water supply.[194]

Compounding these problems, municipal utilities often lack the resources or capacity to address these weaknesses. In partnership with the Department of Homeland Security, federal sector-specific agencies (SSAs) and state and local governments are currently responsible for managing and securing American utilities. For water, the Environmental Protection Agency (EPA) is the principal federal agency responsible for cyber risk management.[195] In practice, however, SSA responsibilities are unclear, and that uncertainty contributes to insufficient coordination between the EPA and other stakeholders in water utilities' security, as well as to cybersecurity funding requests that lack the resources and buy-in necessary for success.

These shortcomings imperil the cybersecurity that is vital to the water infrastructure, which in turn is vital to our lives. Codifying SSA responsibilities, ensuring that SSAs such as the EPA conduct their risk management assignments effectively, and better enabling state and local governments are all critical steps toward improving the capacity of water utilities to prevent and mitigate the growing threats they face from cyberspace.

triggered when a Cyber State of Distress is declared. The funds would not be used for direct financial assistance to affected entities but to increase, scale up, or augment the capabilities of federal civil authorities to provide technical assistance and incident response. This would include enabling standby contracts with private-sector cybersecurity services or incident responders and funding DoD personnel operating under Defense Support to Civil Authorities.

Enabling Recommendations

3.3.1 Designate Responsibilities for Cybersecurity Services under the Defense Production Act

The Defense Production Act provides the U.S. government with expansive authorities to prioritize resources in the event of a natural or man-made disaster, military conflict, or act of terrorism within the United States. However, the most recent executive order pertaining to the act, Executive Order 13603, neither accounts for nor designates responsibilities for "cybersecurity services," including private-sector incident response. These authorities can be better leveraged to provide a more optimal allocation of resources to ensure sufficient capacity for protection against, response to, and recovery from a significant cyber incident. This would empower the United States to better understand and allocate resources for private-sector reserve capacity and procure standby contracts that could be triggered by a significant cyber incident or by an incident that exceeds the federal government's capacity to respond.

To take full advantage of the Defense Production Act for cybersecurity issues, the President should issue or amend an executive order that prioritizes and designates responsibility for "cybersecurity services." This would enhance the U.S. government's ability to rapidly mobilize the private sector in response to a significant cyber incident. This order should ensure that the U.S. government makes all necessary preparations to understand and address gaps in private-sector incident response capacity and prioritization in assisting critical infrastructure in responding to and recovering from a significant cyber incident.

- The executive order should designate DHS as the lead agency to identify cybersecurity-related services that are essential to national security and assess the capacity of these services to support national security needs.
- Under Title VII of the Defense Production Act, the U.S. government should convene the cybersecurity incident response industry to understand the full capacity of their services in steady-state as compared to the capacity that would be required for significant cyber incidents and catastrophic scenarios that have real-world consequences.
- Using this information, the U.S. government can procure standby contracts with cybersecurity incident responders under Title III of the Defense Production Act, which would be triggered for additional assistance in cyber response and recovery efforts in response to a significant or catastrophic cyber incident.

3.3.2 Clarify Liability for Federally Directed Mitigation, Response, and Recovery Efforts

If the United States were to suffer a significant cyber incident, the federal government would undoubtedly require the assistance of private-sector partners in response and recovery. Existing laws to facilitate these activities, such as the Defense Production Act and Federal Power Act, are limited in their ability to provide reliable liability protections for private-sector entities or public utilities that take action, or refrain from taking action, at the direction of the federal government. Because of this lack of protection, private-sector entities or public utilities fearing legal liability and lawsuits may be reluctant to cooperate with the government.

To address this concern, Congress should pass a law specifying that entities taking, or refraining from taking, action at the duly authorized direction of any agency head, or any other federal official authorized by law, should be insulated from legal liability. Covered actions should include any request or order by relevant federal agencies issued to protect against or respond to an emergency or threat relating to a cybersecurity incident impacting national security.

3.3.3 Improve and Expand Planning Capacity and Readiness for Cyber Incident Response and Recovery Efforts

Prior planning is critical for government readiness in responding to and recovering from a significant cyber event. Congress should increase planning capacity within DHS to enable the preparation, review, and updating of key planning documents, standard operating procedures, standby contracts, and nondisclosure agreements necessary for putting into operation plans for cyber incident response and recovery. This planning should allow for immediate execution of response plans and mechanisms during a crisis; take into account national, regional, and SLTT implications; and incorporate and empower Cyber State of Distress declarations, the Cyber Response and Recovery Fund (recommendation 3.3), and Continuity of the Economy planning (recommendation 3.2). Planning should encompass entities that are critical to response and recovery efforts (e.g., private-sector entities, sector-specific agencies, SLTT governments, and international partners).[196] These planning efforts should also include the following steps:

- The federal government should revise the National Cyber Incident Response Plan (NCIRP)—the plan that details how federal, SLTT, and private entities should respond to and recover from significant cyber incidents impacting critical infrastructure[197]—by adding scenario-specific and sector-specific annexes drafted together with sector-specific agencies and Sector Coordinating Councils.
- The annexes of the NCIRP should account for options to mobilize additional resources to augment the government's response, including private-sector incident responders, the DoD under Defense Support to Civil Authorities, the National Guard, and other SLTT assets.
- Planning efforts should be integrated and interoperable with existing emergency response and disaster recovery mechanisms and programs operated by federal and SLTT entities.

3.3.4 Expand Coordinated Cyber Exercises, Gaming, and Simulation

Preparedness planning leads to defined response mechanisms, public awareness, and improved response. In practice, however, plans can be rendered ineffective by unforeseen challenges and limitations.[198] Exercises build understanding of how complex systems will react in a time of disruption or crisis, building cohesion among disparate entities coordinating the response and promoting unity of effort that can translate to seamless integration when an incident does occur.

Congress should support and fund FEMA and CISA in implementing expanded and coordinated cross-sector cyber exercises, gaming, and simulation, as well as sector-specific agencies in smaller, sector-specific exercises. The existing cohort of exercises, including GridEx,[199] Hamilton,[200] and Cyber Storm,[201] cover a portion of what is necessary for overall national cybersecurity, but they should be enhanced and expanded to include joint exercises among the private sector, the federal government, SLTT entities, and, when and where possible, international partners. These exercises should also be used as the primary mechanism by which the U.S. government exercises Continuity of the Economy planning. Such exercises should also emphasize the importance of ensuring resilient communications among key stakeholders and continuous engagement with the general public.

3.3.5 Establish a Biennial National Cyber Tabletop Exercise

Exercises that account for and incorporate all elements of national power are critical both in demonstrating and ensuring the United States' ability to respond to and recover from cyber disruption and in reducing adversaries' confidence that attacks are able to achieve strategic objectives and shape U.S. behavior. While various departments and agencies in the U.S. government regularly conduct exercises on cyber incident response, the United States lacks a persistent senior-level exercise that incorporates the whole-of-government and whole-of-nation approach necessary for effective response and recovery.

Congress therefore should direct the U.S. government to plan and execute on a biennial basis a national-level cyber table-top exercise that involves senior leaders from the executive branch, Congress, state governments, and the private sector, as well as international partners, where appropriate.

- This "National Cyber Tabletop Exercise" should be organized and led by the National Cyber Director (recommendation 1.3) with the support of the DHS, FBI, and DoD, in coordination with sector-specific agencies, state governments, and private-sector partners.
- The exercise should be used as an opportunity to operationalize, troubleshoot, and inform preparedness programs such as Continuity of the Economy planning and to test the effectiveness of response and recovery measures such as the Cyber State of Distress and the Cyber Response and Recovery Fund.
- The exercise should also be used as an opportunity to improve, inform, and guide resilience measures, such as the National Cybersecurity Assistance Fund (recommendation 3.1.2) and other efforts that fall within the National Risk Management Cycle and the National Critical Infrastructure Resilience Strategy (recommendation 3.1.1).

3.3.6 Clarify the Cyber Capabilities and Strengthen the Interoperability of the National Guard

States have increasingly relied on National Guard units under state active duty and Title 32 of the U.S. Code to prepare for, respond to, and recover from cybersecurity incidents that overwhelm state and local assets.[202] While Title 32 has been interpreted to allow for these activities, Department of Defense guidelines leave ambiguities

Army National Guard personnel analyze network traffic during a Cyber Shield 19 training week class at Camp Atterbury, Ind. April 7, 2019. As the nation's largest unclassified cyber defense training exercise, Cyber Shield provides participants with training on industry network infrastructure and cyber protection best practices.

(U.S. Army National Guard / Photo by Staff Sgt. George Davis)

about what activities the National Guard can conduct and be reimbursed for with federal funding.[203] In addition, it is unclear how state cyber incident response forces, including the National Guard in state active-duty status, would integrate with federal personnel and processes when responding to a significant cyber incident, and current federal cyber incident response planning does not sufficiently account for or integrate the role of the National Guard.

- Congress should direct DoD to update existing policies to consider National Guard activities that could be performed and reimbursed under Title 32 of the U.S. Code.[204]
- The National Guard Bureau should promulgate guidance to its constituent cyber units on CISA's and the FBI's cyber roles and responsibilities, the agencies' local presence and capabilities, ways to collaborate during times of stability (e.g., through local multiagency task forces and information-sharing groups), and incident response planning and exercises.

- The Department of Homeland Security should more regularly integrate state cyber incident response forces, including the National Guard in state active-duty status, as part of response and recovery planning and exercises and should define mechanisms to ensure interoperability at times of crisis.

- The role of the National Guard should be assessed and where appropriate incorporated into DHS and executive branch cyber response planning efforts, including the update to the National Cyber Incident Response Plan and annexes.

STRATEGIC OBJECTIVE #3:
ENSURE THE SECURITY OF OUR ELECTIONS AND RESILIENCE OF OUR DEMOCRACY

The U.S. government should ensure the security of our elections and resilience of our democracy. Americans' trust and confidence in their democratic system remain foundational elements of national resilience—and an attractive target for malicious actors. The network of institutions, tools, and personnel that compose our electoral system depend on connectivity and data, introducing new vectors to disrupt the U.S. political system, including at and beyond the ballot box. The federal institutions charged with protecting our electoral process require organizational reform, enduring funding streams, and modern mandates to ensure that states and other partners in our political system, including political parties and campaigns, can improve and maintain their cybersecurity capacity—and ensure that our electoral systems retain a verifiable, auditable paper trail and paper-based balloting backbone. Going beyond elections, the U.S. government must also seek to better understand and counter broader cyber threats targeting our democratic institutions.

Key Recommendation

3.4 Congress should improve the structure and enhance funding of the Election Assistance Commission (EAC), enabling it to increase its operational capacity to support states and localities in defense of the digital infrastructure underpinning federal elections—including ensuring the widest possible employment of voter-verifiable, auditable, paper-based voting systems.

Trust is the lifeblood of American democracy. The American people depend on government institutions, infrastructure, tools, and personnel to provide a fair, open, and safe electoral system in which every vote counts and election results reflect the will of the American voter. The election system's increasing reliance on digital connectivity and data makes it vulnerable to cyberattacks and cyber-enabled information operations such as those seen in 2016 and 2018 and likely already under way in 2020.[205]

Defending against attempts to undermine the American people's trust in their democracy requires improving institutional capacity at the federal, state, local, tribal, and territorial levels and ensuring that our elections utilize a voter-verifiable, auditable, paper-based voting system. States need assistance in the form of enduring, targeted funding to secure and maintain their election infrastructure, and the federal institutions administering such assistance require additional funds and structural reform to do so at the scale and speed of the threat. Election officials should also be resourced with the tools and expertise to develop and rehearse plans for Election Day contingencies, including postponements and recounts. Such contingency plans should be developed in consultation with federal cybersecurity experts from CISA and should include clear criteria established well in advance.

Enhance Support to the Election Assistance Commission to Carry Out Its Mission: The EAC suffers from chronic funding shortages and requires a more robust staff to better execute its responsibilities for improving SLTT election cybersecurity capacity. Further, the EAC commissioners require more technical expertise to enact urgent reforms to protect the integrity of voting systems against malicious cyber activity. By increasing the EAC's capacity and adding a limited but crucial "cybersecurity vote," policymakers will ensure that evolving threats to the integrity of our electoral process are better understood and prioritized. Specifically:

- Congress should amend the Help America Vote Act to create a fifth nonpartisan commissioner with an established cybersecurity background in order to vote exclusively on issues of or relating to cybersecurity.
- Congress should increase the EAC's annual operating budget to enable the hiring of new staff to improve the performance of core responsibilities.
- The EAC should finalize and release its long-delayed update to the Voluntary Voting System Guidelines and increase the breadth and frequency of its recommendations and guidance concerning voting systems and processes.

Streamline and Modernize Sustained Grant Funding for States to Improve Election Systems: While Congress has appropriated funds to improve SLTT election systems, the episodic nature of such funding has prevented states from making plans that rely on it. Congressional grant funding for election security should occur predictably and regularly, and the EAC should disburse those funds and monitor their expenditure. At a minimum, grant funds should be used to ensure that states implement voter-verifiable and paper-based voting systems, as well as post-election audits. Funds should also be used to ensure that election administrators

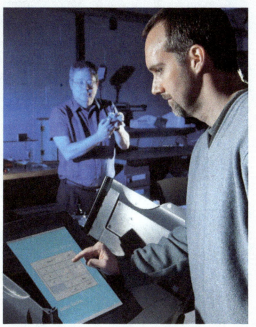

(U.S. Department of Energy)

The Vulnerability Assessment Team at Argonne National Laboratory tests an electronic voting machine for security.

have sufficient provisional ballots for their eligible voting populations to reduce or eliminate the effect of interference with the voter registration rolls. The federal government has a responsibility to resource its requirements, but states must also share in their financial ownership of election administration. Specifically, the U.S. government should:

- Appropriate election security grants sufficient to enable state, local, tribal, and territorial governments to implement voter-verifiable, auditable voting systems, including by replacing outdated voting equipment, building local capacity, and adopting a paper-based backbone.
- Sustain an annual grant appropriation to provide for sufficient provisional ballots, the implementation of post-election audits, and the ongoing maintenance of systems into the future.

- Require states to match federal election grant funds at a 70–30 percent federal-state split and engage in long-term planning for their election infrastructure upgrades, including best practices recommended by organizations like the Center for Internet Security.

Enabling Recommendation

3.4.1 Modernize Campaign Regulations to Promote Cybersecurity

Nation-state adversaries have repeatedly attempted to hack U.S. political campaigns for the dual purposes of gathering intelligence and sowing political discord through the selective disclosure of otherwise private, campaign-specific information.[206] Campaign organizations need more resources to protect themselves, but federal campaign finance law (1) limits the financial support that

national political parties can provide to campaigns, and (2) broadly prohibits corporate contributions to campaigns. While these limitations have been imposed for good reasons and should remain in place, an unintended consequence is that they have functionally limited the cybersecurity support available to campaigns.

In the past few years, the Federal Election Commission has issued several advisory opinions authorizing certain corporations to provide cybersecurity assistance to campaigns. These opinions are narrowly tailored, however, and fail to provide sufficient assurance that similar (or expanded) requests will be approved in the future. By contrast, a statutory amendment would provide much-needed clarity and flexibility regarding this vital issue. Congress therefore should amend the Federal Election

What Is a Malign Influence Campaign?

On May 21, 2016, two groups of demonstrators encountered one another outside an Islamic center in Houston, Texas. One group was attending a gathering called "Stop Islamification [sic] of Texas," while the other had shown up for a "Save Islamic Knowledge" event. Verbal insults and physical confrontations ensued.[207]

Both groups had been drawn to the Islamic center by two sets of social media advertisements purchased for $200 by a Russian information operations cell or "troll farm" called the Internet Research Agency (IRA).[208] During the 2016 election cycle more than 3,000 different advertisements purchased by the IRA made their way into the social media feeds of everyday Americans.[209] These citizens were microtargeted with the same methods used by mainstream consumer advertisers.[210]

The modern digital economy is built on a model of directing consumers to tailored advertisements after observing their behavior. Disturbingly, our adversaries use the very same approach against us and even do so legally. A growing sector of Russian "Manipulation Service Providers" like the IRA create fake accounts on popular social media websites to influence online discourse. These fake accounts can drive the comments, clicks, likes, and shares that social media algorithms interpret as popularity.[211] Other authoritarians are learning from Russia's example; China is rapidly honing its own efforts to influence democratic societies, most brazenly during Taiwan's recent election cycles.[212]

Combating this kind of disinformation will require coordination between the public and private sectors to identify and shut down fake accounts, but the threat will continue to far exceed our capacity to respond. A sustainable solution will require equipping Americans with the media and digital literacy necessary to recognize untrustworthy online content. Such a resilient public—one that understands the value of democracy, the role of its institutions, and the ways in which individuals can help hold those institutions accountable—will find it easier to resist disguised pernicious disinformation intended to undermine trust and lead to disengagement.

Cyberspace Solarium Commission

Campaign Act of 1971 (FECA) to allow corporations to provide free and reduced-cost cybersecurity assistance to political campaigns, so long as such assistance is offered on a nonpartisan basis as assessed by neutral and objective criteria.[213]

Key Recommendation

3.5 The U.S. government should promote digital literacy, civics education, and public awareness to build societal resilience to foreign malign cyber-enabled information operations.

Like American democracy, a safe and secure cyberspace environment depends on the trust and educated stakeholdership of its users. While service providers and product manufacturers are working to develop security frameworks that do not overburden end users, individual Americans are still the most important guarantors of their individual and collective cybersecurity. A third of all breaches still stem from a malign actor's success in persuading individuals to open phishing emails, one of the simplest forms of social engineering.[214]

Similarly, cyber-enabled information operations are increasingly taking their assaults on trust beyond cyberspace and into our broader society. Therefore, we should respond beyond cyberspace, because "[t]he defense of democracy in an age of cyber information war cannot rely on technology alone."[215] Americans must become better equipped to recognize such operations, so that they can mitigate their damage. These information operations endanger our national security by threatening to undermine trust and confidence in American democracy and its institutions—including but also extending beyond our elections.[216] Such operations have previously taken the form of hack-and-release attacks and disinformation campaigns on social media and other outlets.[217] These campaigns seek to convince Americans that their democracy is irrevocably broken, leading them to conflict out of anger or to disengagement out of despair.[218] Improving digital literacy is one way to counter these threats, but alone it is insufficient. Because the intent of so many cyber-enabled information operations is to cause Americans to distrust or lose faith in democracy and its

institutions, digital literacy should be coupled with civics education explaining what democracy is, how individuals can hold their leadership accountable, and why democracy must be nurtured and protected.

For these reasons, the U.S. government must ensure that individual Americans have both the digital literacy tools and the civics education they need to secure their networks *and* their democracy from cyber-enabled information operations.

Promote Digital Literacy and Modernize Civic Education: By promoting modern civics education and digital literacy programs, the U.S. government can assist in enhancing the average American's ability to discern the trustworthiness of online content, and thereby reduce the impact of malicious foreign cyber-enabled information campaigns, without running afoul of concerns about regulating speech. Congress should enable the Department of Education by authorizing a grant program funding nongovernmental organizations (NGOs), private-sector entities, and SLTT education agencies both to study how best to improve digital citizenship and to incorporate effective digital literacy curricula in American classrooms at the K-12 level and beyond. This program should run in tandem with DHS programs and with the collaboration of subject matter experts to develop content on cyber-enabled information operations and other topics of which citizens should be aware. Such curricula should incorporate critical thinking and problem-solving skills, information on implicit vs. explicit messaging, and technology concepts.

Evaluate and Strengthen Efforts to Raise Public Awareness of Cyber Threats: Congress should (1) direct the Government Accountability Office (GAO) to evaluate the effectiveness of government spending on cybersecurity awareness efforts, including the "Stop. Think. Connect." campaign, and (2) authorize and fund DHS, in coordination with the National Institute of Standards and Technology (NIST) and the National Science Foundation (NSF), to establish a grant program seeking research and proposals for effective mechanisms to improve, develop, and implement a public awareness and education initiative on cybersecurity. Successful grantees should prioritize:

- Actionable, consistent public messaging on cybersecurity threats and responses with very specific desired outcomes.
- Wide propagation of cybersecurity warnings among information technology (IT) professionals.
- Modern, vetted, and continually updated "train-the-trainer" resources for academic institutions, trade schools, and other organizations seeking to provide cybersecurity education to the public.
- Demonstrably effective methods for bringing specific and actionable cyber threat information to the attention of the general public.

Enabling Recommendation

3.5.1 Reform Online Political Advertising to Defend against Foreign Influence in Elections

Although foreign nationals are banned from contributing to U.S. political campaigns, they are still allowed to purchase U.S. political advertisements online, making the internet a fertile environment for conducting a malign influence campaign to undermine American elections. In advance of the 2016 U.S. federal elections, Russia launched just such a campaign and purchased thousands of online political ads targeting U.S. elections.[219] That action was and still is possible because the FECA, which establishes rules for transparency in television, radio, and print media political advertising, has not been amended to extend the same political advertising requirements to internet platforms. Applying these standards across all media of communication would, among other things, increase transparency of funding for political advertisements, which would in turn strengthen regulators' ability to reduce improper foreign influence in our elections. There are pending legislative proposals on this critical issue, and Congress should seek to find a consensus.

Multi-factor Authentication

According to the SANS Institute, single-factor authentication (e.g., passwords) is a major threat vector that malicious actors exploit to breach seemingly secure systems. One of the best methods to prevent these types of attacks is multi-factor authentication, or a system that requires a password and an additional method, such as a text or an "authenticator" application, for users to authenticate their identity when logging into a system. Researchers at Google found that even the most basic multi-factor verification methods prevent 96 percent of bulk phishing attacks and more than three-quarters of targeted attacks.[220] Both consumers and businesses should take full advantage of multi-factor authentication to protect their networks, their accounts, and their information.

RESHAPE THE CYBER ECOSYSTEM TOWARD GREATER SECURITY

Denying adversaries benefits is crucial for successful layered cyber deterrence. Whereas building resilience denies adversaries benefits by managing the consequences of attacks, reshaping the cyber ecosystem toward greater security drives down cyber vulnerability at national scale, lowering the likelihood of successful attacks in the first place. In cyber conflict, the cyber ecosystem is the battlefield. Unlike more conventional battlefields, the cyber ecosystem is entirely human-made and therefore can be manipulated in ways other domains may not be. This feature provides a unique opportunity for the United States to shape its cyber ecosystem in ways that make it more difficult for adversaries to achieve their goals and that deny them the benefits of their operations. Today, the cyber ecosystem is more than the technology—information, network, and operational technology—that constitutes the internet. The ecosystem is also the people, processes, and organizations that plug into the technology and the data they combine to produce. This ecosystem has increased the speed of our communications as well as efficiency, functionality, and growth in the economy. But while it is central to the functioning of the nation, it has also introduced significant challenges—causing vulnerability across the United States. Adversaries leverage vulnerabilities in this ecosystem and its expansive reach into our society to gain an asymmetric advantage, developing capabilities to hold our critical infrastructure at risk, disrupt our elections, and spy on and target the American people.

This pillar attempts to drive down vulnerability across the ecosystem by shifting the burden of security away from end users to owners and operators, developers, and manufacturers who can more effectively implement security solutions at the appropriate scale. In some cases, scaling up security means aligning market forces. Where those market forces either are not present or do not adequately address risk, the U.S. government must explore executive action, investment, legislation, and regulation. Specifically, this pillar focuses on five strategic objectives.

First, this pillar seeks to promote the creation of more secure technology—both by incentivizing product manufacturers to scrap a "first to market" mentality in favor of a "secure to market" approach and by ensuring that they have access to trusted suppliers. Technology companies are under intense market pressure to prioritize "first to market" over security, thereby passing on risk to companies and individuals. The aggregated vulnerability assumed by these companies and individuals has created a significant national concern: rampant insecurity that passes costs of billions of dollars to downstream consumers and that has the potential both to disrupt our day-to-day life and to undermine public confidence in and the effectiveness of key institutions.

Second, this pillar endeavors to change behavior, encouraging more secure practices by users and organizations. Standards bodies and regulators in key sectors have developed numerous standards and best practices for organizations' behavior. However, with some notable exceptions, commitment to these standards and practices is largely voluntary. Incentivizing better practices—including those that would shape or offset the behavior of individual employees—means both crafting financial incentives for better behavior, through a vibrant insurance market, and holding bad behavior to account.

Third, this pillar seeks to better leverage large-scale information and communications technology enablers—both by empowering companies that can deploy security across the ecosystem and by encouraging them to deploy it. While the U.S. government's ability to directly influence the ecosystem is limited, companies that provide services and infrastructure essential to the functioning of the internet could have outsized impact on its security. For these entities, some forms of security—what is required to ensure that the services they provide are always available—are already incentivized. The financial benefit of other aspects of security—ensuring the integrity and confidentiality of the data they hold and the networks they administer—is often less obvious, but no less important for managing national vulnerability.

Fourth, as technology supply chains have become more complex and global, the United States has grown more dependent on suppliers susceptible to malign influence, a possibility that creates new vectors to introduce vulnerabilities into the ecosystem. In shaping its cyber ecosystem, the United States must identify industries and technologies critical to national and economic security and take steps to reduce vulnerability at a macroeconomic level (e.g., industrial strategy and market exclusions) and at a microeconomic level (e.g., supply chain risk management).

Fifth, this pillar attempts to build better data security at the systemic level. New industries are being created that rely on the concentration and analysis of private data, but they are emerging in an ecosystem with few norms and complex, and at times even conflicting, laws governing the appropriate use and security of that data. At the same time, breaches of private data offer malicious actors a treasure trove of information. The information stolen from American entrepreneurs, public officials, industry leaders, everyday citizens, and even clandestine operatives is fueling social engineering and espionage campaigns against U.S. firms and agencies. This entanglement of private data security and national security reveals the need for legal and technical norms to protect the information of individuals and firms, minimize the likelihood of their loss or manipulation, and make the "big data" economy safe for everyday Americans.

STRATEGIC OBJECTIVE #1:
INCENTIVIZE GREATER SECURITY IN THE MARKETS FOR TECHNOLOGY

The U.S. government should incentivize the creation of more secure technology. Currently, technology companies are under intense market pressure to prioritize being "first to market" over security, an approach that in turn passes risk on to other companies and individuals.[221] Moving the markets for technologies toward greater security requires delineating clearer expectations and standards for what constitutes secure technology development and maintenance, presenting that information to consumers in an accessible form to help them make informed decisions, and incentivizing suppliers to build security into the development lifecycle of the products they sell.

Key Recommendation

4.1 Congress should establish and fund a National Cybersecurity Certification and Labeling Authority empowered to establish and manage a program for voluntary security certifications and labeling of information and communications technology products.

While agreed-on security standards and best practices are useful in reducing vulnerability in information technology products, they can be employed more effectively to move product developers to use security as a product differentiator. Without accessible and transparent mechanisms, such as certifications (e.g., Energy Star, Underwriters

Laboratory, or Certified Organic products) and labels (e.g., nutrition labels), to compare security between products, critical infrastructure owners and operators cannot easily price security into their purchasing decisions.[222] The lack of differentiation leads to a lack of demand for more secure products; as a result, product developers have little market incentive to make established security standards or security best practices a primary consideration in designing, testing, and developing their products. Short of regulation, the U.S. government is institutionally and legally limited in its ability to attest and certify that products adhere to security standards, and third-party efforts to fill this gap lack sufficient scale, funding, and maturity to enact meaningful change in the marketplace.[223]

To address this gap, Congress should pass a law directing the Department of Commerce, in coordination with the Department of Homeland Security (DHS) and the Department of Defense (DoD), to hold a competitive bid for a nonprofit, nongovernmental organization to be designated and funded as the National Cybersecurity Certification and Labeling Authority. This organization would be charged with establishing and managing a voluntary cybersecurity certification and labeling program for information and communication technologies.[224] This designation should last five years and carry with it sufficient funding for its operational costs and the programmatic activities necessary to carry out its mission. The National Cybersecurity Certification and Labeling Authority should be overseen by a committee chaired by the Department of Commerce and DHS, with membership from DoD, the Department of Energy, and the Federal Trade Commission (FTC). The law should also empower the FTC to set and levy fines if it is found that companies are falsely attesting to a standard for certification, are intentionally mislabeling products, or have failed to maintain the standard to which they have attested.

In order to keep pace with rapidly changing technology and good practices in secure technology development, the National Cybersecurity Certification and Labeling Authority must be supported by empirical efforts both to test products and to continually identify good practices in secure product development. Any certification and labeling work should build on existing endeavors in and outside of government, including such efforts as the Critical Technology Security Centers (recommendation 4.1.1), the Cyber Independent Testing Laboratory, the Digital Standard, and the Software Bills of Material work at the National Telecommunications and Information Administration (NTIA).[225]

Product Certification and Attestation: The National Cybersecurity Certification and Labeling Authority should be established and empowered to publicly certify products that vendors have attested meet and comply with secure product development best practices and other cybersecurity standards identified by the authority. Issued certifications should be publicly accessible and manufacturers should be encouraged to display certification marks on product packaging. For industrial control systems, network technology, and open-source code projects, the proposed Critical Technology Security Centers could serve as testing centers in support of the National Cybersecurity Certification and Labeling Authority.

Accredited Certifying Agents: Like the organics certifying program run by the U.S. Department of Agriculture, the National Cybersecurity Certification and Labeling Program should be empowered to define criteria and a process for accrediting nongovernmental organizations as certifying agents. Agents should be accredited to certify individual classes of products. For example, an entity could apply to be a certifying agent that specifically reviews connected industrial control systems, internet of things (IoT) devices, operating systems, cloud service offerings (recommendation 4.5), or voting machines, among other things.

Comparative Security Scoring: In coordination with the National Institute of Standards and Technology (NIST) and subject matter experts across the federal government, academia, relevant nongovernmental organizations, and the private sector, the National Cybersecurity

Certification and Labeling Authority should be charged with defining and establishing a set of metrics for quantifying and scoring the security of hardware and software. This scoring regime should differentiate between product type and intended operating environment, setting higher scoring metrics for products that have systemic industrial applications.

Partnership on Product Labeling: The National Cybersecurity Certification and Labeling Authority should work with the private sector to standardize language and develop a labeling regime to provide transparent information on the characteristics and constituent components of a software or hardware product, including those that contribute to the security of a product or service. The authority should also establish a mechanism by which product developers can educate users about these characteristics and components, providing this information for both product labeling and public posting.[226]

Integration with Ongoing Efforts: The National Cybersecurity Certification and Labeling Authority should identify and integrate ongoing public, private, and international efforts to develop security standards, frameworks,

Can the 5G Deployment Be Made Fundamentally Secure?

A recurring finding from this Commission's research has been the misalignment of market forces that place profit and cybersecurity in opposition. The deployment of 5G systems will increase the urgency of a national conversation on the cybersecurity responsibilities that private-sector entities owe to their customers, and the Commission hopes it will also demonstrate how misaligned incentives can be corrected to produce outcomes that are good both for business and for security.

The deployment of 5G systems will dramatically increase the "attack surface," or the exposed routes through which malicious actors can threaten our networks. An exponential increase in connected devices will more deeply embed the internet in our lives and may, in turn, lead to a rise in the everyday leakage of private data. Worse still, security vulnerabilities will spread into sectors not traditionally associated with cyberspace (e.g., transportation, agriculture, or health care) and thereby increase the risk of catastrophic systemic failures.

Given the cascading risks that will accompany widespread 5G deployment, the U.S. government has a responsibility to set clear cybersecurity standards in the marketplace. These standards should shape cyberspace hardware and software development toward being both "secure-by-design" and "secure-by-default." A secure-by-design system has security baked into its fundamental construction—and not simply added as a feature when a given product is ready to hit the market. A secure-by-default system would similarly not require consumers to "turn on" any included security features in order to realize their benefits; a consumer would not have to know they're there to trust that they're working.[227] Prioritizing critical cybersecurity design principles like these should be seen by the private sector as a means to profit rather than as a burden.

With this in mind, the U.S. government should push firms (particularly service providers) to create and use trusted 5G components and vendors. It should also work with and incentivize support for small and medium-sized telecom providers, as well as state, local, territorial, and tribal governments, to upgrade outdated and vulnerable cellular infrastructure. Finally, digital products must provide clear, easy-to-digest information on their security features and capabilities; consumers' resulting decisions about purchases would raise the quality of products made available in the marketplace.

By pointing the way to a secure 5G future, the United States can illuminate the path connecting cybersecurity with profitability.

and certifications. This work should build on, but not be limited to, existing efforts at the Department of Commerce to develop software bills of material and the DoD's Cybersecurity Maturity Model Certification.

Update to Federal Procurement Regulations and Guidelines: Within five years the executive branch should consider updating federal procurement regulations and guidelines, including the Federal Acquisition Regulations, to require National Cybersecurity Certification and Labeling Authority certifications and labeling for certain information technology products and services procured by the federal government. The executive branch should be required to report to Congress on its decision to require National Cybersecurity Certification and Labeling Authority certifications and labeling under Federal Acquisition Regulations, the extent of these requirements, or an explanation if no action was taken.

Enabling Recommendations

4.1.1 Create or Designate Critical Technology Security Centers

While various public and private entities currently provide security evaluations and testing, the U.S. government lacks trusted, centralized entities to perform these functions. Congress should direct and appropriate fund for DHS, in partnership with the Department of Commerce, Department of Energy, Office of the Director of National Intelligence, and DoD, to competitively select, designate, and fund up to three Critical Technology Security Centers in order to centralize efforts directed toward evaluating and testing the security of devices and technologies that underpin our networks and critical infrastructure.[228] These Centers would provide the U.S. government with the capacity to test the security of critical technologies and, when appropriate, assist in identifying vulnerabilities, developing mitigation techniques with relevant original equipment manufacturers, and supporting new and ongoing efforts to certify technologies as secure. The Centers could also play an important role as project managers and, in some cases, would provide funding for the broader research

community already working toward similar ends. To the greatest extent possible, these centers should be designated from existing efforts and institutions, such as ongoing industrial control system work at the Idaho National Lab, rather than created as new entities.

The Centers should be focused on technologies critical to the security of the national cyber ecosystem and of critical infrastructure. This initial list of Centers could be expanded in the future to focus on other critical technologies, including IoT devices:

- A *Center for Network Technology Security* to test the security of hardware and software that underpins our cyber ecosystem, including routers, radio equipment, modems, switches, and other core network technology.
- A *Center for Connected Industrial Control Systems Security* to test the security of connected programmable logic controllers, supervisory control and data acquisition servers and systems, and other connected industrial equipment.
- A *Center for Open-Source Software Security* to systematically identify critical open-source libraries and test and fix vulnerabilities in open-source software repositories, which provide the basis for most software in use today.[229]

4.1.2 Expand and Support the National Institute of Standards and Technology Security Work

The U.S. government is uniquely placed to identify and legitimize standards and best practices. In cybersecurity, standards are crucial for helping regulators understand how to regulate, helping companies understand the state of the art, and helping developers understand security expectations. NIST, which is within the Department of Commerce, is the body through which the U.S. government—often in collaboration or consultation with the private sector—identifies, harmonizes, and develops technology standards, guidelines, tools, and measurement capabilities. As the rapid pace of technological change poses new security challenges, the role of NIST will continue to grow. While NIST employs some of the U.S. government's leading experts in cyber and emerging technologies, it lacks the resources necessary to meet the increasing demands on its staff and support expanding mission requirements. Failure to invest in and grow NIST's capacity runs the risk of impeding the development of both U.S. government and private-sector security initiatives.

Congress should increase funding in support of NIST's work on cybersecurity. Specifically, NIST should be appropriately resourced to:

- Routinely update industry-wide frameworks and standards, including the NIST Cybersecurity Framework.
- Develop and harmonize standards for secure technology development, building on ongoing work on the secure software development lifecycle.[230]
- Develop and harmonize standards for specific processes, including standards for vulnerability and patch management, and provide lasting institutional support for the National Vulnerability Database, Common Vulnerabilities and Exposures program, and the Cybersecurity and Infrastructure Security Agency's (CISA) vulnerability disclosure work.

Key Recommendation

4.2 Congress should pass a law establishing that final goods assemblers of software, hardware, and firmware are liable for damages from incidents that exploit known and unpatched vulnerabilities

Software vulnerabilities present cracks in systems that our adversaries seek to exploit. Shortening the lifecycle of vulnerabilities by ensuring that patches are created and implemented in a timely manner would limit their availability to those who seek to exploit them, driving up adversaries' operating costs and denying them the benefits that successful exploitation could bring.[231] However, the discovery and responsible disclosure of vulnerabilities does little to inhibit their use for malicious purposes unless the vulnerabilities are patched. Patch development and distribution—the processes whereby the developer of the software creates a fix to a vulnerability and distributes it to users so that they can update their systems—is key to eliminating the risk that a given vulnerability can pose across the ecosystem.

When a software vulnerability is found, users of that software have little recourse to mitigate their inherited vulnerability beyond taking the vulnerable system offline—an unworkable solution that in many cases would result in business interruption. In these cases, users are entirely reliant on the software vendor to develop and issue a patch. Large-sample empirical

research has found that 50 percent of vulnerabilities remain without a patch for more than 438 days after disclosure, that a quarter of vulnerabilities remain without a committed patch beyond three years, and that there is no correlation between a vulnerability's severity and the length of its lifespan.[232]

To date, there has not been a clearly defined duty of care for final goods assemblers in their repsonsibilities for developing and issuing patches for known vulnerabilities in their products and services, the timeliness of those patches, and maintaining a vulnerability disclosure policy.[233] To encourage final goods assemblers to shorten the vulnerability lifecycle by more quickly developing and issuing patches, the U.S. government should establish a duty of care in law. Congress should therefore enact legislation establishing that final goods assemblers of software, hardware, and firmware are liable for damages from incidents that exploit vulnerabilities that were known at the time of shipment or discovered and not fixed within a reasonable amount of time. The law should establish expectations that final goods assemblers are responsible for producing security patches for as long as the product or service is supported (as disclosed at the time of sale) or for a year after the last function-enhancing patch is released, whichever is later.[234]

As part of these measures's implementation, Congress should direct the Federal Trade Commission to establish a regulation mandating transparency from final goods assemblers. This regulation should levy requirements that make it easier for the end users or purchaser to understand how a final goods assembler finds, logs, discloses, and retains vulnerabilities. The regulation should also require disclosure of known, unpatched vulnerabilities in a good or service at the time of sale.

Definition of "Known Vulnerability": The regulation should account for common methods by which a vulnerability would be made known to a software or hardware developer or manufacturer—including vulnerabilities publicly disclosed through existing public databases, such as the National Vulnerability Database and Common Vulnerabilities and Exposures program;[235] vulnerabilities reported to the software or hardware developer by a third party; and vulnerabilities discovered by the software or hardware developer themselves.

Definition of "Final Goods Assembler": The final goods assembler should be the entity that enters into an end user licence agreement with the user of the product or service and is most responsible for the placement of a product or service into the stream of commerce. Products and services can include not just objects such as smartphones and laptops but also operating systems, applications, and connected industrial control systems. There is one final goods assembler for each product or service, and the definition of final goods assembler should not include resellers who repackage products without modifying them.

Vulnerability Disclosure and Retention: The regulation should require that final goods assemblers, as well as the software and hardware component developers and manufacturers, establish a publicly accessible process for vulnerability reporting, retain records documenting when a vulnerability was made known to or discovered by the company, and maintain a vulnerability disclosure and patching policy for their products that conforms to the requirements set out under this regulation. The regulation should therefore acknowledge and encourage the concept of coordinated vulnerability disclosure— the process by which the discoverer of a vulnerability reports it directly to the vendor responsible for the software's maintenance—building on earlier work by CISA and the NTIA.[236]

Enabling Recommendation

4.2.1 Incentivize Timely Patch Implementation

In 2015, the Verizon *Data Breach Investigations Report* found that 99.9 percent of vulnerabilities in use by attackers had been known for more than a year, most with a patch available.[237] Vulnerability discovery, vulnerability disclosure, and patch development do little to shrink the supply of vulnerabilities available to adversaries if the patches go unimplemented by users. With some exceptions, when a vendor or assembler of software issues a method of remediating a vulnerability, the onus of implementing that remediation falls on the user of that software or hardware. When implementing a security update poses a challenge to the configuration of the user's environment, possibly leading to downtime or the need to reconfigure a system entirely, these patches can often go unimplemented.

Short of regulation, there is likely no one way to incentivize companies to better patch their systems. Instead, the U.S. government should study the potential effectiveness of several actions, including:
- Directing NIST to develop guidance or expectations about how quickly patches should be implemented once released.
- Placing a cap, via standards or certifications of insurance products, on insurance payouts for incidents that involve unpatched systems.

STRATEGIC OBJECTIVE #2:
INCENTIVIZE BETTER ORGANIZATIONAL CYBERSECURITY

The U.S. government should endeavor to change private-sector cybersecurity behavior, encouraging more secure practices by users and organizations. Whereas measures to incentivize greater security in the marketplace for technologies seek to drive down technical vulnerability, incentivizing better organizational cybersecurity behavior seeks to address the human and organizational aspects of national vulnerability. To achieve this, the U.S. government needs to build a greater statistical capacity to develop, test, and understand the effectiveness of good practices and standards. Armed with a greater understanding of good practices, the U.S. government should use all available instruments to craft incentives to change behavior at large scale, including shaping market forces like the insurance market, crafting regulations, and changing federal procurement practices.

Key Recommendation

4.3 Congress should establish a Bureau of Cyber Statistics charged with collecting and providing statistical data on cybersecurity and the cyber ecosystem to inform policymaking and government programs.

While there is broad consensus that cyberattacks on U.S. citizens and businesses are increasing in frequency and severity, the U.S. government and broader marketplace lack sufficient clarity about the nature and scope of these attacks to develop nuanced and effective policy responses. Compounding this problem is a fundamental lack of clarity about what security measures are effective in reducing risk in the technologies, in business enterprises, and even at the level of national policymaking. This confusion limits the ability of the government to evaluate the effectiveness of its cybersecurity programs and prevents private enterprises and insurance providers from being able to adequately price, model, and understand cyber risk. Existing data sets are incomplete and provide only a superficial or cursory understanding of evolving trends in cybersecurity and cyberspace.

To address similar gaps in other policy areas, the United States established statistical agencies to inform both public policymaking and private decision making. These agencies, like the Bureau of Labor Statistics, established the metrics and reporting by which government policy

and private-sector efforts are measured and report those assessments. One of the great successes of many of these statistical agencies has been in delivering useful information to improve the lives of everyday Americans, while anonymizing that information and protecting privacy. The U.S. government should adopt this model for cyberspace.

Congress should establish a Bureau of Cyber Statistics within the Department of Commerce, or another department or agency, that would act as the government statistical agency that collects, processes, analyzes, and disseminates essential statistical data on cybersecurity, cyber incidents, and the cyber ecosystem to the American public, Congress, other federal agencies, state and local governments, and the private sector. Statistical analysis provided by the Bureau would be useful for informing national risk (recommendations 3.1 and 3.1.1), helping the insurance industry create more accurate risk models (recommendation 4.4.1), and helping the U.S. government craft more effective cybersecurity policy and programs.

The Definition and Promulgation of Cybersecurity Metrics: In partnership with NIST, the Bureau would be charged with identifying and establishing meaningful metrics and data necessary to measure cybersecurity and risk reduction in cyberspace. As part of this task, the Bureau would develop, in collaboration with departments and agencies, metrics that would enable better evaluation of the adoption, reach, and effectiveness of federal cybersecurity programs. This information would also be made available to the Office of Management and Budget (OMB) to guide decision making on budgets and priorities for programs.

Data Collection and Aggregation: The Bureau should be empowered and sufficiently funded to establish programs and make purchases required to collect the data necessary to inform its analysis. These tasks include collecting and aggregating open-source data, purchasing private or proprietary data repositories, and conducting surveys. Departments and agencies should assist the Bureau in its work, making available data sets as needed, and to the greatest extent practicable, in furtherance of its work.

Cyber Incident Reporting: In the authorizing legislation, Congress should mandate that relevant departments and agencies, as well as companies that regularly collect cyber incident data as a part of their business, are required to provide aggregated, anonymized, minimized data on cyber incidents to inform statistical analysis on a yearly basis.[238] The law would authorize the Bureau of Cyber Statistics to define key data points, a standardized format, timelines, and mechanisms for complying with these requirements, unless departments and agencies are precluded by a legal constraint or by considerations of operational sensitivity.[239] The law should also insulate these private companies from liability associated with disclosing minimized, anonymized, and aggregated data to the Bureau.

Data Privacy and Protection: Authorizing legislation should ensure that the aggregated and anonymized data collected is insulated from public disclosure, the collection and retention of personally identifiable information is minimized, and, in the case of cyber incidents, the identity of victims is protected. In addition, legislation should establish safeguards against or punitive measures for the disclosure of raw data to regulatory agencies or non-federal entities.

Academic and Private-Sector Exchanges: The Bureau should be funded and equipped to host academics as well as private-sector and independent security researchers as a part of extended exchanges. The purpose of this program should be to ensure that the Bureau can benefit from new methods and techniques of data and statistical analysis and that academia and the public can benefit from the public-interest research sourced from its data sets.

Key Recommendation

4.4 Congress should resource and direct the Department of Homeland Security to resource a federally funded research and development center to work with state-level regulators in developing certifications for cybersecurity insurance products.

A robust and functioning market for insurance products can have the same positive effect on the risk management behavior of firms as do regulatory interventions. Although the insurance industry plays an important role in enabling organizations to transfer a small portion of their cyber risk, it is falling short of achieving the public policy objective of driving better practices of risk management in the private sector more generally. The reasons for this failure are varied but largely come down to an inability on the part of the insurance industry to comprehensively understand and price risk, due in part to a lack of talented underwriters and claims adjusters and the absence of standards and frameworks for how cyber risk should be priced. This has had the combined effect of creating an opaque environment for enterprises attempting to purchase coverage and undermining the effectiveness of insurance as an incentive to push enterprises toward better security behavior.

Because insurance falls under the purview of state regulators, the federal government can do little to directly affect change in the market for insurance specific to a given industry, short of creating large-scale programs akin to the crop insurance program instituted by the Federal Crop Insurance Act. Thus, to bring to maturity and improve the market for cybersecurity insurance, Congress should appropriate funds and direct DHS to resource a Federally Funded Research and Development Center (FFRDC) to develop models for underwriter and claims adjuster training and certification. In addition, the program should develop certification frameworks for cybersecurity insurance products in consultation and coordination with state insurance regulators.

Underwriter Training and Certification: For underwriters to effectively evaluate and analyze risk in a given industry, they must understand it. Certification is available for underwriters in other areas of insurance, including homeowners, flood, life, and health. The FFRDC should work with insurers, state regulators, and experts in cybersecurity risk management to develop curricula and training courses for cyber insurance underwriters required under a cyber insurance underwriter certification.

Claims Adjuster Training and Certification: Like underwriters, claims adjusters are crucial in ensuring that insurance policies can adapt to changing conditions. Like underwriting, other areas of insurance have training and certification available for claims adjusters. The FFRDC should work with insurers, state regulators, and cybersecurity risk management experts to develop training and certification models for cyber claims adjusters.

Cyber Insurance Product Certification: State insurance regulators can and often do set minimum standards that insurance products must meet in order to be offered in their state, thereby "ensuring that insurance policy provisions comply with state law, are reasonable and fair, and do not contain major gaps in coverage that might be misunderstood by consumers and leave them unprotected."[240] Working with state insurance regulators and the public-private working group on pricing and modeling cyber risk (recommendation 4.4.1), the FFRDC should develop cybersecurity product certifications based on a common lexicon and security standards.

Enabling Recommendations

4.4.1 Establish a Public-Private Partnership on Modeling Cyber Risk

For insurance to act as a de facto regulator of organizational behavior, the market for insurance must accurately price risk. Premiums and limits on insurance products must also drive firms that have bought insurance to invest in improving their cyber risk posture. Today, insurance companies lack quality data sets and models to understand, price, and mitigate cyber risk.[241] Although bad or incomplete data is a major barrier to accurately pricing cyber risk, insurers are not incentivized to pool and aggregate their data to build more robust and accurate pricing models.[242]

The executive branch should establish a public-private working group at DHS to convene insurance companies and cyber risk modeling companies to collaborate in pooling and leveraging available statistics and data that can inform innovations in cyber risk modeling. Drawing on insights gained by the defunct Cyber Incident Data and Analysis Working Group at DHS, and informed by the work of the Bureau of Cyber Statistics (recommendation 4.3), this effort should identify areas of common interest so that these entities can benefit from one another's risk modeling efforts, particularly with regard to dependency mapping and the consequences of cyber disruptions. One applicable use-case would be the work of the National Risk Management Center as it intersects with the work of the cybersecurity insurance industry. The working group should:

- Develop frameworks and research methodologies for understanding and accurately pricing cyber risk.
- Conduct research on the applicability and utility of common frameworks, controls, and "essentials" as baseline requirements for reducing premiums in pricing insurance risk, such as the NIST Cybersecurity Framework and the International Organization for Standardization/International Electrotechnical Commission (ISO/IEC) 27000 standards family.
- Identify common areas of interest for pooling anonymized data from which to derive better, more accurate risk models.

4.4.2 Explore the Need for a Government Reinsurance Program to Cover Catastrophic Cyber Events

In December 2016, the U.S. Department of Treasury issued guidance clarifying that cyber events could trigger Terrorism Risk Insurance Act (TRIA) protections. However, the U.S. government is in a position to do more to further define what types of cyber events fall under the TRIA umbrella and what types of events should remain covered by insurance companies themselves. Currently, TRIA coverage is activated only for a "certified act of terrorism." The Further Consolidated Appropriations Act, 2020[243] directs the Comptroller

Can Modern Insurance Improve Cybersecurity?

Insurance can provide financial incentives for individuals and organizations to better manage their risk. From incentivizing the use of seatbelts and airbags in the automotive industry to pushing for fire suppression systems as a part of building codes, the insurance industry has played an important role in identifying risk management standards for individual consumers and large corporations alike. A robust and functioning market for cyber insurance could play a similar role in identifying and regulating behavior to improve cyber risk management.[244]

Today, the market for cyber insurance is failing to deliver on this potential. The reasons for this failure are varied. Insurers struggle to find underwriters and claims adjusters, the individuals charged with pricing and adjusting the price of risk, who understand cyber risk. Where talent exists, insufficient or inconsistent models for risk persist. Confounding these factors is the notion of silent cyber risk—the cyber risk inherited from other insurance offerings, such as general corporate liability or property and casualty coverage. All of these issues lead to a hesitancy on the part of insurers to assume meaningful amounts of risk that would define a healthy cyber insurance market.

Currently, the estimated worldwide value of cyber insurance premiums sits at $7.5 billion.[245] For context, in 2017 property and casualty insurance premiums were worth $275.5 billion in the United States alone.[246] Because insurers can either assume their inherited cyber risk with little threat to their overall solvency or pass this risk along to reinsurers in the form of derivatives, they have little incentive to push the entities they insure to manage that risk. For the insurance industry to effectively serve as a lever to scale up risk management, the industry must mature to supply products aligned with the demands of those seeking to buy them and must increase overall premiums to take on a meaningful amount of risk.

Some of this maturation will come with time, but the U.S. government is well placed to play the same role it has taken with other emerging insurance industries throughout history, facilitating collaboration to develop mature and effective risk assessment models and expertise. Cyber insurance is not a silver bullet to solve the nation's cybersecurity challenges. Indeed, a robust and functioning market for cybersecurity insurance is not an end in and of itself, but a means to improve the cybersecurity of the U.S. private sector and the security of the nation as a whole in cyberspace.

General at the Government Accountability Office (GAO) to assess the current state of insurance for cyber-related incidents. The Commission supports the need to study the cyber insurance market and encourages the GAO to work closely with relevant departments and agencies, including the Department of Commerce, DHS, and Department of the Treasury.

In addition to the aspects of the study outlined in the law, the study should explore:

- Current exemptions for casualty and property insurance policies, including act of war exemptions, and complications of including them in cyber insurance policies.
- The existing scoping of the TRIA to assess whether it is sufficiently broad to cover cyber events perpetrated by nation-states, which most general property and casualty insurance policies currently exclude or attempt to exclude.
- If the triggering threshold for the TRIA—a loss of $200 million, as of the 2020 reauthorization—is the appropriate size to trigger a similar backstop for catastrophic cyber events.
- Comparative models of federal share percentage of a cyber insurance–related backstop.
- What types of cyber events constitute "certified acts of terrorism" and whether this provides a sufficient backstop for insurers, as many major cyber events—particularly those perpetrated by nation-states—may not fit squarely under the definition of "certified act of terrorism."
- What events and which entities would be covered by a backstop, given that terror attacks generally take place in and affect a confined area, while some cyber incidents are not bounded by geography. For example, the study should address whether a cyber-attack on an American company affecting only assets in another jurisdiction would qualify.

4.4.3 Incentivize Information Technology Security through Federal Acquisition Regulations and Federal Information Security Management Act Authorities

The U.S. government is in a powerful position to help develop and generate more sustainable requirements for cybersecurity best practices, as requirements placed on government contractors can become de facto industry standards.[247] Requiring vendors to adhere to standards when doing business with the federal government will compel them to produce product or service offerings that meet those standards, potentially making those more secure offerings available to the broader public.[248]

The executive branch should direct the Federal Acquisition Regulation Council and the Office of Management and Budget to update its cybersecurity regulations in the Federal Acquisition Regulations and cybersecurity guidance under Federal Information Security Management Act at least every five years, to account for changing cybersecurity standards, and explore ways to integrate and fully account for existing models and frameworks, such as the Cybersecurity Maturity Model Certification, in Federal Acquisition Regulations. In addition, the Federal Acquisition Regulation Council should be directed to update Federal Acquisition Regulations to require that:

- Federal civilian agency contractors adhere to the contractor-exclusive Binding Operational Directive issued by DHS.[249]
- Federally procured information technology fully accounts for identified good security practices for building secure software and systems, such as those offered by NIST's Secure Software Development Framework[250] and the ISO/IEC 27000 standards family.[251]
- When developing requirements, the council should take into account lessons learned with NIST Special Publication 800.171, comments from DoD's

Cybersecurity Maturity Model Certification, rulings or comments of the Federal Acquisition Security Council, and the ISO/IEC 27000 standards.

- Providers of information technology submit software transparency and software bills of materials for the systems they provide in support of government missions in line with the certifications and labels developed by the National Cybersecurity Certification and Labeling Authority (recommendation 4.1).[252]
- Upon the development of cybersecurity insurance policy certifications (recommendation 4.4), U.S. government contractors maintain a certified level of cybersecurity insurance and explore whether the Cybersecurity Maturity Model Certification should be updated to require cybersecurity insurance.

4.4.4 Amend the Sarbanes-Oxley Act to Include Cybersecurity Reporting Requirements

In today's cyber-based business environment, the cybersecurity of a publicly traded company is a critical component of its financial condition. In short, cyber risk is a business risk. A company's ability to rapidly detect, investigate, and remediate network intrusions is a useful indicator of the maturity of its security operations, in its ability both to defend against cyberattacks and to mitigate the types of cybersecurity risks that could harm its business operations and financial conditions.

The Sarbanes-Oxley Act[253] was passed in 2002 to improve corporate accountability and oversight in response to a series of corporate failures. The law sets out requirements, enforced through the Securities and Exchange Commission (SEC), for all publicly traded U.S. companies, including stricter disclosure rules and a mandate that senior corporate officers certify the validity of periodic financial reports, in addition to criminalizing

efforts by corporate personnel to improperly influence auditors. In 2018, the SEC issued interpretive guidance of existing regulations, stating that "although no existing disclosure requirement explicitly refers to cybersecurity risks and cyber incidents, companies nonetheless may be obligated to disclose such risks and incidents," including the requirements under Sarbanes-Oxley.[254]

To harmonize and clarify cybersecurity oversight and reporting requirements for publicly traded companies, Congress should amend the Sarbanes-Oxley Act to explicitly account for cybersecurity. Specifically, the amendment should:

- Add a definition of an "information system," to mean "a set of activities, involving people, processes, data, or technology, that enable the issuer to obtain, generate, use, and communicate transactions and information to maintain accountability and measure and review the issuer's performance or progress toward the achievement of objectives."
- Specify corporate responsibility requirements for the security of information systems, including the metrics and records publicly traded companies must keep regarding risk assessments, determinations, and decisions; cyber hygiene; and penetration testing and red-teaming results, including a record of metrics relating to the speed of their detection, investigation, and remediation.[255]
- Mandate that public companies maintain, as part of this requirement, internal records of cyber risk assessments, so that a full evaluation of cybersecurity risks can be judged in acquisition or in legal or regulatory action.
- Require management assessments and attestation of plans to manage risk from information systems and data.

STRATEGIC OBJECTIVE #3:

EMPOWER ICT ENABLERS TO DEPLOY SECURITY ACROSS THE ECOSYSTEM

The U.S. government should undertake efforts to better leverage the scale of information and communications technology (ICT) enablers in cybersecurity—both by empowering companies that can deploy security across the ecosystem and by incentivizing the adoption of the scalable security solutions they offer. While the U.S. government's ability to directly influence the ecosystem is limited, companies that provide services and infrastructure essential to the functioning of the internet could have an outsized impact on its security. For these entities, some forms of security—ensuring the continuous availability of the services they provide—is already incentivized. The financial benefit of other aspects of security—ensuring the integrity and confidentiality of the data they hold and the networks they administer—is often less obvious, but no less important for managing national vulnerability.

Key Recommendation

4.5 The National Cybersecurity Certification and Labeling Authority, in consultation with the National Institute of Standards and Technology, the Office of Management and Budget, and the Department of Homeland Security, should develop a cloud security certification.

Traditional forms of data storage can generate a number of vulnerabilities. First, hosting data on-site opens the entity to the risk of a catastrophic event wiping out its primary and backup data. Such an event could take the form of a fire, an electrical surge, or water damage, as well as a cyberattack. Traditional on-site data storage models not only fail to meet the needs of an increasingly flexible and disparate office culture but also offer a vulnerable target for cyberattack. Cloud-based services[256] offer a more economical and secure alternative to traditional forms of data storage and computing. In addition to eliminating the costs for the business of purchasing hardware, software, and other data center infrastructure, cloud computing providers leverage a set of technologies and policies that bolster the user's security posture.[257] In doing so, cloud services could potentially provide maximum levels of security by operating at scale. With sufficient resources, cloud computing service providers house their data on a worldwide network of regularly updated data centers, maximizing the security of that data.[258] Similarly, large cloud service providers' size and scale enable them to provide more sophisticated security features (from

end-to-end encryption to security key authentication) than would be practical for smaller organizations to implement individually. Unless they invest significant resources into securing their cloud data centers, small to medium-sized data-hosting service providers risk opening their customers to the vulnerabilities of misconfiguration. Today, nearly two hundred thousand insecure cloud configurations are in use. More than 43 percent of cloud databases are not encrypted, and 40 percent of cloud storage services have logging disabled.[259]

As various branches of government and the broader economy increasingly adopt cloud services to strengthen their data security, cloud infrastructure is becoming critically important for the country. In the same way that large distributors provide safer and more reliable sources of drinking water than does a family well, large cloud service providers often serve as a more dependable and resilient source of data hosting and, in some cases, infrastructure. Migration to cloud services therefore stands to drive down risk for small and medium-sized enterprises, but it also serves to concentrate national risk in a relatively small number of entities. As of 2019, 90 percent of companies were on the cloud.[260] In an age when every company is a technology company, cloud service providers that remotely manage a business's IT and networks—and often store large portions or all of an entity's data—hold a vast amount of public trust. This concentration represents an opportunity for policymakers to affect the security of the ecosystem through economies of scale by holding entities that provide cloud services to a higher security standard.

To fully realize the security and economic benefits of the migration to the cloud, the U.S. government needs to ensure that those services are able to provide security value commensurate with the risk they hold in the ecosystem.[261] To accomplish this, DHS, in consultation with NIST and OMB, should work with the National Cybersecurity Certification and Labeling Authority (recommendation 4.1) to develop a secure cloud certification. In developing this certification, the U.S. government should engage with and take lessons from the European Union Agency for Cybersecurity, which is currently in the early stages of developing certifications.[262]

Certifying Agent: The National Cybersecurity Certification and Labeling Authority should serve as the certifying agent for the cloud security certification. In the event that the Authority does not exist, DHS, in consultation with NIST, should serve as the certifying agent. Entities eligible for certification should include any cloud service provider or entity that operates cloud services, with a focus on entities that provide infrastructure as a service and platform as a service. The cloud security certification should last two years, and the National Cybersecurity Certification and Labeling Authority, or authorized certifying agent, should be empowered to conduct initial and subsequent audits of entities that apply for and meet the requirements for certification.

Standards Development: Congress should direct NIST to lead, in coordination with the National Cybersecurity and Certification and Labeling Authority and DHS, a public-private standards-making process for a secure cloud standard. This process should include major cloud service providers and small sector-specific cloud service providers. Initial efforts should focus on standards for general business enterprise IT environments, with subsequent efforts focusing on the application of cloud services in different industrial contexts, environments, and sectors.

Security and Transparency: As part of its certification development process, the National Cybersecurity Certification and Labeling Authority should work with NIST to develop metrics for security offered by which cloud services can be compared to allow users to more easily differentiate between more and less secure offerings, and more clearly communicate what aspects of security are the responsibility of the user rather than the provider. When certifying the security of cloud services, the certifying agent should account for cloud security standards and best practices as well as factors such as extrajudicial state pressure that may be applied to a company to hand over user data or information.

Update FedRAMP: Within five years, the executive branch should consider updating and simplifying the Federal Risk and Authorization Management Program (FedRAMP) requirements to require that all non-national security cloud services procured by the federal government meet the identified standards and possess the cloud security certification. The executive branch should be required to report to Congress on its decision to require National Cybersecurity Certification and Labeling Authority cloud security certifications under FedRAMP, on the extent of these requirements, or an explanation if no action was taken.

Enabling Recommendations

4.5.1 Incentivize the Uptake of Secure Cloud Services for Small and Medium-Sized Businesses and State, Local, Tribal, and Territorial Governments

The benefits of cloud computing for small and medium-sized enterprises and state, local, tribal, and territorial

(SLTT) governments are well documented.[263] In addition to providing greater flexibility and scalability for businesses, cloud service providers enable these entities—which may lack the financial and human capital to invest in strong security controls or modernize their information technology—to outsource their security to an entity that, under the above regulation, would be held to a higher cybersecurity standard.

The cloud security certification may have the adverse effect of eliminating less expensive providers that do not meet that standard. To ensure the continued availability of affordable cloud services to smaller and medium-sized businesses as well as SLTT governments, the U.S. government may need to provide financial incentives. Congress should direct the Department of Commerce, Small Business Administration, and DHS to conduct a six-month study to define the method of incentivizing the adoption of these services, and report their findings and recommendations to Congress. The ultimate goal would be to move, to the greatest extent practicable, small and medium-sized businesses and SLTT governments to cost-effective cloud services.

The report should:
- Identify barriers or challenges for small and medium-sized business and SLTT governments in purchasing or acquiring secure cloud services.
- Assess market availability, market pricing, and affordability for small and medium-sized businesses and SLTT governments, with particular attention to identifying high-risk and underserved sectors or regions.
- Estimate the timeline and cost of tax breaks for small and medium-sized businesses and grants for SLTT governments necessary to incentivize the adoption of secure cloud services, as determined by the certified secure assessment.
- In conducting this study, the U.S. government should focus on the incentivization and adoption of services that meet the certifications and requirements outlined in the recommendation above.

4.5.2 Develop a Strategy to Secure Foundational Internet Protocols and Email

The internet and related technologies were not designed with security as a priority.[264] For example, there are no enforced routing authentication standards underlying Border Gateway Protocol (BGP), a foundational mechanism that enables the internet to function. Likewise, there is no security designed into the Domain Name System (DNS), the internet's address book, which ensures that users get the intended address they request. These flaws allow DNS and BGP hijacking, common ways for attackers to redirect traffic to websites that host malware or collect personal information like passwords. In addition, email represents a common vector for initial compromise leading to cyber incidents. The Domain-based Message Authentication, Reporting, and Conformance (DMARC) standard ensures that email coming from fraudulent domains is blocked, diminishing the rate of success of phishing, spoofing, and spam email. There have been a variety of attempts to address these issues, including at the Federal Communications Commission via their Communications Security Reliability and Interoperability Council, by the NTIA, and by industry itself in standards bodies such as the Internet Engineering Task Force. Despite these efforts, there remain significant concerns over the security of these mechanisms and their potential to be exploited.

To encourage broader implementation of security measures,[265] Congress should pass a law that does the following:
- Requires the NTIA and DHS to develop a strategy and recommendations, in consultation with internet service providers and civil society and academic experts, to define common, implementable guidance for securing the DNS and BGP.
- Requires DHS to develop a strategy and recommendations, in consultation with the information technology sector to implement DMARC at scale, across all U.S.-based email providers.

- Requires DHS and the NTIA to report back to Congress within one year with a plan to implement security across the DNS, BGP, and email.

4.5.3 Strengthen the U.S. Government's Ability to Take Down Botnets

"Robot networks," or botnets, are networks of computers hijacked by criminals and nation-states to promulgate their malicious activity. Criminals use botnets to spread spam and phishing emails, to impersonate users, and to carry out distributed denial-of-service (DDoS) attacks.[266] It is estimated that as much as 30 percent of all internet traffic could be attributable to botnets, and most of that traffic is from DDoS attacks.[267] Currently, law enforcement, working with the private sector, can dismantle botnets when they are used to perpetrate fraud or illegal wiretapping; however, botnets are often used for other nefarious purposes, such as harvesting email accounts and executing DDoS attacks against websites or other computers. In these latter types of cases, the courts may lack the statutory authority to issue an injunction to disrupt the botnet. As the techniques of adversaries adapt (i.e., moving to greater use of virtual private servers), addressing the challenge of dismantling adversary botnets becomes even more complex. To enable the U.S. government to better work with private industry and international partners, action is needed. In consultation with the Department of Justice, Congress should enact Section 4 of the International Cybercrime Prevention Act.[268] This legislation would provide broader authority to disrupt all types of illegal botnets, not just those used in fraud.[269]

How Do You Defeat a Botnet? (It Takes a Village)

From December 2015 to October 2018, a cybercriminal ring used malware known as "Kovter" to infect and access more than 1.7 million computers worldwide and used hidden browsers on those computers to download fake web pages. Ads were then loaded onto those pages to falsify billions of ad views, resulting in businesses paying over $29 million for ads they believed were viewed by actual human users. The botnet was part of a sophisticated infrastructure of command-and-control servers that also monitored whether individually infected computers had been detected by cybersecurity companies as involved in fraud. The botnet was controlled by three Russian nationals located abroad.[270]

The Department of Justice (DoJ) and the Federal Bureau of Investigation (FBI) worked with the nonprofit National Cyber-Forensics and Training Alliance (NCFTA) to bring together multiple private-sector and nonprofit organizations to dismantle the botnet.[271] The NCFTA played a key role by providing a collaborative information-sharing platform that enabled partners to share cyber threat indicators, develop an operational strategy, and coordinate sequenced actions.[272]

Following the arrest of one of the suspects, the FBI worked with private-sector companies to reroute or "sinkhole" traffic to prevent further victimization, executed seizure warrants to take control of 23 internet domains used by the criminals, and worked with server-hosting companies in six countries to preserve and then take down 89 servers used to operate the scheme.[273] The DoJ and the FBI, including several FBI Legal Attachés stationed overseas, also worked closely with foreign partners—specifically, Malaysian, Bulgarian, Estonian, German, French, Dutch, British, and Swiss authorities and Europol—to assist with aspects of the investigation and with apprehending three indicted subjects for arrest and extradition.

Within hours, a criminal cyber infrastructure that had been generating millions of fraudulent electronic bid requests per minute went completely dark. Eight defendants were indicted for their role in orchestrating the botnet and another fraudulent digital advertising scheme, and to date several have appeared and entered guilty pleas in U.S. courts.

STRATEGIC OBJECTIVE #4:
REDUCE CRITICAL DEPENDENCIES ON UNTRUSTED INFORMATION AND COMMUNICATIONS TECHNOLOGY

The United States should identify industries and technologies critical to national and economic security and take steps to reduce vulnerability at a macroeconomic level (e.g., industrial strategy) and at a microeconomic level (e.g., supply chain risk management). Of particular importance, as technology supply chains become more complex and global, the United States has developed a growing dependence on suppliers that may come under malign influence, introducing vulnerability into the ecosystem. To better manage these risks, the United States should develop a more robust capacity to identify and protect against untrusted suppliers while ensuring the presence of viable alternative suppliers for critical technologies through strategic investment.

Key Recommendation

4.6 Congress should direct the U.S. government to develop and implement an information and communications technology industrial base strategy to ensure more trusted supply chains and the availability of critical information and communications technologies.

The United States participates in a global marketplace. Merely limiting the access of untrusted firms and their technologies to our cyber ecosystem not only will be inadequate to contain their risks but, in the absence of suitable alternatives, could instead stifle our economic growth and deprive core aspects of the U.S. economy of access to potentially transformative technologies. Nowhere is this truer than in technologies like 5G, which are pursued by strategic competitors, such as China, that bolster their companies' market share and subsidize their growth as a matter of national policy—effectively dominating a global market without having to respond to market forces.

While existing authorities under the Defense Production Act[274] empower the U.S. government to allocate resources and ensure domestic capacity in industries that directly serve national defense and security, they are limited in addressing areas where the lack of domestic or trusted industrial capacity itself constitutes a national security *and* economic security risk. U.S. government mechanisms to implement Defense Production Act authorities are similarly limited in resourcing and funding, and they provide no clear mandate to address these problems.

Congress should direct the U.S. government to assess the United States' information and communications technology (ICT) supply chain and develop and implement an ICT industrial base strategy to reduce dependency and ensure greater security and availability of these critical technologies. This strategy should focus on ensuring the availability and integrity of trusted components, products, and materials necessary for the manufacture and development of ICTs deemed most critical to national and economic security. As part of this effort, the U.S. government should assess the ability of its current structure, resources, and authorities to inform, develop, and execute such a strategy and provide recommendations to strengthen them. Given the global, interconnected nature of trade and supply chains, the strategy should be formed in coordination with trusted partners and allies. In addition, the strategy should fully utilize the authorities available to the federal government, including but not limited to the Defense Production Act.

Identify and Assess Critical Dependencies: In forming the strategy, the U.S. government should conduct an in-depth analysis of market conditions to comprehensively assess foreign dependencies affecting critical information and communication technologies. This assessment should:

- Clearly identify critical technologies, components, and materials that the industrial base strategy seeks to protect.
- Identify domestic and allied ICT industrial capacity.
- Identify key areas of risk where a foreign adversary could restrict supply of a critical technology or introduce supply chain compromise at large scale.
- Identify barriers to a market-based solution.

Direct Investments for ICT Industrial Capacity and Trusted Supply: The strategy should clearly outline national strategic priorities and estimate what federal resources need to be allocated to address and reduce dependencies on untrusted foreign technology and bolster domestic or allied production to ensure viable alternatives. The strategy should define lines of effort, assign responsibilities, and issue accompanying executive orders or presidential determinations necessary to carry it out. Further, the executive branch should work with Congress to identify additional resources and programmatic, legislative, or structural changes necessary for its implementation.

Direct Strategic Investments in Research and Development: The strategy must identify and address areas where strategic investment in research and development must now be undertaken today to prevent future overreliance on foreign, untrusted technology in high-tech areas. This requires the U.S. government to examine provisions and mechanisms for strategic investment in research and development, identifying any areas in need of updates to meet current needs. As part of strategic research and development investment, and in addition to providing funding, the U.S. government will play an important role in overcoming the understandable reluctance of industry competitors to share space and knowledge.

Amend the Defense Production Act to Enable an ICT Industrial Base Strategy: In addition to the amendments recommended above, Congress should amend

the Defense Production Act to clarify and expand the definition of "national defense" to include mitigating potential dependencies on foreign-sourced information and communications technology. In addition, Congress should consider expanding the definition of "industrial resources" to include those needed to maintain a modern domestic industrial base. These amendments would empower the President to shape domestic production under Title III of the Defense Production Act.

Enabling Recommendations

4.6.1 Increase Support to Supply Chain Risk Management Efforts

Software, hardware, and information technology service supply chains are major means through which foreign actors, particularly China, can seek to introduce vulnerability and risk into the U.S. ecosystem in ways that can neither be accounted for nor mitigated through standard cybersecurity practices. Increasing reliance on foreign-owned or -controlled companies introduces new vulnerabilities into our nation's supply chains.[275] At a national level, the United States can elect to limit market access to untrusted or high-risk vendors where the risk of supply chain compromise is unacceptable, such as through entities list designations, through the International Emergency Economic Powers Act, or by limits on inbound investment through the Committee on Foreign Investment in the United States. At a more tactical level, the U.S. government and the private sector can utilize supply chain risk management techniques to reduce their risk and minimize vulnerability. Those undertaking both efforts require robust intelligence, both classified and open-source, to inform their work, alert them to adversary plans and intentions, and enable them to assess risk when making decisions. However, while the United States has strengthened mechanisms to address supply chain risk over the past few years, there must be a commensurate increase in resources for intelligence organizations that support and enable those mechanisms.

To start correcting this gap, the 2020 National Defense Authorization Act laid the groundwork for strengthening the U.S. intelligence community's capacity to provide better supply chain intelligence: it established a Supply Chain and Counterintelligence Risk Management Task Force within ODNI to improve supply chain intelligence for U.S. government acquisition.[276] The supply chain task force should explore additional avenues to expand this support to critical infrastructure, including:

- Leveraging the ongoing work and findings of the DHS-led ICT Supply Chain Risk Management Task Force[277] to work with the private sector in order to identify both its needs and its mechanisms to improve information sharing on supply chain risk.
- Determining appropriate funding, resourcing, and authorities for U.S. intelligence community efforts to aggregate all-source information relating to supply chains,[278] share strategic supply chain warning and

counterintelligence risk assessments with public and private partners, and serve as the central and shared knowledge resource for threats to supply chain activities or supply chain integrity.[279]

- Understanding and defining additional measures the U.S. government can adopt in making greater use of publicly available and proprietary sources in informing supply chain and foreign investment risk assessments.

4.6.2 Commit Significant and Consistent Funding toward Research and Development in Emerging Technologies

The federal government has a long, storied history of spurring technological revolutions by funding and engaging in basic and applied research. By pursuing discoveries in

Should the United States Have a High-Tech Industrial Strategy?

In the 1980s, the U.S. semiconductor industry faced fierce competition from Japan. Growing dependence on Japanese-sourced semiconductors, and the United States' diminishing industrial capacity, alarmed U.S. officials who understood the fundamental importance of maintaining this capability for both national competitiveness and national defense. Recognizing the need to regain competitiveness, more than a dozen U.S.-based computer chip manufacturers established a consortium called Sematech in partnership with the Reagan administration. With the objective of leapfrogging Japanese chip makers by the 1990s,[280] the Reagan administration successfully supported the effort with public subsidies, over five years appropriating $500 million in funding from the Defense Advanced Research Projects Agency and the Department of Defense (approximately $1.125 billion today, adjusted for inflation).

Today, the United States faces an even greater challenge to its industrial might. Countries like China are growing increasingly dominant in the production and assembly of critical current and next-generation telecommunications equipment. But whereas the Japanese semiconductor industry grew out of genuine free market innovation, Chinese tech giants have benefited significantly from Chinese government support to build their massive market share. In other words, the playing field is uneven and global markets are neither free nor fair.

While the Chinese tech giants have provided a wake-up call that might normally spur the competitors in the telecommunications industry, both U.S. companies and, with some exceptions, those of our trusted allies and partners have fallen so far behind industry leaders that regaining competitiveness may prove impossible without government support. As technology supply chains become more complex and global, the U.S. government must work with partners to ensure that trusted industry can provide the United States and its allies with trusted supply of critical technologies now and into the future.

science and technology well before a path toward commercial viability is certain or even understood, federally backed research is able to drive innovation in the absence of the nearer-term returns on investment traditionally required for commercial R&D—with the internet itself being perhaps the most notable breakthrough. Emerging technologies such as artificial intelligence and quantum information science (quantum computing, quantum key encryption, etc.) pose both opportunities and risks, but we have yet to fully understand how to exploit and prepare for them, much less commercialize or deploy them, without further research. The federal government can best aid both the public and private sectors in their research endeavors through the application of consistent, significant funding to both fuel their efforts and protect them from theft.

In 2016, a federal interagency working group found that one of the barriers to advanced, high-performance computing breakthroughs was a broad lack of consistent funding.[281] In 2019, the National Security Commission on Artificial Intelligence determined that "Federal R&D funding for AI has not kept pace with the revolutionary potential it holds or with aggressive investments by competitors."[282] The long-term, multiyear nature of this research requires institutions to carefully plan research and development campaigns across time.

To ensure continuity of effort, Congress should appropriate consistent funding and task the executive branch, including the National Science Foundation, the Defense Advanced Research Projects Agency, and the Intelligence

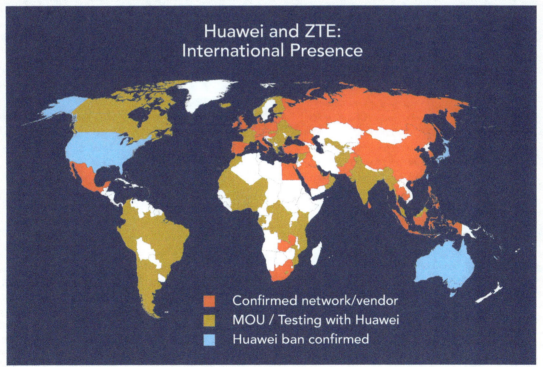

Huawei and ZTE:
International Presence

■ Confirmed network/vendor
■ MOU / Testing with Huawei
■ Huawei ban confirmed

(Yash Mishra, "Here Are the Countries That Allowed Huawei to Build 5G," Huawei Central, August 30, 2019, https://www.huaweicentral.com/here-are-the-countries-that-allowed-huawei-to-build-5g-list/.)

Note: Data as of August 2019. Danish carriers have not selected Huawei or ZTE.

Advanced Research Projects Agency, to develop and implement the Office of Science and Technology Policy's 2021 research and development priorities:[283]

- Building and leveraging a diverse, highly skilled American workforce.
- Creating and supporting research environments that reflect American values.
- Supporting transformative research of high-risk and potentially high-reward technologies.
- Leveraging the power of data.
- Building, strengthening, and expanding strategic multisector partnerships.

4.6.3 Strengthen the Capacity of the Committee on Foreign Investment in the United States

The U.S. government must consider and implement acceptable measures to ensure the resilience of the supply of technologies deemed critical to national security and economic prosperity. This requires taking disparate measures to both stem the flow of foreign investment into U.S. companies and stop the loss of technologies to competitors through state-sponsored industrial espionage. The Committee on Foreign Investment in the United States (CFIUS) is the primary mechanism through which the U.S. government combats these threats. While recent reforms enacted in the Foreign Investment Risk Review Modernization Act (FIRRMA) bolstered the Committee, the executive branch should do more to help it achieve its goals.

Specifically, the executive branch should:
- Direct the Committee to more aggressively review bankruptcy buyouts and restructuring, as well as early-stage venture capital and private equity investment.
- Direct departments and agencies to identify inconsistencies, gaps, or redundancies in programs across the federal government meant to support department and agency CFIUS reviews and compliance work, and identify areas where FIRRMA funds can be used to centralize or consolidate programs as managed services to fill gaps and reduce redundancies.

- Direct departments and agencies to conduct a comprehensive review of budgetary shortfalls for programs and work envisioned under FIRRMA and work with Congress to ensure that departments and agencies have funding sufficient to carry out their respective CFIUS programs.

4.6.4 Invest in the National Cyber Moonshot Initiative

In 2018, the President's National Security Telecommunications Advisory Committee determined that "[t]he United States is at an inflection point: simultaneously faced with a progressively worsening cybersecurity threat environment and an ever-increasing dependence on Internet technologies fundamental to public safety, economic prosperity, and overall way of life. Our national security is now inexorably linked to cybersecurity." The committee called for a "moonshot" initiative to emphasize the "national prioritization, collective action, and accelerated innovation" required to solve this grand challenge, akin to putting a human on the moon.[284]

While the National Cyber Moonshot Team is making progress on the 10-year plan with its six pillars and grand challenges, its success ultimately depends on consistent and enduring attention and support. The initial Cybersecurity Moonshot report reinforces this point, stating that "the level of U.S. Government funding and investment in cybersecurity should exceed current levels by orders of magnitude and must be sustained at wartime-like levels for the decade timespan of the initiative."[285] However, the federal government's fiscal year 2019 and proposed 2020 budgets failed to appropriate funds commensurate with the needs of the National Cyber Moonshot efforts. Congress and the executive branch must therefore actively engage with the National Cyber Moonshot Council to identify and appropriate the funds necessary to achieve the goals of the Moonshot initiative, and to identify and implement methods to permit and encourage private-sector participation at an effective level.

STRATEGIC OBJECTIVE #5:
STRENGTHEN NATIONAL SYSTEMIC DATA SECURITY

The security and privacy of Americans' data should be substantially and systemically improved, especially as data becomes increasingly central to the modern digital economy and our everyday lives. In our current ecosystem, there is insufficient legal consensus on the appropriate use and security of personal and sensitive data, even as data breaches are increasingly delivering a treasure trove of information to malicious actors. The information stolen from American entrepreneurs, public officials, industry leaders, everyday citizens, and even clandestine operatives is fueling social engineering and espionage campaigns against U.S. firms and agencies. This entanglement of private data security and national security reveals the need to establish clear and consistent legal and technical frameworks to protect the information of individuals and firms, minimize the likelihood of their loss or manipulation, and make the "big data" economy safe for everyday Americans.

Key Recommendation

4.7 Congress should pass a national data security and privacy protection law establishing and standardizing requirements for the collection, retention, and sharing of user data.

The creation, storage, transmission, and analysis of data are core components of the modern economy. Seven of the United States' 15 most profitable firms are software or telecommunications companies, and the technology industry as a whole represents more than 10 percent of overall economic output.[286] The private information and behavior of individual consumers and businesses are fueling this industry and powering a new wave of data-centric commerce. This concentration and monetization of Americans' personal and business data is creating new industries and value—but also new opportunities for the unintentional mishandling or the malicious misuse of that data. The loss or exposure of sensitive information is becoming more common and more severe, and each instance provides malign actors with additional opportunities for exploitation, espionage, or attack.

These dynamics have spurred advanced economies around the world into action, from Europe's General Data Protection Regulation to Japan's Act on the Protection of Personal Information to California's Consumer Privacy Act. In the absence of congressional leadership, these competing frameworks threaten to splinter the digital economy, confuse efforts to secure users' personal data, and imperil the ability of American companies to compete globally.

Congress should pass legislation standardizing requirements that are enduring for the safe and appropriate handling of personal data. This is a necessary step to make the modern data-driven economy safe yet flexible for all Americans, provide the regulatory certainty needed for U.S. companies' continued innovation and prosperity, and ensure that the global digital marketplace remains open, interoperable, reliable, and secure.

Specifically, this legislation should establish:
- National minimum common standards for the collection, retention, analysis, and third-party sharing of personal data.
- Definitions of personal data, to include that which can be linked, directly or indirectly, to individuals or households.
- Thresholds for what entities are covered by this legislation.
- Timelines for deleting, correcting, or porting personal data upon request by the appropriate persons.
- A clear mandate for the Federal Trade Commission to enforce these standards with civil penalties.

Any legislation should also explicitly create the expectation that covered entities will exert reasonable care and security regarding the protection of all relevant data they hold. Data security is a necessary first step for data privacy, because if the security of data is not guaranteed, its privacy cannot be either. Legislative proposals on this critical issue are pending, and Congress should seek to find a consensus.

Enabling Recommendation

4.7.1 Pass a National Breach Notification Law

Data breach notification laws require an entity that has been subject to a data breach—regardless of cause—to notify its customers and other parties and take steps to remediate injuries caused by the breach.[287] While such laws have been adopted in some form by all 50 states, the District of Columbia, Guam, Puerto Rico, and the Virgin Islands, there is no national standard for such notification.[288] As a result, Americans' data is subject to a patchwork of varying protections. A national framework is needed to standardize consumers' expectations and provide regulatory certainty to American businesses engaging in interstate and global commerce.

Congress should pass a national breach notification law that:

- Preempts the 54 existing state, district, and territorial data breach notification laws.
- Establishes a threshold for what would be considered a covered "breach."
- Requires the notification and transmission of relevant forensic data to the appropriate law enforcement and cybersecurity authorities and other relevant anonymized data to authorized data-gathering bodies, such as the Bureau of Cyber Statistics proposed above (recommendation 4.3).
- Sets standards and timelines for notifying victims.
- Sets criteria that determine when victims should receive free credit monitoring or other data and identity protections.
- Deconflicts with existing federal regulation for private-sector and other non-federal entities.

Benefits and Challenges of End-to-End Encryption

There is broad consensus across industry and the government on the importance of strong encryption. Advanced encryption of data in motion (i.e., as it is being transmitted) and at rest (i.e., as it is stored) should be a cornerstone of responsible data security. This includes, for example, using mature, well-researched protocols such as Transport Layer Security (TLS) to shield email, web browsing, and other important internet traffic from interception or modification by malicious actors. Strong encryption helps prevent or limit data breaches, and when data is breached it mitigates the harm to businesses, the government, and individuals.

One particular implementation of encryption, known as "end-to-end," is the subject of considerable debate. End-to-end encryption enables the transmission of data in such a way that only the communicating parties have the ability to access the data being secured—intermediaries, such as the company that provides the communication system, do not. Broad implementation of this form of encryption could improve the systemic data security of the overall cyber ecosystem, though it may also conceal the activities of criminals and shield them from government action. The debate over balancing these concerns has run for decades, but recently it has been energized by the rapid adoption of end-to-end encrypted communications. Between WhatsApp, Signal, Telegram, and iMessage, numerous companies around the world are now offering end-to-end encrypted messaging services to more than 100 million Americans and 1.5 billion global citizens.[289]

One reason the debate over end-to-end encryption has been so difficult is that its benefits and costs are so hard to compare. As end-to-end encryption is more comprehensively adopted, and beyond the domestic data security benefit described above, it helps protect democratic values around the globe by making unfettered surveillance more difficult in certain repressive nations where such values are under siege. The United Nations' Office of the High Commissioner for Human Rights has observed that end-to-end encryption is becoming an important tool for pushing back against a rising tide of increasingly lethal high-tech illiberalism and for protecting global freedom of expression.[290] In this way, end-to-end encryption is currently making repression more difficult and less effective, imposing persistent costs on authoritarian governments.

This form of encryption is a double-edged sword, however, as it also challenges democratically authorized and judicially circumscribed access to data that law enforcement agencies require for public safety and security. End-to-end encryption is currently impeding the government's ability to obtain lawful access to electronic evidence in investigations ranging from cyber intrusions and attacks to crimes threatening serious harms, like child exploitation, gang violence and drug trafficking, and domestic and international terrorism. For example, attributing responsibility for malicious cyber activity to particular actors—a necessary precursor to many law enforcement responses—can be difficult and slow without access to relevant encrypted data content.

The quest for solutions to these issues should be informed by the core values that unite citizens of free and open societies. All government access to data should be, as it is in the United States, tightly circumscribed by protections like those in our Fourth Amendment. The United States requires infrastructure that enables citizens to confidently and securely conduct their affairs without unwarranted infringement of their essential liberties and that incorporates methods to protect them from harm. While the Commission does not express a position on the growing adoption of end-to-end encryption, the Commission does assert that both the government and the private sector should look to the future with a dual mandate on which all agree: strong encryption can and must underpin the essential functions of a free, open, interoperable, secure, and resilient global internet, but appropriately authorized and publicly accountable government officials must also be able to pursue criminal elements exploiting the internet to prey upon innocent persons.

This debate is difficult, but the U.S. government should rely on these principles to engage with the trade-offs of end-to-end encryption honestly—while recognizing that market forces and other countries (democratic and not) are rapidly shaping the encryption reality.

OPERATIONALIZE CYBERSECURITY COLLABORATION WITH THE PRIVATE SECTOR

Layered cyber deterrence requires reshaping how the U.S. government coordinates with the private sector to address systemic cyber risk and counter growing cyber threats. The majority of assets, functions, and entities in the cyber domain that are attractive targets for adversaries are owned and operated by the private sector. As a consequence, cyber defense, while a shared responsibility, will depend significantly on the underlying efforts of the owners and operators of private networks and infrastructure. National defense therefore takes a very different shape in cyberspace, where the government mainly plays a supporting and enabling role in security and defense and is not the primary actor. The U.S. government and industry thus must arrive at a new social contract of shared responsibility to secure the nation in cyberspace. This "collective defense" in cyberspace requires that the public and private sectors work from a place of truly shared situational awareness and that each leverages its unique comparative advantages for the common defense.

This pillar attempts to operationalize cybersecurity collaboration with the private sector by organizing and focusing U.S. government efforts on areas where they can have an outsized impact. Doing so requires improving the integration of public and private cyber defense efforts as well as ruthlessly prioritizing support to private entities and concentrating on areas where the U.S. government has an asymmetric advantage. Specifically, this pillar focuses on three strategic objectives.

First, this pillar creates a framework for improving and prioritizing U.S. government cybersecurity support to critical elements of the private sector. Because the federal government's resources and capabilities are limited, it must prioritize its contributions to the defense of systemically important critical infrastructure—that is, critical infrastructure entities that manage systems and assets whose disruption could have cascading, destabilizing effects on U.S. national security, economic security, and public health and safety. While private-sector entities are responsible for the defense and security of their networks, the U.S. government must bring to bear its unique authorities and resources, as well as diplomatic, economic, military, law enforcement, and intelligence capabilities, to support these actors in their defense efforts.

Second, this pillar sets out a plan to focus U.S. government efforts on areas where it can add the most value: namely, on building better situational awareness of cyber threats. Information sharing is an important part of public-private collaboration, but it is not an end in and of itself. It is a means of building better situational awareness of cyber threats, which can then inform the actions of both the private sector and the government. Here the U.S. government has a unique capacity to take in information from disparate sources, including the intelligence community, and integrate that information to produce a more holistic picture of and better insights into the national collective understanding of threats.

Third, this pillar identifies the need for the U.S. government to better integrate its own cyber defense security efforts with those of the private sector. To confront this challenge, the U.S. government must both better understand the system of centers and missions within the federal government and how they can be more fully integrated into the execution of the national cybersecurity mission and facilitate better joint, coordinated campaign planning that includes the private sector. To those ends, the U.S. government should conduct a comprehensive systems analysis review of federal cyber defense and security centers and missions, with a view toward diminishing barriers to collaboration across the federal government and between the public and private sectors.

STRATEGIC OBJECTIVE #1:
IMPROVE GOVERNMENT SUPPORT TO PRIVATE-SECTOR OPERATIONS

The U.S. government should improve government support to private-sector cyber defensive operations. However, the federal government has limited resources and capabilities, and should prioritize the defense of systemically important critical infrastructure—the critical infrastructure entities that manage systems and assets whose disruption could have cascading, destabilizing effects on U.S. national security, economic security, or public health and safety. While the U.S. government has taken steps to assist these high-risk entities through Section 9 of Executive Order 13636, that effort falls short of codifying or fully implementing the social contract of shared responsibility and partnership in cybersecurity—and it also does not empower the U.S. government with the resources and authorities necessary to defend them.

Key Recommendation

5.1 Congress should codify the concept of "systemically important critical infrastructure," whereby entities responsible for systems and assets that underpin national critical functions are ensured the full support of the U.S. government and shoulder additional security requirements consistent with their unique status and importance.

Through Section 9 of Executive Order 13636, the Obama administration took vital steps to recognize that not all critical infrastructure is of equal importance to the preservation of public health and safety, economic security, or national security.[291] The systemically important critical infrastructure (SICI) entities, and their most vital systems and assets, are focal points of leverage for nation-state adversaries, allowing them to scale up the effects of cyber campaigns and thus the risk they can pose to the United States in peacetime and in crisis.[292] Both the private sector and the U.S. government have a vested interest in protecting these systems and assets and have unique responsibilities for their security and resilience. The U.S. government must be assured that these companies are taking their security responsibilities seriously, honoring the public trust that appertains to the services and functions they provide, and participating in fully collaborative joint security efforts. Private-sector entities should likewise trust that the U.S. government is fully leveraging its unique authorities and resources to support their security operations, both in fulfillment of its responsibility to defend against and respond to nation-state

attacks and in recognition of their unique national security importance—and the public good they provide. While Section 9 of Executive Order 13636 recognizes this relationship and acknowledges the social contract that underlies it, it does not endow the U.S. government with any new requirements, resources, or authorities to support SICI; nor does Section 9 designation place any additional expectations on the entities that receive it.

To address this gap, Congress should codify into law the concept of "systemically important critical infrastructure," whereby entities responsible for systemically critical systems and assets are granted special assistance from the U.S. government and shoulder additional security and information-sharing requirements befitting their unique status and importance. While these entities are ultimately responsible for the defense and security of their networks, the U.S. government can and should bring to bear its unique authorities, resources, and intelligence capabilities to support these entities in their defense—and assume greater responsibility in instances in which they are directly threatened by nation-states, designated transnational criminal groups, or terrorist organizations. Separate, distinct designation and requirements should be established for sectors that have a unique relationship with the federal government, such as the Defense Industrial Base.

Identification and Designation: Congress should direct the executive branch, through the Department of Homeland Security (DHS) and in consultation with the appropriate sector-specific agencies, to develop a process to identify key systems and assets underpinning certain critical functions and designate the entities responsible for their management, operations, and security as "systemically important critical infrastructure." These designations should be reviewed and updated as part of the regularly occurring National Risk Management Cycle led by DHS (recommendation 3.2.2). Designated entities should be codified in an unclassified determination issued by the President, while the specific systems and assets that led to the designation should be classified.

In defining the critical functions by which to designate systemically important critical infrastructure, the U.S. government should focus on national critical functions that:
- Directly support or underpin national security programs or government or military operations.
- Constitute essential economic functions or underpin the national distribution of goods and services.
- Support or underpin public health and safety or are so foundational that their disruption could endanger human life on a massive scale.

Insulation from Liability: Entities designated as systemically important critical infrastructure would be shielded from liability in instances when covered systems and assets are targeted, attacked, compromised, or disrupted through a cyberattack by a nation-state, designated transnational criminal group, or terrorist organization. To qualify, designated entities would need to have demonstrated good-faith compliance with all requirements set as a consequence of their designation.

Government Program Requirements: Congress should direct the executive branch to define government programs in which entities designated as systemically important critical infrastructure would be required to participate as a consequence of their designation; this list should be updated regularly. These programs should include federal government information-sharing programs, national risk identification and assessment efforts, and other relevant federal programs meant to assist the private sector in cyber defense and security.

Security Certification: Congress should direct the executive branch to develop a "Security Certification" for systemically important critical infrastructure and a mechanism, devised in consultation with the private sector, for SICI entities to certify their compliance on a consistent basis. DHS and the Department of Defense (DoD), in coordination with sector-specific agencies, should establish common and sector-specific standards and expectations for the governance and execution of security operations for this certification. In establishing these certifications, the executive branch should seek to reduce redundancy and regulatory burden by looking to existing regulatory requirements or existing security regimes rather than establishing new ones.

Prioritized Federal Assistance: The executive branch should define a process by which designated entities can, through DHS, request expedited federal assistance in instances when they have been compromised or attacked by a malicious cyber actor. This process should define the information required to submit a request, the timeline for response, and the criteria used by federal departments and agencies to evaluate and approve requests.

Indications and Warning and Intelligence Support: Congress should explicitly establish in law that sharing intelligence with U.S.-owned entities designated as SICI does not constitute unlawful favoring of one entity over another. In addition, Congress should direct the executive branch to define mechanisms and procedures, through DHS and the Office of the Director of National Intelligence and in consultation with sector-specific agencies, for enhanced collaboration among designated entities, sector-specific agencies, and the U.S. intelligence community.

Enabling Recommendations

5.1.1 Review and Update Intelligence Authorities to Increase Intelligence Support to the Broader Private Sector

The U.S. intelligence community is not currently resourced to fully support the private sector in cyber defense and security. While the intelligence community is formidable in informing security operations in instances when the U.S. government is the defender, it lacks appropriate policies and processes to do so when primary responsibility falls outside of the U.S. government. Intelligence policies and procedures remain outdated; they have not been sufficiently modernized to account for the unique challenges of cyberspace or the flexibility and ingenuity of malicious foreign actors. As a result, the intelligence community continues to be significantly limited in its ability to maintain awareness of evolving cyber threats and provide warning to U.S. entities when they are being targeted. While codifying systemically important critical infrastructure will ensure stronger intelligence support and indications and warning for the most critical systems and assets, the intelligence community will still be limited in its ability to support critical infrastructure that falls outside of that designation. Thus the U.S. government must address more general limitations in its ability to provide intelligence support to all private sector stakeholders and associated organizations, such as information sharing and analysis centers (ISACs) and the Financial Systemic Analysis and Resilience Center (FSARC).

To that end, Congress should direct the executive branch to conduct a six-month comprehensive review of intelligence policies, procedures, and resources to identify and address key limitations in the ability of the intelligence community to provide intelligence support to the private sector. The executive branch should report its findings to Congress upon conclusion of its review, which should include specific recommendations or plans to address challenges identified in the report. The review should:

- Examine U.S. foreign intelligence surveillance authorities to identify and address limitations in collection for cyber defense missions supporting private-sector stakeholders.
- Review policies to identify limitations in the intelligence community's ability to share threat intelligence information with the private sector, including accounting for instances when national security outweighs concerns over preferential treatment.
- Review downgrade and declassification procedures for cyber threat intelligence to improve the speed and timeliness of its release; consider defining criteria and procedures for expedited declassification and release of certain types of intelligence.
- Examine current and projected mission requirements of the National Security Agency's (NSA) Cybersecurity Directorate, identify current funding gaps, and recommend budgetary changes needed to ensure that NSA meets expectations for increased support to the nation's cybersecurity effort.
- Review cyber-related information-sharing consent processes, including consent to monitor agreements, and assess gaps and opportunities for greater standardization and simplification while ensuring privacy and civil liberty protections.
- Review existing statutes governing "national security systems"—including National Security Directive 42, which establishes executive policy on the security of national security telecommunications and information systems—and assess their ability to provide the National Security Agency with sufficient authority to conduct its mission in protecting systems and assets that are critical to national security.

5.1.2 Strengthen and Codify Processes for Identifying Broader Private-Sector Cybersecurity Intelligence Needs and Priorities

Understanding the intelligence needs and gaps of private-sector entities is critical in ensuring that the U.S. government is able to provide focused, actionable intelligence in support of their cybersecurity operations. While the preceding recommendations focus on removing barriers to or limitations in the collection or production of intelligence and its distribution to the private sector, they will be fundamentally hindered if the U.S. government lacks the processes to best serve the private sector and answer its security requirements. However, existing processes to solicit private-sector input into U.S. intelligence needs and collection requirements are inconsistent, too narrow in scope, and lack sufficient detail. For instance, existing processes compile self-identified intelligence gaps but do not account for common vulnerabilities, such as common technology or third-party services, that would be targeted by an intelligent nation-state adversary. This information, if specific enough, can be used to provide indications and warnings and focused intelligence to private-sector entities if and when the intelligence community detects they are being or will be targeted by a malicious actor.

Congress should therefore direct and resource the federal government to establish a formal process to solicit and compile private-sector input to inform national intelligence priorities, collection requirements, and more focused U.S. intelligence support to private-sector cybersecurity operations. This process should:

- Be led by the Office of the Director of National Intelligence and DHS, in coordination with DoD and other sector-specific agencies.
- Identify common technologies or interdependencies—areas of high risk that are likely to be targeted by intelligent nation-state adversaries.
- Seek to identify intelligence gaps, priorities, and needs across the private sector and state, local, tribal, and territorial entities.

- Run parallel with and be tied to National Risk Management Cycle (recommendation 3.1.1) processes for risk identification and assessment, as the same information that informs sector-specific and cross-sector risk can be used to guide U.S. intelligence efforts to provide indications and warnings and more focused intelligence.
- Empower sector-specific agencies and make them accountable to work with their sectors, including sector-coordinating councils and ISACs, to identify specific critical lines of businesses, technologies, and processes and work directly with the intelligence community to convey specific details.
- Codify legal protections for the types of information that would be routinely shared as part of this process, ensuring that such information is protected and insulated from public disclosure.

5.1.3 Empower Departments and Agencies to Serve Administrative Subpoenas in Support of Threat and Asset Response Activities

While the U.S. government has a unique understanding of threat and vulnerability, there are limits to its ability to systematically identify those who are vulnerable or compromised, notify them, and assist them in mitigating or reducing vulnerability. In particular, the inability to identify the owners and operators of known vulnerable or compromised online systems hinders the U.S. government's efforts to notify and, upon request, assist private-sector entities in their security operations. Current authorities are limited exclusively to certain criminal contexts, where evidence of a compromise exists, and do not address instances in which systems are merely vulnerable. To address this gap, Congress should consider granting certain departments and agencies subpoena authority in support of their threat and asset response activities, while ensuring appropriate liability protections for cooperating private-sector network owners.

Congress should extend existing law enforcement administrative subpoena authority, currently defined under 18 U.S. Code § 3486, for the Federal Bureau of Investigation and the United States Secret Service to include violations of the Computer Fraud and Abuse Act, 18 U.S. Code § 1030.

Congress should pass the Cybersecurity Vulnerability Identification and Notification Act of 2019 to grant tailored authority to the Director of the Cybersecurity and Infrastructure Security Agency (CISA) to serve administrative subpoenas so that the owners of online systems with known vulnerabilities can be identified, enabling asset response activities and preventing future intrusion.

STRATEGIC OBJECTIVE #2:
IMPROVE COMBINED SITUATIONAL AWARENESS OF CYBER THREATS

The U.S. government should improve combined situational awareness of cyber threats to better support its own and private-sector cyber defensive efforts. For the better part of a decade, expanding public-private collaboration in cybersecurity was synonymous with sharing threat information. Information sharing is an important part of public-private collaboration, certainly, but it is not an end in and of itself. Rather it enables better situational awareness of cyber threats, which can then inform the actions of both the private sector and the government. Truly shared situational awareness is the foundation on which operational collaboration is built and enabled. The U.S. government should leverage its unique, comparative advantages to improve the national collective understanding of the threat, including the information available to the intelligence community and a capacity to integrate information from disparate sources—both public and private. Similarly, the U.S. government must create the structures and processes to work with private-sector entities that have unique insights of their own and a different, and in some cases more comprehensive, view of threats impacting domestic critical infrastructure.

Key Recommendation

5.2 Congress should establish and fund a Joint Collaborative Environment, a common and interoperable environment for the sharing and fusing of threat information, insight, and other relevant data across the federal government and between the public and private sectors.

While the U.S. government has taken a number of steps to develop situational awareness in cyberspace, there continue to be significant limitations on its ability to develop a comprehensive picture of the threat. Federal departments and agencies each maintain a number of programs that can provide insight into threats affecting U.S. government networks and critical infrastructure. However, the data or information is not routinely shared or cross-correlated at the speed and scale necessary for rapid detection and identification. This fragmented approach presents further challenges in integrating with the private sector, both as a contributor to and as a beneficiary of U.S. government insight, causing confusion and adding significant burden for the private sector in public-private information-sharing efforts. The U.S. government must take steps to shift the burden of integration onto itself, establishing the mechanisms and enforceable procedures to build the situational awareness necessary for its own operations and for forging true operational collaboration with the private sector.

To that end, Congress should establish a "Joint Collaborative Environment", a common, cloud-based environment in which the federal government's unclassified and classified cyber threat information, malware forensics, and network data from monitoring programs are made commonly available for query and analysis—to the greatest extent possible.[293] Initial stages will focus on the integration of programs across the federal government and with owners and operators of systemically important critical infrastructure, while subsequent phases will focus on extending this environment to larger constituencies of critical infrastructure, including ISACs. This program would make real the promise of a "whole-of-government" and public-private approach to cybersecurity, ensuring that network data, cyber threat intelligence, and malware forensics from each department or agency and the private sector are available at machine speed for comprehensive detection and analysis. The Joint Collaborative Environment should support federal cyber centers, an integrated cyber center at CISA (recommendation 5.3), and a planning cell under CISA (recommendation 5.4).

Design, Development, and Planning: Given the complexity of such a program, Congress should allow for a multiyear design and development cycle that proceeds in phases. Initial phases should focus on designing appropriate interoperable standards, affording for integration of all covered data programs, and ensuring that disparate databases or centers can be compatible and interoperable at machine speed and scale. Subsequent phases should focus on sharing high-level insights and more exquisite data—as well as addressing challenges introduced by wider inclusion of private-sector partners.

Program Management: Congress should designate DHS and the NSA to act as the primary program managers and

lead agencies charged with developing and maintaining the environment in unclassified and classified space, respectively. Where feasible, unclassified data should be routinely mirrored to a classified environment, and integrated with classified data, to provide enrichment, to broaden context, and to inform and enable indications and warning. Analytic tools should be deployed across classification levels to leverage all relevant data sets as appropriate.

Designation of Programs: Congress should direct the executive branch to designate, as part of the environment's development process and on a routine basis after it is fully operational, federal programs required to participate, feed into, and/or be interoperable with the environment. These federal programs should include any programs that generate, collect, or disseminate data or information in the detection, identification, analysis, and monitoring of cyber threats, such as:

- Government network-monitoring and intrusion detection programs.
- Cyber threat indicator–sharing programs.
- Government-sponsored network sensors or network-monitoring programs for the private sector or for state, local, tribal, and territorial governments.
- Incident response and cybersecurity technical assistance programs.
- Malware forensics and reverse-engineering programs.

Information-Sharing Protections: The law should direct that any private-sector information-sharing programs participating in the Joint Collaborative Environment are extended protections analogous to those afforded by the Cybersecurity Information Sharing Act of 2015. The availability of data within this environment is contingent on these protections. When appropriate, the environment will share raw, anonymized data to inform the work of the Bureau of Cyber Statistics (recommendation 4.3), in compliance with that bureau's charter.

Data Standardization and Interoperability: Congress should direct the executive branch to establish an interagency council, chaired by the program managers, that sets data standards and requirements for program participation and interoperability. Data standards and interoperability requirements should be formed in a public-private process to ensure the full inclusion of the private sector in program design. Membership should include any department or agency that oversees participating, designated programs. The council would be empowered to recommend budgetary changes necessary for programs to make technical or operational adjustments required for integration and interoperability, to establish and maintain the environment, and to ensure that the environment has adequate security to prevent breaches and to guard against and detect false data insertion.

Modules and Tooling: Congress should appropriate necessary funds to DHS and the NSA to develop, purchase, and deploy tools and analytical software that can be applied and shared to manipulate, transform, and display data and other identified needs.

Data Governance and Privacy: In developing the program, the federal government should establish the procedures and data governance structures necessary to protect the sensitivity of data, comply with federal regulations and statutes, and respect existing consent agreements with the private sector and other non-federal entities. The federal government should take steps to make preexisting and all future consent agreements compliant with inclusion into the environment and bring preexisting agreements and programs into compliance with the program.

Public-Private Partnership: The environment should be designed with the goal of including the participation of the private sector and information sharing and analysis organizations/centers, both to feed into and to benefit from the data and analytical insight the environment would provide. Initially, elements of systemically important critical infrastructure, as part of their designation, will be encouraged to share cyber threat indicators, malware forensics, and data from network sensor programs.

Enabling Recommendations

5.2.1 Expand and Standardize Voluntary Threat Detection Programs

Current voluntary network monitoring and threat detection programs[294] are essential in advancing a better understanding of threats affecting U.S. critical infrastructure. These voluntary programs, through which the U.S. government provides sensors or funding to monitor private-sector networks, can enable the rapid detection and identification of cyber threats—whether they are isolated incidents or part of a larger, coordinated campaign. While programs like DHS's Enhanced Cybersecurity Services Program and the Department of Energy's Cyber Risk Information Sharing Program show great promise, their usefulness has been hindered by a limited scale of deployment and insufficient coverage. In addition, coverage and deployment have not been centrally planned or coordinated to reflect strategic assessment of risk and need. Properly implemented and deployed at sufficient scale, these programs could form the foundation of a virtual "early warning network" in cyberspace, providing a vital missing piece in U.S. government and private-sector situational awareness.

To achieve this goal, the U.S. government should take steps, through the Joint Collaborative Environment's interagency council, to expand and more centrally fund, manage, and deploy these programs and ensure their interoperability with broader federal cyber threat–sharing and integration efforts. In addition, Congress should identify programs that should be excluded from or have special handling in this expansion and standardization, such as law enforcement and domestic counterintelligence collection efforts.

5.2.2 Pass a National Cyber Incident Reporting Law

The government's cyber incident situational awareness, its ability to detect coordinated cyber campaigns, and its risk identification and assessment efforts rely on comprehensive data. However, there are insufficient federal and state laws and policies requiring companies to report incidents that impact or threaten to impact business operations. While mandated reporting for regulatory purposes and voluntary information-sharing protections exist, the federal government lacks a mandate to systematically collect cyber incident information reliably and at the scale necessary to inform situational awareness.

To address this shortcoming, Congress should authorize DHS and Department of Justice (DOJ) to establish requirements for critical infrastructure entities to report cyber incidents to the federal government. In crafting this requirement, DHS and DOJ should collaborate with public- and private-sector entities to identify the types of critical infrastructure entities to which it should apply. This information should be minimized, anonymized, and shared as statistical data with the Bureau of Cyber Statistics (recommendation 4.3).

- DHS and DOJ should, in coordination with sector-specific agencies and the private sector, define the thresholds and types of cyber incidents that would be required to be reported under this law.
- DHS and DOJ should define clear mechanisms, processes, the format, and information required in reporting such an incident. These specifications should include processes necessary to protect privacy and minimize personally identifiable information.
- Reported incidents may not be used to inform or drive punitive measures taken by regulatory agencies; however, reporting under this requirement does not trigger, or obviate, reporting requirements under existing regulations—nor does it shield covered

entities from regulatory action if violations are discovered through other means.
- As the relevant sector-specific agency and contracting party, DoD may define additional mechanisms, process, format, and reporting information and regulations required for the Defense Industrial Base.

5.2.3 Amend the Pen Register Trap and Trace (PRTT) Statute to Enable Better Identification of Malicious Actors

Current electronic surveillance laws do not allow companies to engage in defensive measures to fully identify actors or infrastructure that is being used to target or attack them. This information is often transitory, and immediate action may be needed to ensure that identifying information is preserved. Current ambiguities center on certain cybersecurity techniques such as establishing a "honeypot"—that is, direct action taken by an entity outside of its own network, such as following an actor after a compromise of its own system. Amending PRTT to include existing exemptions to the Wiretap Act found at 18 U.S. Code § 2511(2) would allow an avenue for defenders to receive information about attackers that is currently restricted to "Electronic Communication Providers." To reduce ambiguity and allow the private sector a broader range of defensive techniques, Congress should amend 18 U.S. Code § 3121, referred to as the Pen Register and Trap and Trace statute, to help enable certain "active defense" activities. Amending the PRTT statute would allow cybersecurity companies, or companies with the necessary resources and expertise, to conduct more effective identifying activities on behalf of their companies or customers.

STRATEGIC OBJECTIVE #3:
INTEGRATE PUBLIC- AND PRIVATE-SECTOR CYBER DEFENSE EFFORTS

The U.S. government should improve its capacity to better coordinate its own cyber defense planning and operations and integrate its operations with the private sector. Current federal government operations to defend against cyberattacks are decentralized and tend to be uncoordinated, leading to inefficiencies and the lack of a coherent, strategic approach to defend the nation. Therefore, the interests of critical infrastructure providers and parts of the private sector that are key to cyber defense are not always adequately incorporated into these defensive operations because of a lack of institutionalized processes and procedures for collaboration with federal agencies and a dearth of threat information.

Key Recommendation

5.3 Congress should direct the executive branch to strengthen a public-private, integrated cyber center within CISA in support of the critical infrastructure security and resilience mission and to conduct a one-year, comprehensive systems analysis review of federal cyber and cybersecurity centers, including plans to develop and improve integration.

Over the past decade, the U.S. government has stood up a number of missions, centers, and programs across the federal government to strengthen U.S. cybersecurity. As the number of agencies involved in the cybersecurity mission has expanded, however, there have been difficulties in integrating their operations for coordinated action, common situational awareness, and joint analysis, and the risk of fragmented, uncoordinated efforts has grown. U.S. public-private cybersecurity efforts will continue to be undermined without effective, meaningful cooperation across federal departments and agencies. While the recommendations in this report that call for investment in programs that support and enable joint planning, coordinated action, and shared information and analysis—all vital parts of operational collaboration—can do much to address these issues, they are insufficient if underlying structural procedural issues remain unaddressed. More importantly, these recommendations are no substitute for human-to-human collaboration and close, trusted relationships. For the United States, seamless collaboration means diminishing barriers between agencies and between the public and private sectors with a focus on relationships—underpinned and served by a

strong technical foundation like the Joint Collaborative Environment (recommendation 5.2).

CISA is already a key component in coordinating the cyber defense and security efforts of federal departments and agencies and integrating these efforts with the private sector. Initially conceptualized through a national cybersecurity and communications integration center (NCCIC), the vision for CISA's cyber mission is to be the U.S. government's primary coordinating body charged with forging whole-of-government, public-private collaboration in cybersecurity. However, CISA has been institutionally limited in its ability to fully carry out this mission, hindered by inadequate facilities, insufficient resources, lack of buy-in from other federal departments and agencies, ambiguity from Congress on its role and position in relation to other agencies, and inconsistent support to and integration with the private sector. To truly operationalize cybersecurity collaboration with the private sector, the U.S. government must strengthen an integrated cyber center within CISA, improve its connectivity with other key cyber and cybersecurity centers—including the FBI's National Cyber Investigative Joint

Task Force (NCIJTF), ODNI's Cyber Threat Intelligence Integration Center (CTIIC), DOD's Integrated Cyber Center and Joint Operations Center (ICC/JOC), and NSA's Cybersecurity Directorate (CSD)—and ensure that the systems, processes, and *human element* of collaboration and integration are fully brought to bear in support of the critical infrastructure cybersecurity and resilience mission.

Congress should direct the executive branch to immediately begin to strengthen a public-private, integrated cyber center within CISA in support of the critical infrastructure cybersecurity and resilience mission and in coordination with centers in the FBI, ODNI, and DoD. While this is under way, the executive branch should conduct a one-year, comprehensive systems analysis review of federal cyber and cybersecurity centers, which should include developing plans to better integrate the centers. The review should identify challenges and solutions to more effectively integrate elements of federal cyber centers, the private sector, and CISA with a view toward reinforcing human-to-human collaboration, reducing procedural or technical barriers to integration, implementing other recommendations within this report, and, to the greatest extent possible, increasing meaningful integration of cybersecurity stakeholders. This process should be undertaken by the National Cyber Director (recommendation 1.5), or, in lieu of a National Cyber Director, a working group led by DHS, in coordination with DoD, DOJ, FBI, and ODNI. In particular, this review should address the following actions.

Strengthening CISA's Public-Private Integrated Cyber Center: CISA's role as the primary interface between the federal government and critical infrastructure for cybersecurity places it in a unique position to operationalize the type of public-private collaboration necessary to secure and defend cyberspace and the critical infrastructure that relies on it. In strengthening a public-private integrated cyber center within CISA, the executive branch should identify continuing gaps and shortcomings in CISA's current capacity, structure, funding, and integration

of its work with sector-specific agencies that prevent it from fulfilling its role as the central coordinator among federal centers for critical infrastructure cybersecurity and resilience.

Identifying Areas of Integration and Collocation: The executive branch should assess areas where existing federal cyber centers, or portions of a center's mission, would benefit from greater integration or collocation to support cybersecurity collaboration with critical infrastructure. The review should identify and acknowledge continuing gaps and shortcomings in associated capacity and funding of the FBI and ODNI, identify methods to better integrate efforts with CISA in support of its mission to ensure the security and resilience of critical infrastructure, and identify where federal agencies have distinct statutory authorities (i.e., those of law enforcement, counterintelligence, military, and intelligence operations) best kept distinct and separate from these efforts.

Supporting the National Security Agency's Cybersecurity Directorate (CSD): The executive branch review of federal cyber centers should include a particular focus on NSA's new Cybersecurity Directorate. Sustaining and strengthening the CSD's collaboration with and support to other federal departments and agencies, particularly CISA, is critical in ensuring that the U.S. government's technical expertise and intelligence resources are fully brought to bear in supporting both federal and public-private cybersecurity efforts. The executive branch should identify continuing gaps and opportunities for greater integration of CSD with CISA, other federal cyber centers, and, as needed, the private sector in its role of securing national security systems.

Assessing Centralized, Collocated Public-Private Collaboration: The U.S. government should identify lessons from the United Kingdom's National Cybersecurity Center model, which maintains collocated classified and unclassified environments for private-sector cybersecurity integration. The review should assess whether an integrated cyber center within CISA should be similarly organized into two environments: an unclassified side, which handles general cybersecurity coordination and cooperation with the private sector, and a classified side with appropriate support from CSD, which handles deeper collaboration with systemically important critical infrastructure and the intelligence community on systemic cyber security and resilience and cyber defense operations. The executive branch should assess continuing gaps and limitations in its ability to provide for greater centralization of public-private cybersecurity efforts similar to the NCSC model within a CISA integrated cyber center.

Increasing Public- and Private-Sector Integration: The executive branch review should also recommend procedures and criteria for increasing and expanding the participation and integration of public- and private-sector personnel into U.S. government cyber defense and security efforts. This review should identify continuing limitations or hurdles in the security clearance program for private

sector partners and in integrating private sector partners into a CISA integrated cyber center, including integrating private sector organizations like information sharing and analysis centers (ISAC) and the Financial Systemic Analysis and Resilience Center (FSARC).

Within one year and upon the conclusion of its review, the executive branch should report its findings to Congress and provide recommendations on additional resources or authorities required to implement its plans and to address gaps the review has identified. The executive branch will conduct an annual review thereafter, providing a yearly report to Congress on the status of its efforts, any revised findings or additional resources or authorities required, and its progress in addressing the areas identified in this recommendation. Future reports should include updates on the progress of the Joint Collaborative Environment (recommendation 5.2) in enabling greater federal agency and public-private integration, after the environment comes online.

Key Recommendation

5.4 The executive branch should establish a Joint Cyber Planning Cell under the Cybersecurity and Infrastructure Security Agency to coordinate cybersecurity planning and readiness across the federal government and between the public and private sectors for significant cyber incidents and malicious cyber campaigns.

Successfully defending against malicious cyber incidents, mitigating their consequences, and countering adversary cyber campaigns requires the United States to be able to mount its own coordinated, timely, whole-of-government, public-private cyber defense and security campaigns. Planning is a critical element in fulfilling this mandate. Effective cyber planning ensures that the government both aligns and readies the full range of U.S. government tools in cyberspace and coordinates jointly with private-sector entities, so that they can be employed and integrated seamlessly in response to or in advance of a crisis. Elements of the U.S. government and the private sector, working within their respective sectors

or as individual firms or agencies, often lack the power to independently counter and mitigate a coordinated nation-state cyber campaign. Given this reality, planning is fundamental to enabling and strengthening feedback loops for identifying an effective division of effort and preparing individual agencies and firms to execute responses quickly and with a common understanding of roles, responsibilities, and courses of action.

But efforts to date have not adequately included private-sector stakeholders, and they have been reactive to individual incidents rather than being comprehensive and forward-looking. This inadequate response is largely due to insufficient coordination of the U.S. government's cyber capabilities, authorities, and expertise—which remain distributed across a variety of agencies—and questions on how to appropriately integrate private-sector participation. Furthermore, these agencies have not engaged in the collaborative planning necessary to overcome jurisdictional hurdles, identify gaps, align whole-of-government capabilities, build private-sector buy-in, or institutionalize learning through combined exercises. As a result, when an adversary cyber campaign is identified or an incident does occur, coordinated and comprehensive operations in defense of critical infrastructure are unlikely to be timely or effective.

To address this shortcoming, the executive branch, with the support of Congress, should establish a Joint Cyber Planning Cell ("the Cell") under CISA. The Cell should be composed of a central planning staff and representatives from the federal agencies that wield operational cyber capabilities and/or authorities in defense of critical infrastructure. The Cell will facilitate comprehensive planning of defensive, non-intelligence cybersecurity campaigns across agencies. It will integrate these planning efforts with the private sector, particularly with systemically important critical infrastructure (recommendation 5.1) and in areas where the ability of the private sector to deploy security mitigating a threat rivals or exceeds that of the U.S. government (recommendation 5.4.2). The Cell will be managed and hosted by CISA and informed by the Joint Collaborative Environment (recommendation 5.2). The plans should not include consequence imposition options, but should instead focus on limiting and mitigating malicious cyber campaigns once they have been identified.

Centralized Planning Resources and Support: As part of the Cell's establishment, Congress should ensure that it has sufficient resources both to carry out its mission and to provide support to other agencies that possess relevant equities but do not have adequate operational planning capacity.

Cyber Campaign Planning: The Cell will be charged with coordinating planning for campaigns and operations to respond to and recover from a significant cyber incident or limit, mitigate, or defend against a coordinated, malicious cyber campaign targeting U.S. critical infrastructure. These plans should be developed through a deliberate planning process, accounting for all participating federal agency cyber capabilities and authorities. The planning will integrate representatives from the NCIJTF Office of Campaign Coordination and from the private sector to identify comparative advantages, develop unity of purpose, and understand needs or limitations of government or private-sector action in protecting critical infrastructure.

Planning Procedures: The executive branch should establish procedures for identifying and prioritizing scenarios and contingencies around which the Cell will develop whole-of-government and public-private plans. The executive branch should assign roles and responsibilities to federal agencies necessary to carry out this requirement and establish further directives on how plans will be formed, coordinated, maintained, updated, and routinely exercised.

Execution of Plans: When an adversary campaign is identified or a significant cyber incident occurs, the Cell's deliberate plans would help inform courses of action to be approved through a National Security Council (NSC) decision-making process. As appropriate, the Cell would coordinate the execution of these plans with existing cyber centers, which oversee contributing operations by responsible agencies. Agency elements of plans should be prepared and submitted through a predetermined approval process to appropriate authorities for rapid—and, if required, sustained—execution in response to an attack.

Integration with Consequence Imposition Options: The Cell's planning efforts would integrate with, and be one element of, broader NSC-led options levied against an adversary in response to a malicious cyber campaign. These would include public attribution, criminal charges (such as indictments), sanctions, and other executive actions designed to impose consequences and deter future malicious behavior.

Enabling Recommendations

5.4.1 Institutionalize Department of Defense Participation in Public-Private Cybersecurity Initiatives

Building better public-private collaboration will require more active and deeper collaboration between DoD and other federal departments and agencies and private-sector stakeholders, including owners and operators of systemically important critical infrastructure. DoD brings considerable resources, expertise, and advanced capabilities that, when integrated appropriately with new or existing public-private initiatives, can substantially increase the timeliness and effectiveness of U.S. cyber defense and security efforts. An example is the Pathfinder initiative,[295] which grew out of a 2017 pilot program, Project Indigo, between the U.S. government and the financial sector. These projects enabled the increased sharing of threat data and greater joint collaboration between firms and government stakeholders. A second Pathfinder initiative has since been created for the energy sector.[296] The Pathfinder initiative is a key proof of concept of collaboration between the private sector and critical infrastructure in support of the U.S. cyber defense and security mission. Developing institutional support for Pathfinder-type initiatives not only creates opportunities for increased collaboration across critical sectors, as prioritized by federal departments and agencies, but will also buttress and accelerate nascent efforts and increase their chances of success. These initiatives will also enable these programs to move beyond threat information sharing toward better human-to-human collaboration in developing sector-specific concepts of operations and joint exercises.

Congress should request in the FY2021 National Defense Authorization Act (NDAA) an assessment of the impact of the current Pathfinder initiative, prospects for making existing Pathfinder pilots more robust, and whether and how to expand Pathfinder or similar models of public-private collaboration to other critical infrastructure sectors, particularly systemically important critical infrastructure. The review should also:

- Examine additional comparative models for ensuring dedicated, long-term support to public-private cybersecurity initiatives led by civilian departments and agencies, such as the FBI and CISA.
- Examine DoD support to existing federal cyber centers and assess the need for establishing a meaningfully permanent presence of personnel to encourage greater integration with public- and private-sector cybersecurity efforts.

5.4.2 Expand Cyber Defense Collaboration with Information and Communications Technology (ICT) Enablers

Telecommunications and information technology sectors are likely to hold systemically important critical infrastructure assets, because the disruption of their assets could cause cascading or catastrophic effects. As providers, owners, and operators of core services and of infrastructure key to the functioning of the cyber ecosystem, internet service providers, cloud service providers, information technology software and hardware producers, and cybersecurity companies are uniquely placed to have an outsized impact on national cybersecurity efforts. Currently, U.S. government efforts to provide more and more actionable information to enable ICT enabler security operations have been limited in scope and duration. Likewise, the U.S. government is limited in its capacity to receive information from these enablers. To leverage the reach of these companies, the U.S. government should invest more resources in:

- Providing better support to ICT enablers, including better and more actionable information and classified indicators, and increasing collaboration on broader cyber defense efforts.
- Building institutional mechanisms to better identify, accept, and integrate key cybersecurity information and indicators with information and indicators from other government sources.
- Operationalizing public-private initiatives, like the Enduring Security Framework, between the U.S. government and critical technology enablers such as internet service providers and information technology companies.

PRESERVE AND EMPLOY THE MILITARY INSTRUMENT OF POWER

To best implement layered cyber deterrence, the United States must be prepared to impose costs to deter and, if necessary, fight and win in conflict, as well as counter and reduce malicious adversary behavior below the level of armed conflict. Therefore, this pillar comprises implementing defend forward in day-to-day competition to counter adversary cyber campaigns and impose costs, as well as being prepared to prevail in crisis and conflict. Importantly, the military instrument of cyber power is intended to complement, rather than supplant, other instruments. The result is the coordinated employment of all instruments of national power.

Thus far, the United States has successfully deterred strategic cyberattacks that would rise to the level of an armed attack. However, below that threshold, there is a significant set of adversary behavior that the United States has not prevented. That is why, critical to this pillar is the defend forward concept, originally articulated in the 2018 Department of Defense Cyber Strategy.[297] This approach addresses the set of malicious adversary action that exists on a spectrum between routine activities that states tacitly accept (e.g., espionage) and strategic cyberattacks that would constitute an armed attack. The Commission reimagines and expands the core logic of DoD's concept of defend forward to incorporate both military and non-military instruments of power.

Defend forward follows from the recognition that organizing U.S. cyber forces around simply reacting to adversary activity has been ineffective in preventing adversary cyber campaigns; and initiatives that rely solely on non-military instruments of power have been insufficient to alter adversaries' cost-benefit and risk calculus. Therefore, the United States must ensure that it is organized, resourced, and postured to position and employ forces forward—geographically and virtually—to counter adversary campaigns, pursue adversaries as they maneuver, and impose costs.

An urgent concern is the ability to defend and surge when adversaries utilize cyber capabilities to attack U.S. military systems and functions. To accomplish objectives in support of defend forward, credible deterrence, and the ability to win if deterrence fails, the U.S. government must maintain ready and resilient military capabilities. These include cyber tools to be employed as an independent military capability and as enablers of conventional operations and campaigns. The same technologically advanced military capabilities that form the bedrock of the United States' military advantage also create cyber vulnerabilities that adversaries can and will use to their strategic advantage. In this way, vulnerabilities that adversaries are able to exploit in routine competition below the level of war have potentially dangerous implications for the United States' ability to deter and prevail in conflict above that threshold.

Adversary cyber threats to the U.S. military and the defense industrial base (DIB) continue to cause the loss of national security information and intellectual property. They also generate the risk that, through cyber means, U.S. military systems could be rendered ineffective or their intended uses distorted. Actions such as improving detection and mitigation of adversary cyber threats to the DIB are critical to providing for the proper functioning and resilience of key military systems and functions. These strategic realities create an imperative for the United States to preserve and employ the military instrument of power in and through cyberspace, including the intersection of cyberspace with conventional and nuclear military capabilities, while deliberately managing potential escalation risks. This pillar focuses on two key aspects of this mission: implementing the military component

Desired End States

of defend forward, and securing the resilience of key weapons systems and functions.

Focusing on the military instrument of power, this pillar lays out how to implement the military elements of defend forward, which represents a key—though not the only—element of its whole-of-government implementation. This implementation draws on the central tenets of the Department of Defense's defend forward concept as set forth in the 2018 DoD Cyber Strategy, as well as U.S. Cyber Command's implementation of it through persistent engagement. In February 2019 testimony before the Senate Armed Services Committee, General Paul Nakasone described how U.S. Cyber Command conducts "persistent engagement, which includes partnering with other US Government elements to build resilience into US networks and systems, defending against malicious cyberspace activities as far forward as possible, and contesting adversary attempts to disrupt our nation's key government and military functions."[298] This entails "acting"—conducting cyber operations to gain access, pursue adversaries where they operate and, when warranted, deliver effects against adversary infrastructure and

capabilities—and "enabling"—providing early warning to partners, sharing threat information and, when requested, surging to provide support in the form of personnel and capabilities for contingencies or crises.[299]

Operationalizing defend forward and persistent engagement within the military pillar of the Commission's strategic approach requires three key actions.

First, the United States must plan, resource, and conduct cyber operations and standing campaigns to counter adversaries. This includes countering adversaries' offensive cyber capabilities and infrastructure, organizations that support their cyber operations and campaigns, and the locus of their decision making. Such actions impose direct and indirect costs on adversaries. Direct costs include those that impact adversaries' ability to conduct cyber operations and campaigns. Indirect costs involve forcing adversaries to shift to secondary and tertiary lines of effort and divert resources from other areas. These actions are designed to affect an adversary's overall perception of the costs, risks, and benefits of targeting the United States.

(U.S. Cyber Command Public Affairs)

U.S. service members and civilians along with partner nation service members work to improve tactical-level cyber operations skills against a live opposing force at the Joint Training Facility in Suffolk, VA, during U.S. Cyber Command's annual exercise.

Second, the United States must have capabilities and processes within the cyber force to rapidly respond to emerging geopolitical situations, and ensure that these cyber capabilities can be easily integrated with other military and non-military tools. Specifically, DoD should develop the capacity to provide decision makers with cyber options, including options to support crisis bargaining and response that are independent of and do not rely on existing cyber campaign plans and the forces already committed to them. For U.S. warfighting, in particular, cyber options enable the Joint Force to gain an information advantage, exercise global command and control, and execute strikes at long range.[300]

Third, the United States must operate in cyberspace to provide early warning; gain situational awareness of evolving adversary tactics, techniques, and procedures (TTPs), capabilities, and personas; and conduct operational preparation of the environment (OPE). The cyber domain is dynamic, opportunities are fleeting, and our adversaries are agile and adaptive. A prerequisite to

keeping pace with them and anticipating their behavior, rather than simply reacting and responding to it, is gaining and maintaining access against defined targets and pursuing adversaries as they maneuver.

When these three elements are combined, the military component of defend forward can be integrated as part of a whole-of-government effort with other instruments of national power. These include diplomacy, information, the military, economic and financial tools, intelligence, and law enforcement.

The recommendations supporting this pillar focus on ensuring that the United States protects its ability to employ the military instrument of power, alongside other instruments, across the spectrum of engagement from competition to crisis and conflict. Two recommendations are key: (1) growing the Cyber Mission Force (CMF) capacity commensurate with the scale of the threat and the scope of mission requirements, and (2) promoting the cybersecurity and resilience of critical military systems and functions. Achieving the former requires assessing the force size and mixture of the CMF, and succeeding at the latter demands recurring reporting on the cyber vulnerabilities of all major weapons systems and a cybersecurity and vulnerability assessment of all segments of the nuclear command, control, and communications (NC3) enterprise and of National Leadership Command Capabilities (NLCC).

STRATEGIC OBJECTIVE #1:

GROW THE CAPACITY OF THE CYBER MISSION FORCE (CMF) TO MEET THE SCOPE OF THE THREAT AND GROWING MISSION REQUIREMENTS

The United States should achieve appropriate resourcing, force size, and mix of its cyber forces as well as streamlined decision-making processes to ensure rapid maneuver and flexibility. The CMF, under U.S. Cyber Command, is the locus of the Department of Defense's efforts to counter, disrupt, and impose costs against malicious adversary behavior in cyberspace. Planning and executing cyber operations and campaigns demand a significant investment in time, skill, resources, and human capital. These operations and campaigns also necessitate flexibility in decision making and delegated authority to enable rapid response and maneuver, intelligence capabilities that enable gaining and maintaining access, and a decision-making and operational environment that supports long-term campaigning.

Key Recommendation

6.1 Congress should direct the Department of Defense to conduct a force structure assessment of the Cyber Mission Force (CMF).

As part of the FY2021 National Defense Authorization Act (NDAA), Congress should direct the Department of Defense to conduct a force structure assessment of the U.S. Cyber Command's Cyber Mission Force in light of growing mission requirements and expectations, in terms of both scope and scale. This assessment should include resource and capability implications for the National Security Agency (NSA) in its combat support agency role.

The CMF is currently considered at full operational capability, with 133 teams comprising a total of approximately 6,200 individuals. However, these requirements were defined in 2013, well before the United States experienced or observed some of the key events that have shaped the U.S. government's understanding of the urgency and salience of the cyber threat posed by adversaries, as well as before the development of DoD's defend forward strategy. Today, the teams that make up the CMF are responsible for a range of distinct DoD cyber missions, including defending the DoD information network (DoDIN), providing support to military operations through the geographic combatant commands, and defending the nation to counter malicious

adversary behavior in day-to-day competition. This represents an expansion of the scope of the CMF's mission set (operating off DoDIN) and the scale of its operations (increasing operations in response to a more dangerous threat environment), even though its force structure goal has remained constant.

The FY2020 NDAA made important progress toward the needed assessment, though work remains to be done. Notably, Section 1652 requires a zero-based review of DoD cyber and information technology personnel, while Sections 1655 and 1656 require studies on future DoD cyber warfighting capabilities given existing cyber architecture and acquisition programs, as well as a study on the structure of the Joint Force Cyber Organizations. However, Congress must also ensure that the CMF, in particular, conducts a force structure assessment and troop-to-task analysis that takes into account the increasing scope and scale of CMF missions compared to previous fiscal years and projected into the future. In addition, in its capacity as a combat support agency, the National Security Agency provides critical intelligence support to Title 10 cyberspace operations, particularly at the tactical and operational level. Therefore, an assessment must also be conducted that includes resource requirements in support of this aspect of its mission.

To conduct these missions at scale, as well as ensure that the CMF has sufficient capacity to maintain steady-state operations while surging to respond to an emerging crisis, Congress should request in the next Cyber Posture Review, and quadrennially thereafter, that DoD provide an assessment of the requirements to grow the CMF, including projected force size and mixture necessary to sustain all DoD missions in cyberspace as determined by the department. Key concerns that should be addressed include ensuring that the CMF is appropriately sized, given the requirements of the diverse and significant mission sets it supports, and ensuring that the allocation of teams within the CMF is matched to the prioritization of strategic objectives. The results of this assessment should drive resource allocation, force size and mix, and continued congressional oversight of these efforts. The realities of the current and anticipated future threat and operational environments demand that the CMF and NSA be given resources commensurate with the nature of the challenge faced by the United States.

(U.S. Air Force Graphic by Tech. Sgt. R. J. Biermann)

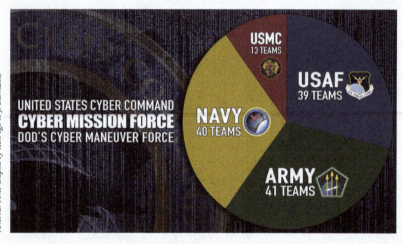

The Cyber Mission Force (CMF) reached full operational capability in 2013 with 133 teams comprising a total of approximately 6,200 individuals.

Enabling Recommendations

6.1.1 Direct the Department of Defense to Create a Major Force Program (MFP) Funding Category for U.S. Cyber Command

To enhance the flexibility and agility of U.S. Cyber Command in a dynamic operating environment, Congress should direct in the FY2021 NDAA that the Department of Defense submit a budget justification display that includes a Major Force Program (MFP) category for the training, manning, and equipping of U.S. Cyber Command. According to 10 U.S. Code § 238, DoD is required to submit to Congress a budget justification display that includes an MFP category for the Cyber Mission Force. However, this law was enacted in 2014, before U.S. Cyber Command was elevated to a unified combatant command. Therefore, there is a need for a new budget justification display that establishes an MFP category for U.S. Cyber Command. A new MFP funding category for U.S. Cyber Command would provide it with acquisition authorities over goods and services unique to the command's needs. It should also provide a process to expeditiously resolve Combatant Command/Service funding disputes, consistent with the intent of DoD Directive 5100.03.[301] This would be analogous to the MFP funding category for U.S. Special Operations Command, which was created to support comparable needs for operational adaptability.

6.1.2 Expand Current Malware Inoculation Initiatives

As part of defend forward and persistent engagement, as well as in support of broader DoD missions, DoD/U.S.

Cyber Command conducts threat hunting to discover, among other things, adversary malware. Working with the Department of the Treasury, the Department of Homeland Security (DHS), the Federal Bureau of Investigation (FBI), NSA, and the private sector, U.S. Cyber Command has participated in recent efforts to expose adversary malware by making it public in information-sharing venues such as VirusTotal.[302] To contribute to the readiness of U.S. defense and critical infrastructure, efforts should be made to accelerate sharing of the most recent malicious code captured in the wild through appropriate interagency channels, including through the Joint Collaborative Environment (recommendation 5.2). Doing so allows the private sector an opportunity to develop response plans and potentially inoculate their systems to avoid harm. While the private sector has created a number of malware reporting venues available to the public, federal entities have begun to participate only in the past few years.

U.S. Cyber Command has unique capabilities and authorities for threat hunting, making its input to these databases critical for national security. In addition, NSA plays an essential role in malware analysis in support of this initiative. These malware inoculation efforts have made important contributions to reducing vulnerabilities. However, the timing and sequencing of their public release have often been met with frustration from the private sector, given the lack of coordination between the two entities. These efforts should continue and be accelerated, and U.S. Cyber Command should ensure coordination with DHS, the FBI, and stakeholders in the private sector in the release of information, particularly with owners and operators of systemically important critical infrastructure (SICI; recommendation 5.1). Improvements in the timing, granularity, and actionability of information should be synchronized with existing efforts across interagency partners and with the new enhanced coordination mechanisms proposed elsewhere in this report so that the private sector can be confident that it has a shared picture of the threat landscape. Without a coherent framework for the release

of threat information across agencies, the private sector will be forced to de-duplicate, rationalize, and reconcile the disparate outputs of the various federal stakeholders. There should also be a bias toward action to get perishable data out to victims in the private sector as quickly as reasonably possible, rather than waiting to complete a slow process of coordination prior to release.

6.1.3 Review the Delegation of Authorities for Cyber Operations

To enable support for more streamlined decision-making processes, and flexible and rapid maneuver, Congress should request that DoD provide in the next Cyber Posture Review an analysis of and recommendations for the conditions under which further delegation of cyber-related authorities is appropriate to U.S. Cyber Command, as well as to other DoD components including NSA, the Defense Information Systems Agency (DISA), and the DoD Cyber Crime Center (DC3).

The pace of cyberspace operations may require delegated authorities and seamless decision making to pursue and deliver effects against adversary targets. A number of cyber-related authorities currently exist within DoD, but not all are delegated to a single organization. Relevant authorities within the scope of Title 10 for conducting counter-cyber operations include not only authorities to deliver offensive cyber effects but also those that support planning and executing these operations. These encompass information operations (IO), which include authorities to create, procure, and deploy personas; military information support operations (MISO); military deception (MILDEC); and counterintelligence. Currently, cyber-related authorities are diffused across different elements of DoD (functional combatant commands, geographic combatant commands, and the various services).

DoD should also review the option of further delegating information warfare authorities to U.S. Cyber Command and the specific conditions under which such delegation would be appropriate. The purpose of this assessment is to prevent both unnecessary friction that might delay rapid and cohesive action to implement defend forward and inappropriate constraints on U.S. Cyber Command's ability to quickly respond to and thwart adversary behavior in day-to-day competition. U.S. Cyber Command operations would still be subject to rigorous oversight and approval processes.

Relevant authorities to review for delegation to NSA should include those authorities that enable the agency to rapidly tip relevant foreign intelligence collection to private entities that constitute the Defense Industrial Base and their service providers to support the latter's own defensive operations.

6.1.4 Reassess and Amend Standing Rules of Engagement (SROE) and Standing Rules for Use of Force (SRUF) for U.S. Forces

DoD, as part of the next Cyber Posture Review, should produce a study that assesses and provides recommendations for amendments as necessary to the Standing Rules of Engagement (SROE) and Standing Rules for Use of Force (SRUF) for U.S. forces, as these rules are more than a decade old. This study should be context-specific, taking into account the forces' assigned mission sets. Given the unique aspects of operating in cyberspace, particularly below a use-of-force threshold, it is imperative that SROE/SRUF guidance be relevant to actions in and through cyberspace.

Specific issues that could be addressed as part of this study include the fact that there are no "high seas" in cyberspace; the need to conform to current DoD structure and organization (e.g., the Unified Campaign Plan); the reassignment of authorities delegated to U.S. Strategic Command to U.S. Cyber Command in the case of cyberspace activities; the applicability of the default and restrictive nature of SROE/SRUF as applied to actions in cyberspace above and below the threshold of armed conflict; the delineation of authority between geographic combatant commands and functional combatant commands with respect to supplemental rules for actions

in and through cyberspace; and the definitions within the context of cyberspace of such terms as *territory*, *authority to pursue*, and *hostile intent*.

6.1.5 Cooperate with Allies and Partners to Defend Forward

Allies and partners are essential to the effective implementation of layered cyber deterrence and the concept of defend forward. At the strategic level, they are a key source of U.S. comparative advantage. At the operational and tactical levels, implementing defend forward requires operating in allied and partner cyberspace (part of "gray" space).[303] The United States will, whenever possible, get support from allies and partners for this effort. While DoD is already collaborating closely with allies and partners, this effort should include other interagency stakeholders. Therefore, DoD, the Department of State, and other relevant interagency partners should continue and expand efforts with allies and partners to gain permission (when practical) to implement defend forward—particularly in undertaking hunt forward activities, in which U.S. cyber forces are able to conduct threat hunting and pursue adversaries on allied and partner networks, but also in conducting deceptive countermeasures, enabling early warning, and providing resources to support hardening defenses.

The Department of State should focus on the traditional diplomatic channels in support of defend forward, while DoD should lead through military-to-military relationships. In addition, given the preexisting and deep intelligence-sharing partnership among Five Eyes allies (Australia, Canada, New Zealand, the United Kingdom, and the United States), DoD (including the NSA) and the intelligence community should further collaborate with these Five Eyes allies, supplementing the signals intelligence architecture and mission with one supporting military cyber operations. Doing so would increase the scale of the infrastructure that could support defend forward, as well as enable the United States to leverage any unique capabilities of its allies to conduct certain types of operations and missions.

6.1.6 Require the Department of Defense to Define Reporting Metrics

In light of DoD's expanding mission set, it is imperative to assess the extent to which cyber campaigns and operations conducted in support of the defend forward strategy are achieving their intended effects. The FY2020 NDAA made important progress in this effort, with Section 1634 requiring DoD to report on quantitative and qualitative metrics. However, key recommendations on metrics remain, the most critical of which includes ensuring that DoD is measuring defend forward outcomes across strategic, operational, and tactical levels—not just the number of operations conducted or their immediate tactical effects. Therefore, DoD should ensure that when modifying its reporting system pursuant to Section 1634 of the FY2020 NDAA, the department defines and reports to Congress department-specific metrics to measure defend forward outcomes across strategic, operational, and tactical levels and includes this data in the existing quarterly briefings to appropriate congressional committees. These measures should include the direct and indirect costs imposed on adversaries, the impact of defend forward operations and campaigns on adversary behavior, how adversary cyber operations have quantifiably affected DoD's ability to conduct or succeed across cyber and non-cyber missions, and DoD's assessment of the ability of adversary cyber operations to impact future campaigns.

6.1.7 Assess the Establishment of a Military Cyber Reserve

Congress should request in the FY2021 NDAA an assessment from DoD on the need for, and requirements of, a military cyber reserve, its possible composition, and its structure (i.e., a retainer model, a nontraditional reserve, a strategic technological reserve, or other models). The purpose of this military cyber reserve would be to play a central role in mobilizing a surge capacity, utilizing preexisting links between the private sector (particularly SICI) and DoD.

A DoD military cyber reserve assessment should contain a number of key elements, including the following:

- Explore how different types of reserve models, including less traditional models with more flexible requirements, could address broader issues of talent management (e.g., retaining talent transitioning from active duty into the reserve).
- Assess how a cyber reserve could deliberately recruit key people in the private sector to participate, enabling DoD to call on cyber talent that currently resides in the private sector as a surge capacity in times of crisis.
- Examine ways to facilitate recruiting and retaining civilian talent with no prior military expertise who are interested in serving.
- Assess the impact a cyber reserve would have on drawing civilian talent from the private sector and any similar non-DoD governmental capacity.
- Address how DoD might use existing mechanisms to bring in technical expertise when needed to respond to a crisis and identify shortcomings in cyber expertise that might be addressed through more targeted hiring practices.

6.1.8 Establish Title 10 Professors in Cyber Security and Information Operations

The Department of Defense should establish a Title 10 Professor in Cyber Security and Information Operations, housed at the Senior Education Professional Military Education (PME) institutions within each service branch and at the National Defense University (NDU), to communicate and investigate cyber strategy and policy at the national level as it affects the armed forces. A foundational strength of the U.S. armed forces is their education in operations as a professional military force. In response to the evolution of the cyber mission in contingency planning, PME institutions must evolve to meet the challenge of operating in the information environment. Cyber security and information operations are increasingly vital to military planning and guidance: therefore, this senior faculty position is key to adapting service PME to the changing landscape.

These professors would be responsible for establishing and implementing the curriculum for both cyber and information warfare national strategy at the Command, Staff, and Planners Colleges of each service branch. They would also play a crucial role in institutionalizing

and coordinating cyber and information warfare education across each service branch, including through distance education. These positions should not replace existing programs of cyber education within the PME or NDU systems.

STRATEGIC OBJECTIVE #2:

ENSURE THE SECURITY AND RESILIENCE OF CRITICAL CONVENTIONAL AND NUCLEAR WEAPONS SYSTEMS AND FUNCTIONS

As adversaries' cyber threats become more sophisticated, the United States should be able to address the challenges in protecting its essential military systems and functions. While continued automation and connectivity are essential to DoD's military capabilities, they also present numerous access points for adversaries' cyber intrusions and attacks. The scope and the challenge of securing critical military networks and systems are immense. It goes beyond protecting the cybersecurity of the DoDIN to include defending the Defense Industrial Base (DIB) against adversary efforts to steal national security intellectual property and securing critical conventional and nuclear weapons systems and functions.

Key Recommendation

6.2 Congress should direct the Department of Defense to conduct a cybersecurity vulnerability assessment of all segments of the NC3 and NLCC systems and continually assess weapon systems cyber vulnerabilities.

Congress should include language in the FY2021 NDAA that requires the DoD to conduct a cybersecurity vulnerability assessment of all segments of the nuclear command, control, and communications enterprise and National Leadership Command Capabilities. Following this assessment, DoD should begin to report annually to Congress on the status of the ongoing cyber vulnerability assessments of all DoD major weapon systems and NC3 and NLCC enterprises. This report must include assessments of legacy platforms and cyber vulnerabilities *across* networked systems in broader mission areas.

DoD has recently taken critical steps to improve weapons systems cybersecurity. Moreover, as directed by Congress

in the FY2016 NDAA, the department has begun to assess the cyber vulnerabilities of each major weapon system. While this effort represents important steps, barriers to effective cybersecurity still remain, such as the lack of a permanent process to periodically assess the cybersecurity of fielded systems. Further, even as current efforts focus on the vulnerabilities of individual weapons platforms, it is crucial to also evaluate how a cyber intrusion or attack on one system could affect the entire mission. The process of identifying interdependent vulnerabilities should go beyond assessing technical vulnerabilities to also taking a risk management approach that seeks to improve the overall resilience of the system as well as to identify secondary and tertiary dependencies, with a focus on rapid remediation of identified vulnerabilities. With DoD systems more connected than ever before, cybersecurity measures must take a more integrated approach and take into account the impacts of cyber vulnerabilities across systems. Routine testing should be conducted to stress-test mission critical systems and processes in light of an evolving threat environment, and the results should be communicated to Congress. In addition to assessing vulnerabilities of fielded systems, DoD must enforce cybersecurity requirements for systems that are in development early in the acquisition lifecycle, ensuring that they remain baked into the front end of this process and are not "bolted on" later.[304]

The 2018 Government Accountability Office report on DoD's efforts thus far concluded that to "improve the state of weapon systems cybersecurity, it is essential that DOD sustain its momentum in developing and implementing key initiatives."[305] Thus, Congress should direct DoD to institutionalize a continuous assessment process and annually report these vulnerabilities to sustain its momentum in implementing key initiatives.

Even more concerning is the potential cyber threat to the U.S. nuclear deterrent and the survivability and resilience of NC3 systems and NLCC programs facing the full spectrum of cyber threats. These threats are particularly alarming because they can undermine the stability of nuclear deterrence and create the conditions for inadvertent nuclear war. The greatest risk is that precisely because cyber interactions take place below the threshold of armed conflict, the combination of cyber risks and NC3 systems can, in effect, lower that threshold. With this in mind, Congress should direct DoD to routinely assess every segment of the NC3 and NLCC enterprise for adherence to cybersecurity best practices, vulnerabilities, and evidence of compromise. Further, this analysis should not be limited to technical penetrations and vulnerabilities. Attention should also be given to influence operations that aim to distort decision making while leaving NC3 proper intact.

Cyberspace Solarium Commission

Enabling Recommendations

6.2.1 Require Defense Industrial Base Participation in a Threat Intelligence Sharing Program

A shared picture of the threat environment within the DIB is essential to proactively and comprehensively address cyber threats and vulnerabilities to this key sector.[306] Information sharing programs exist, but are insufficient. For example, the DoD Cyber Crime Center and the DIB Cybersecurity Program are largely voluntary, although DIB entities have mandatory reporting requirements. The NSA's newly created Cybersecurity Directorate mission includes an important role in protecting the DIB.[307]

The companies most capable of participating in existing information sharing programs are large prime contractors; however, DoD also relies on small to medium-sized companies, as well as subcontractors. This gives rise to two issues. First, DoD lacks a complete view of its supply chain. Therefore, prime contractors should be incentivized to disclose their subcontractors to DoD. Second, smaller entities with fewer resources to devote to cybersecurity may provide an opening for adversaries to access information paramount to national security. Drawing on DoD's Cyber Maturity Model Certification (CMMC) regulation, the requirements associated with participation in a threat intelligence sharing program should be tied to a firm's level of maturity. In addition, the government should communicate—particularly to small and medium-sized companies—the incentives for participation.

Congress should legislatively require companies that make up the Defense Industrial Base, as part of the terms of their contract with DoD, to participate in a threat intelligence sharing program that would be housed at the DoD component level. A DIB threat intelligence sharing program should contain a number of key elements, including:

- Incentives for certain types of specifically delineated information sharing, such as incident reporting.

- A shared and real-time picture of the threat environment; joint, collaborative, and co-located analytics; and investments in technology and capabilities to support automated detection and analysis.
- Consent by DIB entities for the NSA to query in foreign intelligence collection databases on DIB entities and provide focused threat intelligence to them, as well as enable all elements of DoD, including the NSA, to directly tip intelligence to the affected entity.
- Further empowerment of and resources to the NSA's Cybersecurity Directorate, given that it is a new entity with a critical mission.
- Coordinated intelligence sharing with relevant domestic law enforcement and counterintelligence agencies, including the FBI, Air Force Office of Special Investigations, Naval Criminal Investigative Service, U.S. Army Counterintelligence, and DoD Cyber Crime Center.

The program's ideal end state is to leverage U.S. government intelligence collection to create a better understanding of adversaries' intelligence collection requirements. This action would help DoD and the intelligence community anticipate where adversaries will seek to collect against DIB targets, and then communicate that information to DIB network owners and operators so that they can proactively defend against impending adversary activities.

6.2.2 Require Threat Hunting on Defense Industrial Base Networks

Improving the detection and mitigation of adversary cyber threats to the DIB is imperative to ensuring that key military systems and functions are resilient and can be employed during times of crisis and conflict. Congress should therefore direct regulatory action that the executive branch should pursue in order to require companies that make up the Defense Industrial Base, as part of the terms of their contract with DoD, to create a mechanism for mandatory threat hunting on DIB networks. Malicious code, indicators of compromise,

and insights on the evolving threat landscape should be shared with companies when operationally feasible. This program could be modeled as a Pathfinder program with different options for implementing threat hunting, such as allowing DoD to conduct threat hunting on DIB networks with prior notification and coordination with DIB network owners, or incentivizing the DIB to seek out DoD-approved third-party entities to conduct threat hunting. These options should also take into account variations in maturity across the DIB, leveraging DoD's CMMC security requirements.

A program for threat hunting on DIB networks should also include the following:

- DoD threat assessment programs on DIB networks.
- Incentives for companies to feed data collected and generated from threat hunting activities on DIB networks to DoD and the NSA's Cybersecurity Directorate.
- Coordination of DoD efforts with DHS and the FBI in furtherance of the latter's domestic cybersecurity and counterintelligence responsibilities.

6.2.3 Designate a Threat-Hunting Capability across the Department of Defense Information Network

Given the high consequence of cyber threats for the entire DoD Information Network (DoDIN), including NC3 and NLCC, as well as across the combatant commands, a dedicated threat-hunting capability is key to ensuring the security and resilience of these systems. In addition, because the NSA is the enterprise security architect and builds the cryptography—fundamental to the security of the U.S. military enterprise—that underlies these networks and systems, particularly NC3, its role in this capacity should be formalized.

Therefore, DoD should provide for a force structure element to conduct threat hunting and related activities across the entire DoDIN, covering the full range of non-nuclear to nuclear force employment. Specifically, DoD should develop a campaign plan for a threat-hunting capability that takes a risk-based approach and that analyzes threat intelligence as well as assessments of likely U.S. and allied targets of adversary interest. Based on this analysis, the threat-hunting capability should proactively conduct threat hunting against those identified networks and assets to seek evidence of compromise, identify vulnerabilities, and deploy countermeasures to enable early warning and thwart adversary action. Given the potentially high consequence of cyber threats to NC3 and NLCC, priority should be assigned to identifying threats to these networks and systems, and threat hunting on them should recur with a frequency commensurate with the risk.

It is important to note that many threats will traverse the boundaries of combatant commands, including U.S. Cyber Command, U.S. Strategic Command, and the geographic combatant commands. To ensure seamless and flexible maneuver of this force structure element, DoD should develop a process to reconcile the authorities and permissions to enable threat hunting across all DoDIN networks, systems, and programs owned and operated by multiple DoD stakeholders.

How Will the Future Age of Quantum Computing Change Cybersecurity?

On October 23, 2019, Google announced that its Sycamore processor had achieved "quantum supremacy," the point at which a quantum computer can verifiably outperform a classical computer as predicted hypothetically. Sycamore surpassed this milestone by performing a computation in about 200 seconds that would take "a state-of-the-art classical supercomputer" about 10,000 years.[308] It was a historic achievement, but also another step along the long road to a quantum computer capable of practical applications.

In the future, researchers will use practical quantum computers to develop exotic chemicals, materials, and pharmaceuticals. They will expand our understanding of biology, physics, and the universe itself. Quantum computers will also revolutionize how we use encryption.

In cyberspace encryption is an essential tool, critical to securing modern commerce, communications, and even classified national security information. Popular encryption schemes today underpin the ability of people and organizations to establish confidence in identities and the authenticity of software; information is encoded before being stored or transmitted to another party, to be decoded only if an authorized user or recipient has the correct "key" to unlock the encryption scheme. Today, classical computers working together and testing 1 trillion keys per second to break that same encryption key would need as much as 10.79 quintillion years, or 785 million times the age of the known universe. However, a quantum computer could perform the same task in about six months.[309]

The United States needs to start preparing itself for the day when quantum computing becomes practical enough to unlock promising new opportunities—as well as all the secrets we have ever encrypted against mere classical computers. The federal government has a central role to play in ensuring that U.S. research remains ahead of that of other countries, particularly China. Both the public and private sectors will need a long-term plan to not only reap the benefits of quantum computing but also fortify an internet of classical computing devices to survive an era of quantum threats.

6.2.4 Assess and Address the Risk to National Security Systems Posed by Quantum Computing

The United States should continue to invest in quantum information science, which offers immense opportunities to improve U.S. military operational capabilities. At the same time, it must also defend itself from the development of these technologies by a foreign adversary. For instance, quantum technologies may present significant risks to U.S. national security systems.[310] Quantum computing, in particular, has the potential to outperform even the most powerful modern supercomputers in specific tasks. If sufficiently powerful quantum computing can be applied to the decryption of encoded messages, the encryption and authentication protocols currently in use by all sensitive military and national security systems could potentially be broken. Using this technology, a foreign adversary could neutralize critical security measures used to protect the United States' most sensitive communications, systems, and assets. In part to pursue these applications, a number of nations across the globe, including China, have invested significant resources in both public and private efforts to develop a viable quantum computer. However, while the United States has begun to take initial steps to develop "quantum-resistant" encryption that would safeguard its sensitive systems, it has yet to fully and comprehensively assess the risks

of quantum computing to national security systems or estimate costs associated with upgrades or replacement.

To fully understand and prepare to counter the risks of quantum computing to national security systems, Congress should include language in the FY2021 NDAA that requires DoD (NSA) to comprehensively assess the threats and risks posed by quantum technologies to national security systems and develop a plan to secure those systems. This assessment should include the following:

- Specific recommendations for addressing identified risks and anticipated resource requirements.
- A proposed framework for how to prioritize the defense of different national security systems and a timeline for implementation.
- An assessment of ongoing efforts to develop quantum-resistant cryptographic standards, including expected timelines for that development, budget shortfalls in public-private efforts to reach such a standard, and the feasibility of alternate quantum-resistant models, such as quantum cryptography.

After the initial assessment, Congress should require an annual report from DoD on the status of ongoing assessments and efforts to address identified risks.

APPENDIX A
ROLL-UP OF RECOMMENDATIONS

PILLAR 1: REFORM THE U.S. GOVERNMENT'S STRUCTURE AND ORGANIZATION FOR CYBERSPACE

Key Recommendation 1.1: Issue an Updated National Cyber Strategy

> Enabling Recommendation 1.1.1: Develop a Multitiered Signaling Strategy

> Enabling Recommendation 1.1.2: Promulgate a New Declaratory Policy

Key Recommendation 1.2: Create House Permanent Select and Senate Select Committees on Cybersecurity

> Enabling Recommendation 1.2.1: Reestablish the Office of Technology Assessment

Key Recommendation 1.3: Establish a National Cyber Director

Key Recommendation 1.4: Strengthen the Cybersecurity and Infrastructure Security Agency

> Enabling Recommendation 1.4.1: Codify and Strengthen the Cyber Threat Intelligence Integration Center

> Enabling Recommendation 1.4.2: Strengthen the FBI's Cyber Mission and the National Cyber Investigative Joint Task Force

Key Recommendation 1.5: Diversify and Strengthen the Federal Cyberspace Workforce

> Enabling Recommendation 1.5.1: Improve Cyber-Oriented Education

PILLAR 2: STRENGTHEN NORMS AND NON-MILITARY TOOLS

Key Recommendation 2.1: Create a Cyber Bureau and Assistant Secretary at the U.S. Department of State

> Enabling Recommendation 2.1.1: Strengthen Norms of Responsible State Behavior in Cyberspace

> Enabling Recommendation 2.1.2: Engage Actively and Effectively in Forums Setting International Information and Communications Technology Standards

> Enabling Recommendation 2.1.3: Improve Cyber Capacity Building and Consolidate the Funding of Cyber Foreign Assistance

> Enabling Recommendation 2.1.4: Improve International Tools for Law Enforcement Activities in Cyberspace

> Enabling Recommendation 2.1.5: Leverage Sanctions and Trade Enforcement Actions

> Enabling Recommendation 2.1.6: Improve Attribution Analysis and the Attribution-Decision Rubric

> Enabling Recommendation 2.1.7: Reinvigorate Efforts to Develop Cyber Confidence-Building Measures

PILLAR 3: PROMOTE NATIONAL RESILIENCE

Key Recommendation 3.1: Codify Sector-specific Agencies into Law as "Sector Risk Management Agencies" and Strengthen Their Ability to Manage Critical Infrastructure Risk

> Enabling Recommendation 3.1.1: Establish a Five-Year National Risk Management Cycle Culminating in a Critical Infrastructure Resilience Strategy

Enabling Recommendation 3.1.2: Establish a National Cybersecurity Assistance Fund to Ensure Consistent and Timely Funding for Initiatives That Underpin National Resilience

Key Recommendation 3.2: Develop and Maintain Continuity of the Economy Planning

Key Recommendation 3.3: Codify a "Cyber State of Distress" Tied to a "Cyber Response and Recovery Fund"

Enabling Recommendation 3.3.1: Designate Responsibilities for Cybersecurity Services under the Defense Production Act

Enabling Recommendation 3.3.2: Clarify Liability for Federally Directed Mitigation, Response, and Recovery Efforts

Enabling Recommendation 3.3.3: Improve and Expand Planning Capacity and Readiness for Cyber Incident Response and Recovery Efforts

Enabling Recommendation 3.3.4: Expand Coordinated Cyber Exercises, Gaming, and Simulation

Enabling Recommendation 3.3.5: Establish a Biennial National Cyber Tabletop Exercise

Enabling Recommendation 3.3.6: Clarify the Cyber Capabilities and Strengthen the Interoperability of the National Guard

Key Recommendation 3.4: Improve the Structure and Enhance Funding of the Election Assistance Commission

Enabling Recommendation 3.4.1: Modernize Campaign Regulations to Promote Cybersecurity

Key Recommendation 3.5: Build Societal Resilience to Foreign Malign Cyber-Enabled Information Operations

Enabling Recommendation 3.5.1: Reform Online Political Advertising to Defend against Foreign Influence in Elections

PILLAR 4: RESHAPE THE CYBER ECOSYSTEM TOWARD GREATER SECURITY

Key Recommendation 4.1: Establish and Fund a National Cybersecurity Certification and Labeling Authority

Enabling Recommendation 4.1.1: Create or Designate Critical Technology Security Centers

Enabling Recommendation 4.1.2: Expand and Support the National Institute of Standards and Technology Security Work

Key Recommendation 4.2: Establish Liability for Final Goods Assemblers

Enabling Recommendation 4.2.1: Incentivize Timely Patch Implementation

Key Recommendation 4.3: Establish a Bureau of Cyber Statistics

Key Recommendation 4.4: Resource a Federally Funded Research and Development Center to Develop Cybersecurity Insurance Certifications

Enabling Recommendation 4.4.1: Establish a Public-Private Partnership on Modeling Cyber Risk

Enabling Recommendation 4.4.2: Explore the Need for a Government Reinsurance Program to Cover Catastrophic Cyber Events

Enabling Recommendation 4.4.3: Incentivize Information Technology Security through Federal Acquisition Regulations and Federal Information Security Management Act Authorities

Enabling Recommendation 4.4.4: Amend the Sarbanes-Oxley Act to Include Cybersecurity Reporting Requirements

Key Recommendation 4.5: Develop a Cloud Security Certification

Enabling Recommendation 4.5.1: Incentivize the Uptake of Secure Cloud Services for Small and Medium-Sized Businesses and State, Local, Tribal, and Territorial Governments

Enabling Recommendation 4.5.2: Develop a Strategy to Secure Foundational Internet Protocols and Email

Enabling Recommendation 4.5.3: Strengthen the U.S. Government's Ability to Take Down Botnets

Key Recommendation 4.6: Develop and Implement an Information and Communications Technology Industrial Base Strategy

Enabling Recommendation 4.6.1: Increase Support to Supply Chain Risk Management Efforts

Enabling Recommendation 4.6.2: Commit Significant and Consistent Funding toward Research and Development in Emerging Technologies

Enabling Recommendation 4.6.3: Strengthen the Capacity of the Committee on Foreign Investment in the United States

Enabling Recommendation 4.6.4: Invest in the National Cyber Moonshot Initiative

Key Recommendation 4.7: Pass a National Data Security and Privacy Protection Law

Enabling Recommendation 4.7.1: Pass a National Breach Notification Law

PILLAR 5: OPERATIONALIZE CYBERSECURITY COLLABORATION WITH THE PRIVATE SECTOR

Key Recommendation 5.1: Codify the Concept of "Systemically Important Critical Infrastructure"

Enabling Recommendation 5.1.1: Review and Update Intelligence Authorities to Increase Intelligence Support to the Broader Private Sector

Enabling Recommendation 5.1.2: Strengthen and Codify Processes for Identifying Broader Private-Sector Cybersecurity Intelligence Needs and Priorities

Enabling Recommendation 5.1.3: Empower Departments and Agencies to Serve Administrative Subpoenas in Support of Threat and Asset Response Activities

Key Recommendation 5.2: Establish and Fund a Joint Collaborative Environment for Sharing and Fusing Threat Information

Enabling Recommendation 5.2.1: Expand and Standardize Voluntary Threat Detection Programs

Enabling Recommendation 5.2.2: Pass a National Cyber Incident Reporting Law

Enabling Recommendation 5.2.3: Amend the Pen Register Trap and Trace Statute to Enable Better Identification of Malicious Actors

Key Recommendation 5.3: Strengthen an Integrated Cyber Center within CISA and Promote the Integration of Federal Cyber Centers

Key Recommendation 5.4: Establish a Joint Cyber Planning Cell under the Cybersecurity and Infrastructure Security Agency

Enabling Recommendation 5.4.1: Institutionalize Department of Defense Participation in Public-Private Cybersecurity Initiatives

Enabling Recommendation 5.4.2: Expand Cyber Defense Collaboration with Information and Communications Technology Enablers

PILLAR 6: PRESERVE AND EMPLOY THE MILITARY INSTRUMENT OF POWER

Key Recommendation 6.1: Direct the Department of Defense to Conduct a Force Structure Assessment of the Cyber Mission Force

Enabling Recommendation 6.1.1: Direct the Department of Defense to Create a Major Force Program Funding Category for U.S. Cyber Command

Enabling Recommendation 6.1.2: Expand Current Malware Inoculation Initiatives

Enabling Recommendation 6.1.3: Review the Delegation of Authorities for Cyber Operations

Enabling Recommendation 6.1.4: Reassess and Amend Standing Rules of Engagement and Standing Rules for Use of Force for U.S. Forces

Enabling Recommendation 6.1.5: Cooperate with Allies and Partners to Defend Forward

Enabling Recommendation 6.1.6: Require the Department of Defense to Define Reporting Metrics

Enabling Recommendation 6.1.7: Assess the Establishment of a Military Cyber Reserve

Enabling Recommendation 6.1.8: Establish Title 10 Professors in Cyber Security and Information Operations

Key Recommendation 6.2: Conduct a Cybersecurity Vulnerability Assessment of All Segments of the NC3 and NLCC Systems and Continually Assess Weapon Systems' Cyber Vulnerabilities

Enabling Recommendation 6.2.1: Require Defense Industrial Base Participation in a Threat Intelligence Sharing Program

Enabling Recommendation 6.2.2: Require Threat Hunting on Defense Industrial Base Networks

Enabling Recommendation 6.2.3: Designate a Threat-Hunting Capability across the Department of Defense Information Network

Enabling Recommendation 6.2.4: Assess and Address the Risk to National Security Systems Posed by Quantum Computing

APPENDIX B
LEGISLATIVE PROPOSALS

Listed below are the recommendations of the Commission that have corresponding draft legislative proposals. These legislative proposals reflect the Commission staff's best effort to capture the spirit of the Commission recommendations. The proposals have not been adopted by the Commission, and are not representative of any Commissioner's views. The proposals represent one possible manner of implementing the Commission's recommendations. Legislative proposals are available online at www.solarium.gov

PILLAR 1: REFORM THE U.S. GOVERNMENT'S STRUCTURE AND ORGANIZATION FOR CYBERSPACE

Recommendation 1.2: Create House Permanent Select and Senate Select Committees on Cybersecurity

Recommendation 1.3: Establish a National Cyber Director

Recommendation 1.4.1: Codify and Strengthen the Cyber Threat Intelligence Integration Center

Recommendation 1.5: Diversify and Strengthen the Federal Cyberspace Workforce

PILLAR 2: STRENGTHEN NORMS AND NON-MILITARY INSTRUMENTS OF POWER

Recommendation 2.1: Create a Cyber Bureau and Assistant Secretary at the U.S. Department of State

Recommendation 2.1.4: Improve International Tools for Law Enforcement Activities in Cyberspace [Provide MLAT Subpoena Authority and Increase FBI Cyber ALATs]

Recommendation 2.1.5: Leverage Sanctions and Trade Enforcement Actions [Codify Executive Order 13848]

PILLAR 3: PROMOTE NATIONAL RESILIENCE

Recommendation 3.1: Codify Sector-specific Agencies into Law as "Sector Risk Management Agencies" and Strengthen Their Ability to Manage Critical Infrastructure Risk

Recommendation 3.1.1: Establish a Five-Year National Risk Management Cycle Culminating in a Critical Infrastructure Resilience Strategy

Recommendation 3.1.2: Establish a National Cybersecurity Assistance Fund to Ensure Consistent and Timely Funding for Initiatives That Underpin National Resilience

Recommendation 3.2: Develop and Maintain Continuity of the Economy Planning

Recommendation 3.3: Codify a "Cyber State of Distress" Tied to a "Cyber Response and Recovery Fund"

Recommendation 3.3.2: Clarify Liability for Federally Directed Mitigation, Response, and Recovery Efforts

Recommendation 3.3.5: Establish a Biennial National Cyber Tabletop Exercise

Recommendation 3.3.6: Clarify the Cyber Capabilities and Strengthen the Interoperability of the National Guard

Recommendation 3.4: Improve the Structure and Enhance Funding of the Election Assistance Commission

Recommendation 3.4.1: Modernize Campaign Regulations to Promote Cybersecurity

Recommendation 3.5: Build Societal Resilience to Cyber-Enabled Information Operations [Educational and Awareness Grant Programs]

Recommendation 3.5.1: Reform Online Political Advertising to Defend against Foreign Influence in Elections

PILLAR 4: RESHAPE THE CYBER ECOSYSTEM TOWARD GREATER SECURITY

Recommendation 4.1: Establish and Fund a National Cybersecurity Certification and Labeling Authority

Recommendation 4.1.1: Create or Designate Critical Technology Security Centers

Recommendation 4.2: Establish Liability for Final Goods Assemblers

Recommendation 4.3: Establish a Bureau of Cyber Statistics

Recommendation 4.4: Resource a Federally Funded Research and Development Center to Develop Cybersecurity Insurance Certifications

Recommendation 4.4.4: Amend the Sarbanes-Oxley Act to Include Cybersecurity Reporting Requirements

Recommendation 4.5: Develop a Cloud Security Certification

Recommendation 4.5.1: Incentivize the Uptake of Secure Cloud Services for Small and Medium-Sized Businesses and State, Local, Tribal, and Territorial Governments

Recommendation 4.5.2: Develop a Strategy to Secure Foundational Internet Protocols and Email

Recommendation 4.5.3: Strengthen the U.S. Government's Ability to Take Down Botnets

Recommendation 4.6: Develop and Implement an Information and Communications Technology Industrial Base Strategy

Recommendation 4.7: Pass a National Data Security and Privacy Protection Law

Recommendation 4.7.1: Pass a National Breach Notification Law

PILLAR 5: OPERATIONALIZE CYBERSECURITY COLLABORATION WITH THE PRIVATE SECTOR

Recommendation 5.1: Codify the Concept of "Systemically Important Critical Infrastructure"

Recommendation 5.1.1: Review and Update Intelligence Authorities to Increase Intelligence Support to the Broader Private Sector

Recommendation 5.1.2: Strengthen and Codify Processes for Identifying Broader Private-Sector Cybersecurity Intelligence Needs and Priorities

Recommendation 5.1.3: Empower Departments and Agencies to Serve Administrative Subpoenas in Support of Threat and Asset Response Activities

Recommendation 5.2: Establish and Fund a Joint Collaborative Environment for Sharing and Fusing Threat Information

Recommendation 5.2.2: Pass a National Cyber Incident Reporting Law

Recommendation 5.2.3: Amend the Pen Register Trap and Trace Statute to Enable Better Identification of Malicious Actors

Recommendation 5.3: Strengthen an Integrated Cyber Center within CISA and Promote the Integration of Federal Cyber Centers

Recommendation 5.4.1: Institutionalize Department of Defense Participation in Public-Private Cybersecurity Initiatives

PILLAR 6: PRESERVE AND EMPLOY THE MILITARY INSTRUMENTS OF POWER

Recommendations 6.1 & 6.1.3: Direct the Department of Defense to Conduct a Force Structure Assessment of the Cyber Mission Force / Review the Delegation of Authorities for Cyber Operations

Recommendation 6.1.1: Direct the Department of Defense to Create a Major Force Program Funding Category for U.S. Cyber Command

Recommendation 6.1.7: Assess the Establishment of a Military Cyber Reserve

Recommendation 6.2: Conduct a Cybersecurity Vulnerability Assessment of All Segments of the NC3 and NLCC Systems and Continually Assess Weapon Systems Cyber Vulnerabilities

Recommendation 6.2.1: Require Defense Industrial Base Participation in a Threat Intelligence Sharing Program

Recommendation 6.2.2: Require Threat Hunting on Defense Industrial Base Networks

Recommendation 6.2.4: Assess and Address the Risk to National Security Systems Posed by Quantum Computing

EXECUTIVE SUMMARY:

Establish a Means to Monitor and Support Implementation of Report Recommendations

APPENDIX C
GLOSSARY

Editor's note: Many of the terms and definitions listed below are context dependent. Therefore, the definitions provided capture only the understanding of the Commissioners in the scope of their deliberations and this report; they are not intended to provide legal or political interpretations or technical standards.

access	Entry into an information or operational technology system.
advanced persistent threat (APT)	A sophisticated adversary that (i) pursues its objectives repeatedly over an extended period of time, (ii) adapts to defenders' efforts to resist it, and (iii) is determined to maintain the level of interaction needed to execute its objectives.
artificial intelligence (AI)	The theory, development, and simulation of computer systems able to perform tasks normally requiring human intelligence.
attack vector	Mechanism or method used by an attacker to gain access to a target's computer system and/or deliver an effect.
attribute	Any distinctive feature, characteristic, or property of an object that can be identified or isolated quantitatively or qualitatively by either human or automated means.
attribution	Identification of technical evidence of a cyber event and/or the assignment of responsibility for a cyber event. The technical source may be different from the responsible actor.
backdoor	An intentionally designed vulnerability that enables access to a computer system.
Border Gateway Protocol	A protocol designed to optimize routing of information exchanged through the internet.
bot	A computer that has been compromised with malware to perform activities under the remote command and control of an administrator.
botnet	A network of compromised computers (or bots) under unified command and control.
business continuity	The documentation of a predetermined set of instructions or procedures that describes how an organization's mission/business processes will be sustained during and after a significant disruption.
byte	A unit of digital information consisting of 8 bits (binary digits: each bit corresponds to a choice between two alternatives).
client	A remote application or system that is used to connect to a server.
cloud computing	A model for enabling ubiquitous, convenient, on-demand network access to a shared pool of configurable computing resources (e.g., networks, servers, storage, applications, and services) that can be rapidly provided to users with minimal management effort or service provider interaction.
Committee on Foreign Investment in the United States	U.S. government's interagency committee authorized to review certain transactions involving foreign investment in the United States and certain real estate transactions, in order to determine the effect of such transactions on the national security of the United States.

compromise	Unauthorized access to a computer, network, data, or system.
computer emergency/ incident response team (CERT/CIRT)	A group of individuals, usually consisting of security analysts, organized to develop, recommend, and coordinate immediate mitigation actions for containment, eradication, and recovery resulting from computer security incidents. Often a government entity.
computer network attack (CNA)	Actions taken through the use of computer networks to disrupt, deny, degrade, or destroy information resident in computers and computer networks, or in transit, or the computers and networks themselves.
computer network defense (CND)	Actions taken to defend against unauthorized activity within computer networks. CND includes monitoring, detection, analysis, and response and restoration activities.
computer network exploitation (CNE)	Enabling operations and intelligence collection capabilities conducted through the use of computer networks to gather data from target or adversary information systems or networks.
confidentiality	The preservation of authorized restrictions on information access and disclosure, including means for protecting personal privacy and proprietary information.
Continuity of Government (COG)	An effort to establish executive branch preparedness for and resilience to threats to the National Capital Region.
Continuity of Operations (COOP)	An effort within individual executive departments and agencies to ensure that Primary Mission Essential Functions (PMEFs) continue to be performed during a wide range of emergencies, including localized acts of nature, accidents, and technological or attack-related emergencies.
Continuity of the Economy (COTE)	An effort to ensure that critical data and technology would be available, with priority for critical functions across corporations and industry sectors, to get the economy back up and running after a catastrophic event.
critical infrastructure	Systems and assets, physical and virtual, so vital to the United States that their incapacitation or destruction would have a debilitating impact on security, national economic security, national public health or safety, or any combination of those matters.
Critical Infrastructure Resilience Strategy	A proposed strategy that will set programmatic and budgetary priorities for a five-year national risk management cycle.
Critical Technology Security Centers	Proposed entities/programs that provide the U.S. government with the capacity to test the security of critical technologies and, when appropriate, assist in identifying vulnerabilities, as well as developing and pushing mitigation techniques with relevant original equipment manufacturers.
cryptocurrency	A type of digital currency in which encryption techniques are used to secure transactions and control the creation of additional units while operating independently of a central bank.
cyber	Relating to, involving, or characteristic of computers, computer networks, information and communications technology (ICT), virtual systems, or computer-enabled control of physical components.
cyber actor/cyber operator	A person who employs the functions of computer networks, systems, devices, or services.

cyberattack	Action taken in cyberspace that creates noticeable denial effects (i.e., degradation, disruption, or destruction) in cyberspace or manipulation that leads to denial that appears in a physical domain.
cyber campaign	A cyber operation or series of cyber operations conducted by a single responsible party with the intention of achieving a strategic objective.
cybercrime	A cyber operation that is primarily motivated by reasons other than national security or geopolitical objectives.
cyber disruption	An event that is likely to cause or is causing the temporary loss of normal cyber operations or services.
cyber effect	The manipulation, disruption, denial, degradation, or destruction of data, computers, information or communication systems, networks, physical or virtual infrastructure controlled by computers or information systems, or information resident on them or in transit.
cyber espionage	Cyber operation whose primary purpose is to steal information for national security or commercial purposes.
Cyber Response and Recovery Fund	A new fund, administered by the Federal Emergency Management Agency but directed by the Cybersecurity and Infrastructure Security Agency. Cyber Recovery Fund disbursement would be triggered by a "cyber state of distress" declaration. The funds could be used for a variety of purposes, including direct assistance to entities through purchases of equipment and services for their rapid response and recovery.
cyber risk	Risk of financial loss, legal liability, reputational damage, regulatory action, operational disruption, or damage from the failure of the digital technologies employed for informational and/or operational functions introduced to a manufacturing system via electronic means from the unauthorized access, use, disclosure, disruption, modification, or destruction of the manufacturing system.
cybersecurity	Prevention of damage to, protection of, and restoration of computers, electronic communications systems, electronic communications services, wire communication, and electronic communication. This includes ensuring the availability, integrity, authentication, confidentiality, and nonrepudiation of the information contained therein.
cyberspace	A global domain within the information environment consisting of the interdependent networks of information technology infrastructures and resident data, including the internet, telecommunications networks, computer systems, and embedded processors and controllers.
cyber state of distress	A proposed federal declaration that would trigger additional financial and material assistance. The declaration would be used exclusively for responding to, or preemptively preparing for, cyber incidents that are more serious than "routine" but do not warrant an emergency declaration.
cyber threat	A capability and intent that intentionally compromises the confidentiality, integrity, reliability, or availability of digital devices, systems, networks, or data in transit or at rest.
database	A structured repository of data that is organized to provide efficient retrieval.

data breach	The unauthorized movement or disclosure of sensitive information to a party, usually outside the organization, that is not authorized to have or see that information.
data hosting	The activity or business of providing hardware, systems, software, and infrastructure to store and manage access to data.
data governance	A set of processes or rules that ensure the integrity of data and that data management best practices are met.
data/data set	Quantitative or qualitative raw material used to represent information, or from which information can be derived.
decryption	The process of transforming cipher text into readable text using a cryptographic algorithm and key.
deepfake	A digital picture or video that has been maliciously edited using an algorithm in a way that makes the video appear authentic.
defend forward	The proactive observing, pursuing, and countering of adversary operations and imposing of costs in day-to-day competition to disrupt and defeat ongoing malicious adversary cyber campaigns, deter future campaigns, and reinforce favorable international norms of behavior, using all of the instruments of national power. This is a reimagining and expansion of the defend forward concept as initially conceived of in the 2018 DoD Cyber Strategy, which focuses solely on the military instrument.
defensive cyber campaign	A coordinated set of actions across the U.S. government, utilizing any or all available instruments of U.S. national power, to respond to an adversary cyber campaign, mitigate its potential effects, and impose consequences.
defensive cyber operations	Missions to preserve the ability to utilize one's own network capabilities and protect data, computers, cyberspace-enabled devices, and other designated systems by defeating ongoing or imminent malicious cyberspace activity. Also called DCO.
denial-of-service attack (*see also:* distributed denial-of-service attack)	A type of cyber action designed to prevent users from accessing a network-connected service by sending legitimate requests from one source to overload a network's resources.
deterrence	Dissuading someone from doing something by making them believe that the costs to them will exceed their expected benefit.
digital citizenship	The position or status of being an internet user, particularly as it pertains to knowledge of responsible behaviors pertaining to internet use, including internet safety, digital footprint, online media balance, cyberbullying, online privacy and communication, information literacy, creative credit and copyright, and other related topics.
digital literacy	The ability to use information and communication technologies to find, evaluate, create, and communicate information, requiring both cognitive and technical skills.
direct recording electronic (DRE) voting machine	A device that records votes by means of a ballot display provided with mechanical or electro-optical components that can be activated by the voter (typically buttons or a touch-screen), that processes data by means of a computer program, and that records voting data and ballot images in memory components.

disinformation	False information deliberately spread to deceive.
distributed denial-of-service attack (*see also:* denial-of-service attack)	A denial of service technique that uses numerous hosts to perform the attack.
Domain-based Message Authentication, Reporting & Conformance	An email authentication, policy, and reporting protocol that verifies the authenticity of the sender of an email and blocks and reports fraudulent accounts.
domain name	A unique name composed of alphanumeric characters that identifies a website and appears in the address bar of the web browser.
Domain Name System	A system that stores information associated with domain names in a distributed database on networks.
election infrastructure	Information and communications technology and systems used by or on behalf of the federal government or a state or local government in managing the election process, including voter registration databases, voting machines, voting tabulation equipment, and equipment for the secure transmission of election results.
encryption	A procedure to convert plain text into cipher text.
end-to-end encryption	Communications encryption in which data is encrypted when being passed through a network, but routing information remains visible.
exfiltration	The transfer of data from an information system.
exploit	Software that takes advantage of a vulnerability to undermine a computer's security.
exploitation	The act of extracting and gathering intelligence data.
fifth-generation wireless network (5G)	A set of wireless software and hardware technologies that will produce a significant improvement in data speed, volume, and latency (delay in data transfer) over fourth-generation (4G and 4G LTE) networks.
final goods assembler	The entity that is most responsible for the placement of a product or service into the stream of commerce.
firewall	Devices or systems that act as a protective barrier controlling the flow of network traffic between networks or between a host and a network.
firmware	Software programmed into read-only memory (ROM).
gateway	A node that attaches to two (or more) computer networks that have similar functions but dissimilar implementations and that enables either one-way or two-way communication between the networks.
hacker	Unauthorized user who attempts to gain or successfully gains access to an information system.

hardware	The physical components of an information system.
honeypot	A computer security mechanism to detect, deflect, or counteract unauthorized access to computer systems by acting as a decoy to attract or bait internet users seeking to obtain unauthorized access.
Hunt and Incident Response Team	A set of teams within the Cybersecurity and Infrastructure Security Agency that provides onsite incident response, free of charge, to organizations that require immediate investigation and resolution of cyberattacks.
hunt forward	U.S. efforts with allies and partners to conduct threat hunting and pursue adversaries on allied and partner networks.
implant	Hardware or software designed to enable unauthorized functions on a compromised computer system.
industrial control system (ICS)	An information system, both hardware and software, specifically designed to control industrial processes such as manufacturing, product handling, production, and distribution.
information operations	The integrated employment of the core capabilities of electronic warfare, computer network operations, psychological operations, military deception, and operations security, in concert with specified supporting and related capabilities, to influence, disrupt, corrupt, or usurp adversarial human and automated decision-making process, information, and information systems.
information security (INFOSEC)	The protection of information and information systems from unauthorized access, use, disclosure, disruption, modification, or destruction in order to provide confidentiality, integrity, and availability.
information system (IS)	A discrete set of information resources organized for the collection, processing, maintenance, use, sharing, dissemination, or disposition of information.
information technology (IT)	All categories of ubiquitous technology used for the gathering, storing, transmitting, retrieving, or processing of information (e.g., microelectronics, printed circuit boards, computing systems, software, signal processors, mobile telephony, satellite communications, and networks).
innovation base of the United States	The American network of knowledge, capabilities, and people—including those in academia, National Laboratories, and the private sector—that turns ideas into innovations, transforms discoveries into successful commercial products and companies, and protects and enhances the American way of life.
insider threat	The threat that an insider will use their authorized access, wittingly or unwittingly, to do harm to the organization.
integrity	The guard against improper information modification or destruction, including assurance of information nonrepudiation and authenticity.
internet	The single, interconnected, worldwide system of commercial, governmental, educational, and other computer networks that share (i) the protocol suite specified by the Internet Architecture Board (IAB) and (ii) the name and address spaces managed by the Internet Corporation for Assigned Names and Numbers (ICANN).

Internet of Things (IoT)	A concept that describes everyday physical objects being connected to the internet and identifying themselves to other devices.
in the wild	A term that can be used to describe malware in general use (thereby making attribution difficult) or an unpatched or unknown vulnerability discovered in an information system.
intrusion	A computer system compromise, in which an intruder gains, or attempts to gain, access to a system or system resource without having authorization to do so.
intrusion detection system (IDS)	A software application that can be implemented on host operating systems or as network devices to monitor activity that is associated with intrusions or insider misuse, or both.
Joint Cyber Planning Cell	A proposed cell within the Cybersecurity and Infrastructure Security Agency that would facilitate comprehensive operational planning of defensive, non-intelligence cybersecurity campaigns across agencies.
machine learning	A subfield of computer science in which computers learn without being explicitly programmed and automate analytic model building.
malicious code	Software or firmware intended to perform an unauthorized process that will have adverse impact on the confidentiality, integrity, or availability of an information system.
malware	A computer program that is clandestinely placed onto a computer with the intent to compromise the privacy, accuracy, or reliability of the computer's data, applications, or operating system.
multi-factor authentication	Authentication using two or more factors to achieve authentication. Factors include something you know, something you have, or something you are.
national critical functions	The functions of government and the private sector that are so vital to the United States that their disruption, corruption, or dysfunction would have a debilitating effect on security, national economic security, national public health or safety, or any combination of these elements.
National Cybersecurity Assistance Fund	A proposed fund administered by the Federal Emergency Management Agency that would distribute grants to public and private entities for solutions, projects, and programs where a) there is a clearly defined, critical risk to be mitigated, b) market forces do not provide sufficient private sector incentives to mitigate the risk without government investment, and c) there is clear federal need, role, and responsibility in mitigating the risk
National Cybersecurity Certification and Labeling Authority	A proposed organization that would be charged with certifying critical information technologies against frameworks based on identified and vetted security standards and with supporting and endorsing product labeling, building on existing work on Software Bills of Material at the National Telecommunications and Information Administration.
national security industrial sector	The worldwide industrial complex that enables research and development, as well as the design, production, delivery, and maintenance of military weapons systems, subsystems, and components or parts, to meet U.S. military requirements (also referred to as the defense industrial base).
network resilience	A computing infrastructure that provides continuous business operation, rapid recovery if failure does occur, and the ability to scale up to meet rapid or unpredictable demands.

nonrepudiation	Assurance that the sender is provided with proof of delivery and that the recipient is provided with proof of the sender's identity so that neither can later deny having processed the data.
non-state actor	An organization or individual that is not affiliated with a nation-state.
norm	A collective expectation for the proper behavior of actors with a given identity.
offensive cyber operations	Cyberspace operations intended to project power by the application of force in or through cyberspace.
operational technology	Hardware and software that detects or causes a change through the direct monitoring and/or control of physical devices, processes, and events in the enterprise.
packet	The logical unit of network communications produced by the transport layer.
patch	A software component that, when installed, directly modifies files or device settings related to a different software component without changing the version number or release details for the related software component.
penetration testing	Security testing in which evaluators mimic real-world attacks in an attempt to identify ways to exploit, gain unauthorized access, or circumvent an application, system, or network.
persistent engagement	The concept by which U.S. Cyber Command implements defend forward. It is based on the idea that adversaries are in constant contact in cyberspace. Its elements are enabling partners and acting as far forward as possible.
phishing	A technique for attempting to acquire sensitive data through a fraudulent solicitation in email or on a web site, in which the perpetrator masquerades as a legitimate, reputable, or known-to-the-user person or business.
post-election audit	Any review conducted after polls close for the purpose of determining whether the votes were counted accurately (a results audit) or whether proper procedures were followed (a process audit), or both.
protocol	A set of rules to implement and control some type of association between systems.
public key infrastructure (PKI)	A software-based system designed to provide confidentiality, integrity, and authenticity in communications; it relies on asymmetric cryptography.
quantum computer	A collection of interacting quantum mechanical systems, such as superconductors or trapped ions, that can be manipulated to process information.
ransomware	Malware installed on a victim's device that mounts either an extortion attack that holds the victim's data hostage or threatens to publish the victim's data until a ransom is paid.
reconnaissance	An action to discover malicious tools or vulnerabilities in a targeted system or network.
red team	A group of people authorized and organized to emulate a potential adversary's attack or exploitation capabilities against an enterprise's security posture.
resilience	The capacity to withstand and quickly recover from attacks that could compel, deter, restrain, or otherwise shape U.S. behavior.
router	A device that determines the best path for forwarding a data packet toward its destination.

sandbox	A system that allows an untrusted application to run in a highly controlled environment where the application's permissions are restricted to an essential set of computer permissions.
sector risk management agency	A proposed designation for a federal agency that codifies the minimum roles and responsibilities of a sector-specific agency.
sector-specific agencies	Federal agencies that have institutional knowledge and specialized expertise about a critical infrastructure sector.
significant consequences	Effects that may include loss of life, significant damage to property, significant national security consequences, or significant economic impact on the United States.
significant cyber incident	A cyber incident that is (or group of related cyber incidents that together are) likely to result in demonstrable harm to the national security interests, foreign relations, or economy of the United States or to the public confidence, civil liberties, or public health and safety of the American people.
social engineering	The practice of manipulating legitimate users to allow increased access to a system by an illegitimate user.
software	A computer program written in a computing language.
spam	Electronic junk mail or the abuse of electronic messaging systems to indiscriminately send unsolicited messages.
spoofing	A fraudulent or malicious practice in which communication is sent from an unknown source disguised as a source known to the receiver.
supervisory control and data acquisition (SCADA)	A generic name for a computerized system that is capable of gathering and processing data and applying operational controls over long distances.
supply chain	A system of organizations, people, activities, information, and resources, possibly international in scope, that provides products or services to consumers.
supply chain compromise	An occurrence within the supply chain whereby an adversary jeopardizes the confidentiality, integrity, or availability of a system or the information that the system processes, stores, or transmits.
supply chain management	A cross-functional approach to procuring, producing, and delivering products and services to customers.
supply chain risk management	A systematic process for managing supply chain risk by identifying susceptibilities, vulnerabilities, and threats throughout the supply chain and developing mitigation strategies to combat those threats whether presented by the supplier, the product and its subcomponents, or the supply chain itself (e.g., initial production, packaging, handling, storage, transport, mission operation, and disposal).
systemically important critical infrastructure (SICI)	A proposed designation of critical infrastructure entities that manage systems and assets whose disruption could have cascading, destabilizing effects on U.S. national security, economic security, and public health and safety.
threat	An event or condition that has the potential for causing harm.

trojan horse	A computer program that appears to have a useful function, but also has a hidden and potentially malicious function that evades security mechanisms, sometimes by exploiting legitimate authorizations of a system entity that invokes the program.
troll	A person or group of people that invites discord on the internet by starting arguments or posting inflammatory, extraneous, or off-topic messages in an online community with the deliberate intent of provoking readers into an emotional response or otherwise disrupting normal on-topic discussion.
unauthorized access	Logical or physical access gained without permission to a network, system, application, data, or other resources.
virus	Code that runs on a computer without the user's knowledge, infecting the computer when the code is accessed and executed. It spreads via interaction.
voter-verifiable paper audit trail (VVPAT)	Hardware, added to an existing DRE voting machine, that provides a physical record of a voter's electronic selection. *See also:* direct recording electronic voting machine.
whole-of-government	U.S. government agencies working across boundaries and through interagency cooperation to achieve shared goals and/or an integrated government response.
whole-of-nation	Concerted and cooperative efforts among partners across agencies and the private sector to facilitate ease of operation and/or reach common goals.
zero-day attack	A cyber exploit that relies on exploiting an unknown or undisclosed vulnerability in the design or implementation of a system to violate its security.

Many of the definitions in this glossary are taken or adapted from the following sources:

- Defense Innovation Board, *The 5G Ecosystem: Risks & Opportunities for DoD* (April 2019)

- "Glossary," ISACA, 2020, https://www.isaca.org/resources/glossary

- Office of the Chairman of the Joint Chiefs of Staff, *DOD Dictionary of Military and Associated Terms* (January 2020)

- "Explore Terms: A Glossary of Common Cybersecurity Terminology," National Initiative for Cybersecurity Careers and Studies, November 28, 2018, https://niccs.us-cert.gov/about-niccs/glossary

- "Glossary," National Institute of Standards and Technology, Computer Security Resource Center, https://csrc.nist.gov/glossary

- "Glossary of Security Terms," SANS, 2020, https://www.sans.org/security-resources/glossary-of-terms/

Other U.S. government sources were also consulted.

APPENDIX D
ABBREVIATIONS

5G	fifth-generation
AI	artificial intelligence
ALAT	Assistant Legal Attaché
APT	advanced persistent threat
BGP	Border Gateway Protocol
CAATSA	Countering America's Adversaries Through Sanctions Act
CBMs	confidence-building measures
CDI	Cyber Deterrence Initiative
CFIUS	Committee on Foreign Investment in the United States
CI	critical infrastructure
CIDAWG	Cyber Incident Data and Analysis Working Group
CISA	Cybersecurity and Infrastructure Security Agency
CITF	Cyber Instability Task Force
CMF	Cyber Mission Force
CMMC	Cyber Maturity Model Certification
COTE	Continuity of the Economy
CSD	Cybersecurity Directorate
CSET	Cyberspace Security and Emerging Technologies
CSP	communication service provider
CTIIC	Cyber Threat Intelligence Integration Center
CTMS	Cyber Talent Management System
DARPA	Defense Advanced Research Projects Agency
DC3	Department of Defense Cyber Crime Center
DDoS	distributed denial-of-service
DFC	United States International Development Finance Corporation
DHS	Department of Homeland Security

DIB	Defense Industrial Base
DISA	Defense Information Systems Agency
DNS	Domain Name System
DoD	Department of Defense
DoDIN	Department of Defense Information Network
DOJ	Department of Justice
DSB	Defense Science Board
EAC	Election Assistance Commission
EOP	Executive Office of the President
EU	European Union
FBI	Federal Bureau of Investigation
FECA	Federal Election Campaign Act of 1971
FedRAMP	Federal Risk and Authorization Management Program
FEMA	Federal Emergency Management Agency
FFRDC	Federally Funded Research and Development Center
FIRRMA	Foreign Investment Risk Review Modernization Act
FSARC	Financial Systemic Analysis and Resilience Center
FY	fiscal year
GAO	Government Accountability Office
GPS	Global Positioning System
G7	Group of Seven
G20	Group of Twenty
ICC/JOC	Integrated Cyber Center and Joint Operations Center
ICT	information and communications technology
ILEA	International Law Enforcement Academy
INL	Idaho National Lab
IO	information operations

Cyberspace Solarium Commission

IoT	Internet of Things	NSTAC	National Security Telecommunications Advisory Committee
IP	intellectual property	NTIA	National Telecommunications and Information Agency
IRA	Internet Research Agency	ODNI	Office of the Director of National Intelligence
ISAC	information sharing and analysis center	OEWG	Open-Ended Working Group
IT	information technology	OPE	operational preparation of the environment
ITU	International Telecommunications Union	OMB	Office of Management and Budget
JCPC	Joint Cyber Planning Cell	OSCE	Organization for Security and Co-operation in Europe
MFP	Major Force Program	OTA	Office of Technology Assessment
MILDEC	military deception	PLA	People's Liberation Army
MISO	Military Information Support Operations	PME	Professional Military Education
ML	machine learning	PRTT	Pen Register Trap and Trace
MLAA	Mutual Legal Assistance Agreement	R&D	research and development
MLAT	Mutual Legal Assistance Treaty	SFOPS	State, Foreign Operations, and Related Programs
MOU	memorandum of understanding	SICI	systemically important critical infrastructure
NATO	North Atlantic Treaty Organization	SLTT	state, local, tribal, and territorial
NCCIC	National Cybersecurity and Communications Integration Center	SROE	Standing Rules of Engagement
NCD	National Cyber Director	SRUF	Standing Rules for Use of Force
NCFTA	National Cyber-Forensics and Training Alliance	SSA	sector-specific agency
NCIJTF	National Cyber Investigative Joint Task Force	STEM	science, technology, engineering, and mathematics
NC3	nuclear command, control, and communications	TLS	Transport Layer Security
NDAA	National Defense Authorization Act	TTPs	tactics, techniques, and procedures
NGO	nongovernmental organization	U.K.	United Kingdom
NICE	National Initiative on Cybersecurity Education	UN	United Nations
NIST	National Institute of Standards and Technology	UN GGE	United Nations Group of Governmental Experts on Developments in the Field of Information and Telecommunications in the Context of International Security
NLCC	National Leadership Command Capabilities	U.S.	United States
NSA	National Security Agency	USAID	United States Agency for International Development
NSC	National Security Council		
NSDD	National Security Decision Directive		
NSF	National Science Foundation		
NSPM	National Security Presidential Memorandum		

GOVERNMENT STRUCTURE FOR CYBERSECURITY

Relationship of Commission Recommend

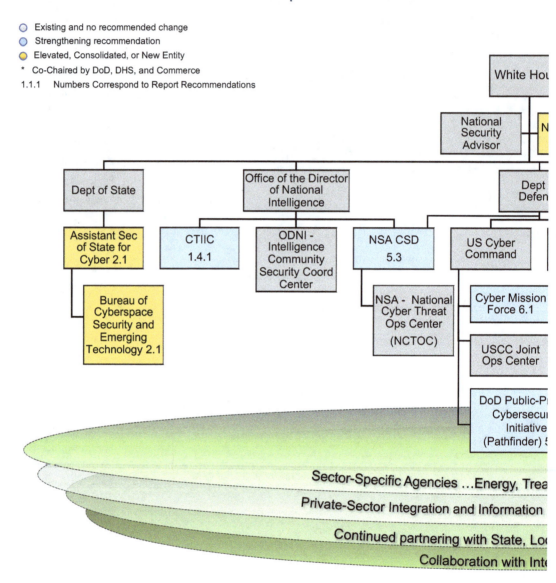

- ○ Existing and no recommended change
- ○ Strengthening recommendation
- ○ Elevated, Consolidated, or New Entity
- * Co-Chaired by DoD, DHS, and Commerce
- 1.1.1 Numbers Correspond to Report Recommendations

ndations to Existing Cyber Organizations

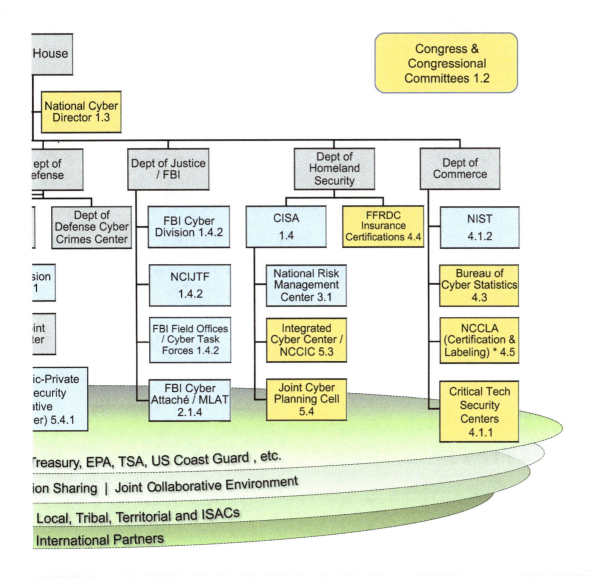

APPENDIX F
SITUATING LAYERED CYBER DETERRENCE

Layered deterrence builds on studies published over the past five years that explore how to secure American interests in cyberspace. It draws on these reports and studies and adds important new elements to provide a comprehensive blueprint for reducing the severity and frequency of cyberattacks. Two elements make the strategy distinct. First, layered cyber deterrence integrates multiple deterrent mechanisms (i.e., layers) to change the cost-benefit calculus of adversaries. It incorporates the Department of Defense (DoD) concept of defend forward, while managing escalation risks. Second, layered cyber deterrence's whole-of-nation approach surpasses previous attempts to expand the deterrent capabilities available to the nation. The strategy encourages a collaborative, persistent, mutually beneficial deterrent posture that defends American society.

STUDY	WHAT IS SIMILAR	WHAT IS DIFFERENT IN LAYERED CYBER DETERRENCE
2019 National Infrastructure Advisory Council's Transforming U.S. Cyber Threat Partnership	Describes the need to partner with the owners and operators of the most critical infrastructure and improve intelligence sharing between government and industry.	Places greater emphasis on the private-sector role in supporting the government.
2018 U.S. National Cyber Strategy	Defines the threat as state and non-state and describes how it affects the whole of American society.	Combines multiple deterrent and compellent logics while emphasizing public-private collaboration and integrating defend forward.
2018 Department of Defense Cyber Strategy	Defines "defend forward" as a proactive approach to addressing malicious adversary behavior.	Broadens the range of strategic options available (i.e., multiple instruments of power) and describes how to approach securing cyberspace through a whole-of-nation framework.
2018 United States Cyber Command Vision	Defines "defend forward" as operating as closely as possible to the origin of adversary activity and persistently contesting malicious actors consistent with international law.	Adopts a whole-of-nation approach, rather than focusing solely on persistent engagement.
2018 Department of Homeland Security Cybersecurity Strategy	Focuses on a prioritized and comprehensive risk-based approach to securing critical systems.	Integrates national resilience and protecting critical infrastructure into a larger framework that builds on multiple deterrent and compellent logics and maps how to create incentives for public-private collaboration.

STUDY	WHAT IS SIMILAR	WHAT IS DIFFERENT IN LAYERED CYBER DETERRENCE
2018 Defense Science Board's Task Force on Cyber as a Strategic Capability	Discusses the cyber threat as it relates not just to offensive capabilities but also to weaponized social media and disinformation.	Focuses on a broader array of threat actors and ways to defend American interests in cyberspace.
2018 National Security Telecommunications Advisory Committee (NSTAC) Report on a Cyber Moonshot	Highlights the need to unify efforts across the government and create new executive bodies to oversee cybersecurity initiatives.	Creates a strategic logic (i.e., ends, ways, means) that prioritizes and coordinates policy recommendations addressing challenges highlighted in the NSTAC report.
2017 National Defense Strategy and National Security Strategy	Emphasizes great power competition.	Describes how to secure U.S. networks during great power competition.
2017 Defense Science Board Task Force on Cyber Deterrence	Prioritizes ensuring the resilience of key weapon systems as part of a larger deterrent strategy.	Integrates multiple deterrent layers combining different instruments of power—including non-military means—and describes how to mobilize the larger society to reduce attack surfaces (i.e., deny benefits).
2016 Commission on Enhancing National Cybersecurity	Calls for incentivizing behaviors in the private sector that increase overall cybersecurity.	Describes how to increase collaboration between the public and private sectors.
2015 DoD Cyber Strategy	Advocates creating international partnerships and "building bridges to the private sector" as key components of generating options to defend American interests in cyberspace.	Integrates a broad range of deterrent and compellent options (i.e., three layers) and describes how to increase national resilience and reshape the cyber ecosystem through private-sector collaboration.

APPENDIX G
ENGAGEMENTS

ACADEMIA

American University
  School of International
  Service

Auburn University
  McCrary Institute

Ben Gurion University

Columbia University
  Columbia Law School
  School of International and
  Public Affairs (SIPA)

George Mason University
  Antonin Scalia Law School,
  National Security Law &
  Policy Program

George Washington University

Georgetown University
  Edmund A. Walsh School of
  Foreign Service

Georgia Institute of Technology

Harvard University
  Belfer Center
  Harvard Kennedy School

Johns Hopkins University
  School of Advanced
  International Studies

King's College London (KCL)

London School of Economics and
  Political Science

Massachusetts Institute of
  Technology
  Computer Science & Artificial
  Intelligence Laboratory
  Lincoln Laboratory

Internet Policy Research
  Initiative

Purdue University

Stanford University
  Center for Security Studies

Tel Aviv University

University of California, Berkeley
  Center for Long Term
  Cybersecurity

University of California, San Diego

University of Cincinnati

University of Michigan

University of Oxford

University of Texas at Austin
  The University of Texas
  School of Law

University of Toronto

Virginia Polytechnic Institute and
  State University

U.S. GOVERNMENT

Central Intelligence Agency

City and County of San Francisco

City of Austin, Texas

City of New York, Cyber
  Command

Commonwealth of Pennsylvania

Executive Office of the President
  National Security Council
  Office of the U.S. Trade
  Representative

Federal Bureau of Investigation
  (FBI)
  New York Field Office

Lawrence Livermore National
  Laboratory

National Cyber Investigative Joint
  Task Force

National Defense Cyber Alliance

National Security Agency

Office of the Director of National
  Intelligence
  Cyber Threat Intelligence and
  Integration Center
  Office of National Intelligence
  Manager for Cyber

State of Colorado
  Colorado National Guard
  Department of Public Safety

State of Tennessee
  Bureau of Investigation

State of Texas
  Department of Information
  Resources
  Texas National Guard

State of Washington
  Washington National Guard

U.S. Department of Commerce
  National Institute of
  Standards and Technology
  National Telecommunications
  and Information
  Administration

U.S. Department of Defense
  Army Cyber Command
  Army Futures Command
  Defense Advanced Research
  Projects Agency
  Defense Innovation Unit
  Defense Science Board

Fleet Cyber Command
U.S. Cyber Command
United States Naval War College
U.S. Department of Energy
U.S. Department of Homeland Security
Cybersecurity and Infrastructure Security Agency
Federal Emergency Management Agency
U.S. Secret Service
U.S. Department of Justice
U.S. Department of State
U.S. Department of the Treasury

INTERNATIONAL GOVERNMENT

Embassy of the Czech Republic
Embassy of the Kingdom of the Netherlands
Embassy of Ukraine
Embassy of the United Kingdom
European Commission, Directorate-General for Migration and Home Affairs
European Union Institute for Security Studies (EUISS)
EU Cyber Direct
European Union, European External Action Service (EEAS)
Government of Israel, National Cyber Directorate
Government of the United Kingdom
Cabinet Office
Department for Digital, Culture, Media & Sport

Foreign and Commonwealth Office
Ministry of Defense
National Cyber Security Centre
National Security Directorate
Parliament, House of Commons, Foreign Affairs Committee
North Atlantic Treaty Organization (NATO)
NATO Cooperative Cyber Defense Center of Excellence (CCDCOE)
Republic of Estonia
Information System Authority (RIA)
Ministry of Defense
Ministry of Economic Affairs and Communications (MKM)
Ministry of Foreign Affairs
Government Office

CORPORATE AND NONGOVERNMENTAL ORGANIZATION (NGO)

Adaptive Strategies, LLC
AECOM
American Gas Association
American Petroleum Institute
American Public Power Association
The Aspen Institute
Association of State Criminal Investigative Agencies (ASCIA)
Atlantic Council
Auto Alliance (Alliance of Automobile Manufacturers)

Automotive Information Sharing and Analysis Center (Auto-ISAC)
Bank of America
Bayshore Networks
Beazley PLC
Bloomberg
BluVector
Brendler Consulting
Business Roundtable
BSA | The Software Alliance
Carnegie Endowment for International Peace
Cato Institute
Center for a New American Security (CNAS)
Center for Internet Security
Center for Strategic and International Studies (CSIS)
Centrify
CenturyLink
Chatham House
Claroty
Comcast
Consumer Technology Association
Council on Foreign Relations
Coveware
CrowdStrike
Cyber Tech Accord
Cyber Threat Alliance
CyberCube
Cybereason
CyberPeace Institute
Cytegic
Defending Digital Campaigns

DIGITALEUROPE

DiploFoundation

DLL Group

DLT Solutions

Downstream Natural Gas
Information Sharing and
Analysis Center

Dragos

EastWest Institute

Expanse

Expel

Financial Crimes Enforcement
Network

Financial Services Information
Sharing and Analysis Center
(FS-ISAC)

Financial Systemic Analysis &
Resilience Center (FS-ARC)

ForeScout Technologies

ForgePoint Capital

German Marshall Fund of the
United States

Grimm (SMFS, Inc.)

Gula Tech Adventures

The Hague Centre for Strategic
Studies

Hathaway Global Strategies LLC

Health Information Sharing and
Analysis Center

Hewlett Packard

Hogan Lovells

HSBC

I Am the Cavalry

Information Technology Industry
Council

Institute for Critical Infrastructure
Technology

IOActive

Jigsaw

JPMorgan Chase

Kleiner Perkins Caufield & Byers

Liberty Ventures

Luta Security

M&T Bank

MassMutual

MassCyberCenter

Mazda North American
Operations

Micro Focus

Microsoft

The MITRE Corporation
Center for National Security

Morgan Stanley

National Association of Insurance
Commissioners

National Association of
Secretaries of State

National Association of State
Chief Information Officers

National Association of State
Election Directors

National Governors Association

National Rural Electric
Cooperative Association

New America

Next Peak LLC

Nippon Telegraph and Telephone
Corporation

Palantir

Palo Alto Networks

Pavisade

PricewaterhouseCoopers (PWC)

Proofpoint

R Street Institute

RAND Corporation
Pardee RAND Graduate
School

Rapid7

Royal United Services Institute for
Defence and Security Studies
(RUSI)

Scythe

SIGA OT Solutions

Software & Information Industry
Association

Sovereign Ventures

Splunk

Square

Team8

techUK

Third Way

Threat Warrior

Trail of Bits

TruSTAR

U.S. Chamber of Commerce

Verified Voting

Vidder, Inc.

Water Information Sharing and
Analysis Center

Wells Fargo

West Wing Advisory Services

White & Case LLP

Wickr

The William and Flora Hewlett
Foundation

The Wilson Center

APPENDIX H
COMMISSIONERS

COMMISSIONERS

Frank J. Cilluffo
Director of Auburn University's
Charles D. McCrary Institute for
Cyber and Critical Infrastructure
Security

Andrew Hallman
Principal Executive of the Office
of the Director of National
Intelligence performing the duties
of the Principal Deputy Director of
National Intelligence

Thomas A. "Tom" Fanning
Chairman, President, and Chief
Executive Officer of Southern
Company

John C. "Chris" Inglis
U.S. Naval Academy Looker
Professor for Cyber Security
Studies and Former Deputy
Director of the National Security
Agency

James R. "Jim" Langevin
U.S. Representative for Rhode Island's 2nd District

Samantha F. Ravich
Chair of the Center on Cyber and Technology Innovation at the Foundation for Defense of Democracies

Patrick J. Murphy
Former Acting Secretary and Under Secretary of the U.S. Army & Former U.S. Representative for Pennsylvania's 8th District

Benjamin E. "Ben" Sasse
U.S. Senator for Nebraska

David L. Norquist
Deputy Secretary of Defense

Suzanne E. Spaulding
Senior Adviser for Homeland Security at the Center for Strategic and International Studies and former Under Secretary for the National Protection and Programs Directorate at the Department of Homeland Security

David Pekoske
Administrator of the Transportation Security Administration & Senior Official Performing the Duties of the Deputy Secretary of Homeland Security

Christopher Wray
Director of the Federal Bureau of Investigation

The executive branch Commissioners contributed superb assessments, insights, and recommendations to the report and actively participated in the Commission's deliberations, but, in accordance with executive branch legal guidance, abstained from its final approval.

APPENDIX I
STAFF LIST

Executive Team   Mark Montgomery, Executive Director

Deborah Grays, Chief of Staff

Senior Leadership   Erica Borghard, Senior Director and Task Force One Lead

John Costello, Senior Director and Task Force Two Lead

Val Cofield, Senior Director and Task Force Three Lead

Cory Simpson, Senior Director and Directorate Four Lead

Benjamin Jensen, Senior Research Director and Lead Writer

Full-Time Staff   Laura Bate, Director for Cyber Engagement

Phoebe Benich, Cyber Strategy and Policy Analyst

Tatyana Bolton, Policy Director

Gregory Buck, Deputy Chief of Staff

Madison Creery, Cyber Strategy and Policy Analyst

Matthew Ferren, Cyber Strategy and Policy Analyst

Chris Forshey, Facility Security Officer

Michael Garcia, Director of External Engagement and Outreach

Charles Garzoni, Director for Defensive Strategy

Karrie Jefferson, Director for Cyber Engagement

Ainsley Katz, Cyber Strategy and Policy Analyst

Alison King, Strategic Communications and Congressional Advisor

Timothy Kocher, Cyber Strategist

Noah Komnick, Cyber Strategist

Harry Krejsa, Director and Deputy Team Lead

Sang Lee, Director for Cyber Engagement

Robert Morgus, Director for Research and Analysis

Diane Pinto, Cyber Strategy and Policy Analyst

Matthew Smith, Cyber Strategist

Brandon Valeriano, Senior Advisor

Dave Zikusoka, Policy Director

Legal Advisors	Stefan Wolfe, General Counsel
	Corey Bradley, Deputy General Counsel
	Cody Cheek, Legal Advisor
	David Simon, Chief Counsel for Cybersecurity and National Security
	Veronica Glick, Deputy Chief Counsel for Cybersecurity and National Security
	Joshua Silverstein, Deputy Chief Counsel for Cybersecurity and National Security
Production Support	Alice Falk, Editor
	Laurel Prucha Moran, Graphic Designer
Senior Advisors (Part-Time)	Steven Chabinsky
	Frank DiGiovanni
	Thomas Donahue
	Michael Fischerkeller
	Jason Healey
	Jackie Kerr
	Nina Kollars
	Jon Lindsay
	Shawn Lonergan
	Christopher Painter
	Mark Raymond
	Phil Reitinger
	Harvey Rishikof
	Christopher Schell
	Jacquelyn Schneider
	Bobbie Stempfley
	Evan Wolff
	JD Work

Contributing Experts

Robert Bair
Ronald Banks
Amy Bianchino
Aaron Brantly
Bob Butler
Bobby Chesney
Peter Dombrowski
Martha Finnemore
Stephen Flynn
David Forscey
Jane Fountain
Kara Frederick
Heidi Gardner
Lindsey Gorman
Neil Jenkins
Alexander Klimburg
Robert Knake
Herb Lin
Austin Long
Ryan Maness
Zane Markel
Joseph Nye
Jonathan Reiber
Josh Rovner
Benjamin Schechter
Lindsey Sheppard
Rebecca Slayton
Jessica "Zhanna" Malekos Smith
Josephine Wolff

The Commission would like to acknowledge the critical support of the following agency and Commissioner Staff Members

Melissa Bunney
Eugene Burrell
Clark Cully
Brett Fetterly
Kelly Gaffney
Matthew Gorham
Michele Guido
Amy Hess
Steven Kelly
Christopher Krebs
Nick Leiserson
Trevor Logan
Thomas McDermott
Charles Morrison
Thomas Muir
Devi Nair
David Radcliffe
Kenneth Rapuano
Steve Smith
Samuel Spector
Bryan Ware
Burke "Ed" Wilson
Thomas Wingfield

APPENDIX J
SOLARIUM EVENT SUPPORT

Red Team Members   Keith Alexander

Dmitri Alperovitch

Ann Barron-DiCamillo

Edward Cardon

Steven Chabinsky

Richard Clarke

J. Michael Daniel

Jen Easterly

Richard Harknett

Jamil Jaffer

Catherine Lotrionte

John Mallery

Jim Miller

Lisa Monaco

John Nagengast

Christopher Painter

Greg Rattray

Laura Rosenberger

Robert "Rooster" Schmidle

NOTES

EXECUTIVE SUMMARY

1   Language inspired by House Report on the Homeland Security Act of 2002, legislation passed after the attacks of September 11; https://www.congress.gov/107/crpt/hrpt609/CRPT-107hrpt609.pdf.

2   See the documentary *No Maps for These Territories*, directed by Mark Neale (Vancouver, CA: Docurama, 2000).

3   The White House, "National Cyber Strategy of the United States of America" (September 2018), https://www.whitehouse.gov/wp-content/uploads/2018/09/National-Cyber-Strategy.pdf.

4   Benjamin Jensen, Brandon Valeriano, and Ryan Maness, "Fancy Bears and Digital Trolls: Cyber Strategy with a Russian Twist," Journal of Strategic Studies, no. 42 (2019): 212–34.

5   David Alexander, "Hagel, Ahead of China Trip, Urges Military Restraint in Cyberspace," *Reuters,* March 28, 2014, https://www.reuters.com/article/us-usa-defense-cybersecurity/hagel-ahead-of-china-trip-urges-military-restraint-in-cyberspace-idUSBREA2R1ZH20140328.

THE CHALLENGE

6   "Alert (TA17-181A): Petya Ransomware," U.S. Department of Homeland Security – Cybersecurity and Infrastructure Security Agency, July 1, 2017, https://www.us-cert.gov/ncas/alerts/TA17-181A.

7   "Global Ransomware Attack Causes Turmoil," *BBC News*, June 28, 2017, https://www.bbc.com/news/technology-40416611.

8   Polina Devitt, Jack Stubbs, and Oksana Kobzeva, "Russia's Rosneft Says Hit by Cyber Attack, Oil Production Unaffected," *Reuters,* June 27, 2017, https://www.reuters.com/article/us-russia-rosneft-cyberattack-idUSKBN19I1N9.

9   Benjamin Jensen, "The Cyber Character of Political Warfare," *Brown Journal of World Affairs* 24, no. 1 (2017): 159–71.

10 On thinking of strategic competition in terms of networks, see Charles Cleveland, Benjamin Jensen, Arnel David and Susan Bryant, *Military Strategy in the 21st Century: People, Connectivity and Competition* (New York: Cambria Press, 2018); Anne-Marie Slaughter, "How to Succeed in the Networked World: A Grand Strategy for the Digital Age," *Foreign Affairs*, December 2016, https://www.foreignaffairs.com/articles/world/2016-10-04/how-succeed-networked-world; Zeev Maoz, *Networks of Nations: The Evolution, Structure, and Impact of International Networks, 1816–2001*, Structural Analysis in the Social Sciences 32 (Cambridge: Cambridge University Press, 2010).

11 Major works that see cyber operations as a modern source of coercion and political warfare include Jensen, "The Cyber Character of Political Warfare"; Erica D. Borghard and Shawn W. Lonergan, "The Logic of Coercion in Cyberspace," *Security Studies* 26, no. 3 (2017): 452–81; Jon R. Lindsay and Erik Gartzke, "Coercion through Cyberspace: The Stability-Instability Paradox Revisited," in *Coercion: The Power to Hurt in International Politics*, ed. Kelly M. Greenhill and Peter Krause (Oxford: Oxford University Press, 2016), 179–203; Erik Gartzke and Jon R. Lindsay, "Weaving Tangled Webs: Offense, Defense, and Deception in Cyberspace," *Journal of Security Studies* 24, no. 2 (2015): 316–48; Brandon Valeriano, Benjamin Jensen, and Ryan C. Maness, *Cyber Strategy: The Evolving Character of Power and Coercion* (Oxford: Oxford University Press, 2018); Joseph S. Nye Jr., "Deterrence and Dissuasion in Cyberspace," *International Security* 42, no. 3 (2017): 44–71, https://www.mitpressjournals.org/doi/pdf/10.1162/ISEC_a_00266.

12 Lindsay and Gartzke, "Coercion through Cyberspace."

13 Wayne M. Morrison, "The Made in China 2025 Initiative: Economic Implications for the United States" (Congressional Research Service, April 12, 2019), https://fas.org/sgp/crs/row/IF10964.pdf.

14 The White House, "National Cyber Strategy of the United States of America" (September 2018), https://www.whitehouse.gov/wp-content/uploads/2018/09/National-Cyber-Strategy.pdf.

15   Lisa Ferdinando, "DoD Officials: Chinese Actions Threaten U.S. Technological, Industrial Base," U.S. Department of Defense, June 21, 2018, https://www.defense.gov/Newsroom/News/Article/Article/1557188/dod-officials-chinese-actions-threaten-us-technological-industrial-base/.

16   Daniel R. Coats, "Statement for the Record: Worldwide Threat Assessment of the US Intelligence Community" (Office of the Director of National Intelligence, January 29, 2019), https://www.odni.gov/files/ODNI/documents/2019-ATA-SFR---SSCI.pdf.

17   For an overview of cyber operations attributed to China along these lines, see Citizen Lab reporting: https://citizenlab.ca/tag/china/.

18   Justin Sherman and Robert Morgus, "Authoritarians Are Exporting Surveillance Tech, and with It Their Vision for the Internet," Council on Foreign Relations, December 5, 2018, https://www.cfr.org/blog/authoritarians-are-exporting-surveillance-tech-and-it-their-vision-internet.

19   Brian Barrett, "How China's Elite APT10 Hackers Stole the World's Secrets," *Wired*, December 20, 2018, https://www.wired.com/story/doj-indictment-chinese-hackers-apt10/.

20   Plea Agreement, *United States v. Su Bin*, No. SA CR 14-131 (C.D. Cal. Mar. 22, 2016), https://www.justice.gov/opa/file/834936/download.

21   John Aglionby, Emily Feng, and Yuan Yang, "African Union Accuses China of Hacking Headquarters," *Financial Times*, January 29, 2018, https://www.ft.com/content/c26a9214-04f2-11e8-9650-9c0ad2d7c5b5.

22   Mark Clayton, "Exclusive: Cyberattack Leaves Natural Gas Pipelines Vulnerable to Sabotage," *Christian Science Monitor*, February 27, 2013, https://www.csmonitor.com/Environment/2013/0227/Exclusive-Cyberattack-leaves-natural-gas-pipelines-vulnerable-to-sabotage.

23   *The IP Commission Report: The Report of the Commission on the Theft of American Intellectual Property* (National Bureau of Asian Research, May 2013), http://www.ipcommission.org/report/ip_commission_report_052213.pdf.

24   Rob Barry and Dustin Volz, "Ghosts in the Clouds: Inside China's Major Corporate Hack," *Wall Street Journal*, December 30, 2019, https://www.wsj.com/articles/ghosts-in-the-clouds-inside-chinas-major-corporate-hack-11577729061?mod=searchresults&page=1&pos=2.

25   Ben Sasse, "Senator Sasse: The OPM Hack May Have Given China a Spy Recruiting Database," *Wired*, July 9, 2015, https://www.wired.com/2015/07/senator-sasse-washington-still-isnt-taking-opm-breach-seriously/.

26   "Attorney General William P. Barr Announces Indictment of Four Members of China's Military for Hacking into Equifax," U.S. Department of Justice, February 10, 2020, https://www.justice.gov/opa/speech/attorney-general-william-p-barr-announces-indictment-four-members-china-s-military.

27   "The Marriott Data Breach," Consumer Information, December 4, 2018, https://www.consumer.ftc.gov/blog/2018/12/marriott-data-breach.

28   Zach Whittaker, "Sources Say China Used iPhone Hacks to Target Uyghur Muslims," *Tech Crunch*, August 31, 2019, https://techcrunch.com/2019/08/31/china-google-iphone-uyghur/.

29   Daniel R. Coats, "Statement for the Record: Worldwide Threat Assessment of the US Intelligence Community" (Office of the Director of National Intelligence, January 29, 2019), 5, 7, https://www.odni.gov/files/ODNI/documents/2019-ATA-SFR---SSCI.pdf.

30   Keir Giles, "Russia's 'New' Tools for Confronting the West: Continuity and Innovation in Moscow's Exercise of Power" (Chatham House, March 2016), https://www.chathamhouse.org/sites/default/files/publications/2016-03-russia-new-tools-giles.pdf.

31   Kenneth Geers, *Cyber War in Perspective: Russian Aggression against Ukraine* (CCDCOE, NATO Cooperative Cyber Defense Centre of Excellence, 2015), https://ccdcoe.org/uploads/2018/10/CyberWarinPerspective_full_book.pdf; Benjamin Jensen, Brandon Valeriano, and Ryan Maness, "Fancy Bears and Digital Trolls: Cyber Strategy with a Russian Twist," *Journal of Strategic Studies* 42, no. 2 (2019): 212–34; Aaron F. Brantly, Nerea M. Cal, and Devlin P. Winkelstein, "Defending the Borderland: Ukrainian Military Experiences with IO, Cyber, and EW" (Army Cyber Institute at West Point, 2017), https://cyberdefensereview.army.mil/Portals/6/Documents/UA%20Report%20Final%20AB.pdf.

32   Coats, "Worldwide Threat Assessment of the US Intelligence Community" (2019), 5–6.

33   Garrett M. Graff, "A Guide to Russia's High Tech Tool Box for Subverting US Democracy," *Wired*, August 13, 2017, https://www.wired.com/story/a-guide-to-russias-high-tech-tool-box-for-subverting-us-democracy/.

34 Emily Tamkin, "10 Years After the Landmark Attack on Estonia, Is the World Better Prepared for Cyber Threats?," *Foreign Policy*, April 27, 2017, https://foreignpolicy.com/2017/04/27/10-years-after-the-landmark-attack-on-estonia-is-the-world-better-prepared-for-cyber-threats/.

35 John Markoff, "Before the Gunfire, Cyberattacks," *New York Times*, August 12, 2008, https://www.nytimes.com/2008/08/13/technology/13cyber.html.

36 Robert M. Lee, Michael J. Assante, and Tim Conway, "Analysis of the Cyber Attack on the Ukrainian Power Grid" (Electricity Information Sharing and Assistance Center (E-ISAC), March 18, 2016), https://www.nerc.com/pa/CI/ESISAC/Documents/E-ISAC_SANS_Ukraine_DUC_18Mar2016.pdf.

37 Ellen Nakashima and Shane Harris, "How the Russians Hacked the DNC and Passed Its Emails to WikiLeaks," *Washington Post*, July 13, 2018, https://www.washingtonpost.com/world/national-security/how-the-russians-hacked-the-dnc-and-passed-its-emails-to-wikileaks/2018/07/13/af19a828-86c3-11e8-8553-a3ce89036c78_story.html.

38 Ellen Nakashima, "Russian Military Was behind 'NotPetya' Cyberattack in Ukraine, CIA Concludes," *Washington Post*, January 12, 2018, https://www.washingtonpost.com/world/national-security/russian-military-was-behind-notpetya-cyberattack-in-ukraine-cia-concludes/2018/01/12/048d8506-f7ca-11e7-b34a-b85626af34ef_story.html.

39 Michael Riley, Jennifer A. Dlouhy, and Bryan Gruley, "Russians Are Suspects in Nuclear Site Hackings, Sources Say," *Bloomberg*, July 6, 2017, https://www.bloomberg.com/news/articles/2017-07-07/russians-are-said-to-be-suspects-in-hacks-involving-nuclear-site.

40 Rebecca Smith, "Russian Hackers Reach U.S. Utility Control Rooms, Homeland Security Officials Say," *Wall Street Journal*, July 23, 2018, https://www.wsj.com/articles/russian-hackers-reach-u-s-utility-control-rooms-homeland-security-officials-say-1532388110.

41 On Russian efforts to manipulate the 2018 election, see Donie O'Sullivan, "Russians Targeted Senate and Conservative Think Tanks, Microsoft Says," *CNN*, August 22, 2018, https://www.cnn.com/2018/08/21/politics/microsoft-russia-american-politicians/index.html.

42 Eugene Rumer, "The Primakov (Not Gerasimov) Doctrine in Action," Carnegie Endowment for International Peace, June 5, 2019, https://carnegieendowment.org/2019/06/05/primakov-not-gerasimov-doctrine-in-action-pub-79254.

43 *Foreign Cyber Threats to the United States: Hearing before the U.S. Senate Committee on Armed Services*, 115th Cong., 1st sess., 2017, https://www.armed-services.senate.gov/hearings/17-01-05-foreign-cyber-threats-to-the-united-states.

44 "Nine Iranians Charged with Conducting Massive Cyber Theft Campaign on Behalf of the Islamic Revolutionary Guard Corps," U.S. Department of Justice, March 23, 2018, https://www.justice.gov/usao-sdny/pr/nine-iranians-charged-conducting-massive-cyber-theft-campaign-behalf-islamic; Eamon Javers, "US Charges Iranians with Cyber Attacks on Banks and Dam," CNBC, March 24, 2016, https://www.cnbc.com/2016/03/24/us-charges-iranians-with-cyber-attacks-on-banks-and-dam.html.

45 John Leyden, "Hack on Saudi Aramco Hit 30,000 Workstations, Oil Firm Admits," *The Register*, August 29, 2012, https://www.theregister.co.uk/2012/08/29/saudi_aramco_malware_attack_analysis/.

46 U.S. Department of Justice, "Nine Iranians Charged with Conducting Massive Cyber Theft Campaign."

47 Ben Elgin and Michael Riley, "Now at the Sands Casino: An Iranian Hacker in Every Server," *Bloomberg*, December 12, 2014, https://www.bloomberg.com/news/articles/2014-12-11/iranian-hackers-hit-sheldon-adelsons-sands-casino-in-las-vegas.

48 Ms. Smith, "Saudi Arabia Again Hit with Disk-Wiping Malware Shamoon 2," *CSO*, January 24, 2017, https://www.csoonline.com/article/3161146/saudi-arabia-again-hit-with-disk-wiping-malware-shamoon-2.html.

49 Zaid Shoorbajee, "Shamoon Resurfaces, Targeting Italian Oil Company," *CyberScoop*, December 14, 2018, https://www.cyberscoop.com/shamoon-saipem-palo-alto-networks/.

50 Sarah Hawley, Ben Read, Cristiana Brafman-Kittner, Nalani Fraser, Andrew Thompson, Yuri Rozhansky and Sanaz Yashar, "APT39: An Iranian Cyber Espionage Group Focused on Personal Information," FireEye, January 29, 2019, https://www.fireeye.com/blog/threat-research/2019/01/apt39-iranian-cyber-espionage-group-focused-on-personal-information.html.

51 Lorenzo Franceschi-Bicchierai, "The Iranian Hacking Campaign to Break into Activists' Gmail Accounts," *Vice*, August 27, 2015, https://www.vice.com/en_us/article/qkvyyx/inside-the-iranian-hackers-campaign-to-break-into-activists-gmail-accounts.

52 Lily Hay Newman, "Facebook Removes a Fresh Batch of Iran-Linked Fake Accounts," *Wired*, May 28, 2019, https://www.wired.com/story/iran-linked-fake-accounts-facebook-twitter/.

53 Jay Greene, Tony Romm, and Ellen Nakashima, "Iranians Tried to Hack U.S. Presidential Campaign in Effort That Targeted Hundreds, Microsoft Says," *Washington Post*, October 4, 2019, https://www.washingtonpost.com/technology/2019/10/04/iran-tried-hack-us-presidential-candidates-journalists-effort-that-targeted-hundreds-microsoft-finds/.

54 Nalani Fraser, Jacqueline O'Leary, Vincent Cannon and Fred Plan, "APT38: Details on New North Korean Regime-Backed Threat Group," FireEye, October 3, 2018, https://www.fireeye.com/blog/threat-research/2018/10/apt38-details-on-new-north-korean-regime-backed-threat-group.html; Jay Rosenberg and Christiaan Beek, "Examining Code Reuse Reveals Undiscovered Links Among North Korea's Malware Families," McAfee, August 9, 2018, https://securingtomorrow.mcafee.com/other-blogs/mcafee-labs/examining-code-reuse-reveals-undiscovered-links-among-north-koreas-malware-families/; Ryan Sherstobitoff and Asheer Malhotra, "Analyzing Operation GhostSecret," McAfee, April 24, 2018, https://securingtomorrow.mcafee.com/other-blogs/mcafee-labs/analyzing-operation-ghostsecret-attack-seeks-to-steal-data-worldwide/; Sergei Shevchenko, Hirman Muhammad bin Abu Bakar, and James Wong, "Taiwan Heist: Lazarus Tools and Ransomware," BAE Systems, October 16, 2017, https://baesystemsai.blogspot.com/2017/10/taiwan-heist-lazarus-tools.html.

55 Choe Sang-Hun, "North Korean Hackers Stole U.S.-South Korean Military Plans, Lawmaker Says," *New York Times*, October 10, 2017, https://www.nytimes.com/2017/10/10/world/asia/north-korea-hack-war-plans.html; Hyeong-wook Boo, "An Assessment of North Korean Cyber Threats," *Journal of East Asian Affairs* 31, no. 1 (2017): 97–117; Kong Ji Young, Lim Jong In, and Kim Kyoung Gon, "The All-Purpose Sword: North Korea's Cyber Operations and Strategies," in *2019 11th International Conference on Cyber Conflict: Silent Battle, CyCon 2019*, ed. Massimiliano Signoretti et al. (Tallinn: NATO CCD COE Publications, 2019), 1–20.

56 Ian Talley and Dustin Volz, "U.S. Targets Korean Hacking as Rising National-Security Threat," *Wall Street Journal*, September 16, 2019, https://www.wsj.com/articles/u-s-targets-north-korean-hacking-as-rising-national-security-threat-11568545202; Carol Morella and Ellen Nakashima, "U.S. Imposes Sanctions on North Korean Hackers Accused in Sony Attack, Dozens of Other Incidents," *Washington Post*, September 13, 2019, https://www.washingtonpost.com/national-security/us-sanctions-north-korean-hackers-accused-in-sony-attack-dozens-of-other-incidents/2019/09/13/ac6b0070-d633-11e9-9610-fb56c5522e1c_story.html.

57 David E. Sanger and Nicole Perlroth, "U.S. Said to Find North Korea Ordered Cyberattack on Sony," *New York Times*, December 17, 2014, https://www.nytimes.com/2014/12/18/world/asia/us-links-north-korea-to-sony-hacking.html.

58 Ju-min Park and Meeyoung Cho, "South Korea Blames North Korea for December Hack on Nuclear Operator," *Reuters*, March 17, 2015, https://www.reuters.com/article/us-nuclear-southkorea-northkorea/south-korea-blames-north-korea-for-december-hack-on-nuclear-operator-idUSKBN0MD0GR20150317

59 Krishna N. Das and Jonathan Spicer, "How the New York Fed Fumbled over the Bangladesh Bank Cyber-Heist," *Reuters*, July 21, 2016, https://www.reuters.com/investigates/special-report/cyber-heist-federal/.

60 Ellen Nakashima and Phillip Rucker, "U.S. Declares North Korea Carried Out Massive WannaCry Cyberattack," *Washington Post*, December 19, 2017, https://www.washingtonpost.com/world/national-security/us-set-to-declare-north-korea-carried-out-massive-wannacry-cyber-attack/2017/12/18/509deb1c-e446-11e7-a65d-1ac0fd7f097e_story.html.

61 Michelle Nichols, "North Korea Took $2 Billion in Cyberattacks to Fund Weapons Program: U.N. Report," *Reuters*, August 5, 2019, https://www.reuters.com/article/us-northkorea-cyber-un/north-korea-took-2-billion-in-cyberattacks-to-fund-weapons-program-u-n-report-idUSKCN1UV1ZX.

62 Darien Huss, "North Korea Bitten by Bitcoin Bug," Proofpoint, December 2017, https://www.proofpoint.com/sites/default/files/pfpt-us-wp-north-korea-bitten-by-bitcoin-bug-180129.pdf; Luke McNamara, "Why Is North Korea So Interested in Bitcoin?," FireEye, September 2017, https://www.fireeye.com/blog/threat-research/2017/09/north-korea-interested-in-bitcoin.html.

63 Michelle Nichols, "North Korea Took $2 Billion in Cyberattacks to Fund Weapons Program: U.S. Report," *Reuters*, August 5, 2019, https://www.reuters.com/article/us-northkorea-cyber-un/north-korea-took-2-billion-in-cyberattacks-to-fund-weapons-program-u-n-report-idUSKCN1UV1ZX.

64 Manny Fernandez, David E. Sanger, and Marina Trahan Martinez, "Ransomware Attacks Are Testing Resolve of Cities across America," *New York Times*, August 22, 2019, https://www.nytimes.com/2019/08/22/us/ransomware-attacks-hacking.html.

65   "ISIL Now 'A Covert Global Network' Despite Significant Losses, United Nations Counter-Terrorism Head Tells Security Council," *United Nations Meetings Coverage*, August 2018, https://www.un.org/press/en/2018/sc13463.doc.htm; Coats, "Worldwide Threat Assessment of the US Intelligence Community" (2019).

66   Christopher Bing and Joel Schectman, "Special Report: Inside the UAE's Secret Hacking Team of U.S. Mercenaries," *Reuters*, January 30, 2019, https://www.reuters.com/article/us-usa-spying-raven-specialreport/special-report-inside-the-uaes-secret-hacking-team-of-u-s-merce-naries-idUSKCN1PO19O; Jon Gambrell, "UAE Cyber Firm DarkMatter Slowly Steps out of the Shadows," *Bloomberg*, February 1, 2018, https://www.bloomberg.com/news/articles/2018-02-01/uae-cyber-firm-darkmatter-slowly-steps-out-of-the-shadows.

67   Ibid; Lorenzo Franceschi-Bicchierai, "Controversial Government Spyware Crops Up in 21 Countries, Report Says," *Mashable*, February 18, 2014, https://mashable.com/2014/02/18/controversial-government-spyware-hacking-team/#3Z120eTa8Eqj; Bill Marczak, John Scott-Railton, Sarah McKune, Bahr Abdul Razzak, and Ron Deibert, "Hide and Seek: Tracking NSO Group's Pegasus Spyware to Operations in 45 Countries," *The Citizen Lab*, September 18, 2018, https://citizenlab.ca/2018/09/hide-and-seek-tracking-nso-groups-pegasus-spyware-to-operations-in-45-countries/.

68   "Treasury Sanctions Evil Corp, the Russia-Based Cybercriminal Group behind Dridex Malware," U.S. Department of the Treasury, December 5, 2019, https://home.treasury.gov/news/press-releases/sm845.

69   "GameOver Zeus Botnet Disrupted: Collaborative Effort among International Partners," U.S. Federal Bureau of Investigation, June 2, 2014, https://www.fbi.gov/news/stories/gameover-zeus-botnet-disrupted.

70   "U.S. Leads Multi-National Action against 'Gameover Zeus' Botnet and 'Cryptolocker' Ransomware, Charges Botnet Administrator," U.S. Department of Justice, June 2, 2014, https://www.justice.gov/opa/pr/us-leads-multi-national-action-against-gameover-zeus-botnet-and-cryptolocker-ransomware.

71   "JPMorgan Hack Exposed Data of 83 Million, among Biggest Breaches in History," *Reuters*, October 2, 2014, https://www.reuters.com/article/us-jpmorgan-cybersecurity/jpmorgan-hack-exposed-data-of-83-million-among-biggest-breaches-in-history-idUSKCN0HR23T20141003.

72   Joseph Marks, "ISIL Aims to Launch Cyberattacks on U.S.," *Politico*, December 29, 2015, https://www.politico.com/story/2015/12/isil-terrorism-cyber-attacks-217179.

73   "GozNym Cyber-Criminal Network Operating out of Europe Targeting American Entities Dismantled in International Operation," U.S. Department of Justice, May 16, 2019, https://www.justice.gov/opa/pr/goznym-cyber-criminal-network-operating-out-europe-targeting-american-entities-dismantled.

74   "DDoS Attack That Disrupted Internet Was Largest of Its Kind in History, Experts Say," *The Guardian*, October 26, 2016, https://www.theguardian.com/technology/2016/oct/26/ddos-attack-dyn-mirai-botnet.

75   Lily Hay Newman, "Atlanta Spent $2.6M to Recover from a $52,000 Ransomware Scare," *Wired Magazine*, April 23, 2018, https://www.wired.com/story/atlanta-spent-26m-recover-from-ransomware-scare/.

76   Manny Fernandez, Mihir Zaveri, and Emily S. Rueb, "Ransomware Attack Hits 22 Texas Towns, Authorities Say," *New York Times*, August 2019, https://www.nytimes.com/2019/08/20/us/texas-ransomware.html; Luke Broadwater, "Baltimore Transfers $6 Million to Pay for Ransomware Attack; City Considers Insurance against Hacks," *Baltimore Sun*, August 2019, https://www.baltimoresun.com/politics/bs-md-ci-ransomware-expenses-20190828-njgznd7dsfaxbbaglnvnbkgjhe-story.html.

77   Keman Huang, Michael Siegel, and Stuart Madnick, "Cybercrime-as-a-Service: Identifying Control Points to Disrupt" (MIT Management Sloan School, November 2017), https://cams.mit.edu/wp-content/uploads/2017-17.pdf; Robert Wainwright and Frank Cilluffo, "Responding to Cybercrime at Scale: Operation Avalanche—A Case Study" (Center for Cyber and Homeland Security, March 2017), http://www.iaem.com/documents/Responding-to-Cybercrime-at-Scale-Mar2017.pdf.

78   Omar Abbosh and Kelly Bissell, "Securing the Digital Economy: Reinventing the Internet for Trust" (Accenture, 2019), 16, https://www.accenture.com/us-en/insights/cybersecurity/_acnmedia/Thought-Leadership-Assets/PDF/Accenture-Securing-the-Digital-Economy-Reinventing-the-Internet-for-Trust.pdf.

79   "Cybercrime Tactics and Techniques: Ransomware Retrospective" (Malwarebytes, August 2019), https://resources.malwarebytes.com/
     files/2019/08/CTNT-2019-Ransomware_August_FINAL.pdf.

80   "High-Impact Ransomware Attacks Threaten U.S. Businesses and Organizations," U.S. Federal Bureau of Investigation, October 2, 2019,
     https://www.ic3.gov/media/2019/191002.aspx.

81   Fernandez, Sanger, and Trahan Martinez, "Ransomware Attacks Are Testing Resolve of Cities across America."

82   For analyses of the balance of public and private innovation ecosystems, see Maryann P. Feldman and Richard Florida, "The Geographic
     Sources of Innovation: Technological Infrastructure and Product Innovation in the United States," *Annals of the Association of American
     Geographers* 84, no. 2 (June 1994): 210–29; Richard R. Nelson, ed., *National Innovation Systems: A Comparative Analysis* (New York: Oxford
     University Press, 1993).

83   "Cybersecurity Supply/Demand Heat Map," CyberSeek, Burning Glass, CompTIA, and the National Initiative for Cybersecurity
     Education, accessed February 18, 2020, https://www.cyberseek.org/heatmap.html.

84   "Hacking the Skills Shortage: A Study of the International Shortage in Cybersecurity Skills" (McAfee and Center for International and
     Strategic Studies, July 2016), https://www.mcafee.com/enterprise/en-us/assets/reports/rp-hacking-skills-shortage.pdf.

85   Lauren C. Williams, "Shanahan: 'We Get Out-Recruited' for Cyber Talent," FCW, May 8, 2019, https://fcw.com/articles/2019/05/08/
     shanahan-cyber-talent-sasc.aspx.

86   Dustin Fraze, "Cyber Grand Challenge (CGC) (Archived)," Defense Advanced Research Projects Agency, https://www.darpa.mil/program/
     cyber-grand-challenge.

87   Paul Mozur, "Beijing Wants A.I. to Be Made in China by 2030," *New York Times*, July 20, 2017, https://www.nytimes.com/2017/07/20/
     business/china-artificial-intelligence.html.

88   Alina Polyakova, "Weapons of the Weak: Russia and AI-Driven Asymmetric Warfare," The Brookings Institution, November 15, 2018,
     https://www.brookings.edu/research/weapons-of-the-weak-russia-and-ai-driven-asymmetric-warfare/.

89   "Clinton's Words on China: Trade Is the Smart Thing," *New York Times*, March 9, 2000, https://www.nytimes.com/2000/03/09/world/
     clinton-s-words-on-china-trade-is-the-smart-thing.html.

90   Hilary McGeachy, "U.S.-China Technology Competition: Impacting a Rules-Based Order" (United States Studies Centre, May 2, 2019),
     available at https://www.ussc.edu.au/analysis/us-china-technology-competition-impacting-a-rules-based-order.

91   Eurasia Group, "Eurasia Group White Paper: The Geopolitics of 5G (November 15, 2018), https://www.eurasiagroup.net/siteFiles/Media/
     files/1811-14%205G%20special%20report%20public(1).pdf.

92   Dan Strumpf, "Where China Dominates in 5G Technology," *Wall Street Journal*, February 26, 2019, https://www.wsj.com/articles/
     where-china-dominates-in-5g-technology-11551236701.

93   McGeachy, "U.S.-China Technology Competition."

94   Steven Fieldstein, "The Global Expansion of AI Surveillance" (Carnegie Endowment for International Peace, September 17, 2019), available
     at https://carnegieendowment.org/2019/09/17/global-expansion-of-ai-surveillance-pub-79847; "Vietnam: Withdraw Problematic Cyber
     Security Law," Human Rights Watch, June 7, 2018, https://www.hrw.org/news/2018/06/07/vietnam-withdraw-problematic-cyber-
     security-law; "Vietnam: Big Brother Is Watching Everyone," Human Rights Watch, December 20, 2018,
     https://www.hrw.org/news/2018/12/20/vietnam-big-brother-watching-everyone; Abdi Latif Dahir, "China Is Exporting Its
     Digital Surveillance Methods to African Governments," *Quartz Africa*, November 1, 2018, https://qz.com/africa/1447015/
     china-is-helping-african-countries-control-the-internet/.

95   Isolated attempts to reverse this dynamic and reinvigorate the government's technological capabilities include the Strategic Capabilities
     Office (SCO), DoD's Defense Innovation Unit (DIU), AFWERX, SOFWERX, Army Futures Command, the U.S. Army Reserve 75th
     Innovation Command, and the Defense Digital Services.

96   Shane Greenstein, *How the Internet Became Commercial* (Princeton, NJ: Princeton University Press, 2015).

HISTORICAL LEGACY AND METHODOLOGY

97   William B. Pickett, ed., *George F. Kennan and the Origins of Eisenhower's New Look: An Oral History of Project Solarium*, Monograph Series 1 (Princeton, NJ: Princeton University Press, 2004).

98   Michèle A. Flournoy and Shawn W. Brimley, "Strategic Planning for National Security: A New Project Solarium," *Joint Forces Quarterly* 41, no. 2 (2006): 80–86, https://pdfs.semanticscholar.org/6252/45e247df30b3ba835021c6b1271c9653f1c5.pdf.

99   Raymond Millen, "Eisenhower and US Grand Strategy," *Parameters* 44, no. 2 (Summer 2014): 35–47, https://publications.armywarcollege.edu/pubs/3715.pdf; Robert H. Bowie and Richard H. Immerman, *Waging Peace: How Eisenhower Shaped an Enduring Cold War Strategy* (New York: Oxford University Press, 1998).

100 John Lewis Gaddis, *Strategies of Containment: A Critical Appraisal of American National Security Policy during the Cold War* (New York: Oxford University Press, 2005); Steven Metz, "Eisenhower and the Planning of American Grand Strategy," *Journal of Strategic Studies* 14, no. 1 (March 1991): 49–71, https://doi.org/10.1080/01402399108437439.

101 "Paul Baran and the Origins of the Internet," RAND Corporation, accessed November 6, 2019, https://www.rand.org/about/history/baran.html.

102 Charles Cleveland et al., *Military Strategy in the 21st Century: People, Connectivity and Competition* (New York: Cambria Press, 2018).

103 Paul Baran, *On Distributed Communications* (Santa Monica, CA: RAND Corporation, 1964), available at https://www.rand.org/pubs/research_memoranda/RM3767.html; Willis H. Ware, *Security Controls for Computer Systems: Report of Defense Science Board Task Force on Computer Security* (1970; reprint, Santa Monica, CA: RAND Corporation, 1979), available at https://www.rand.org/pubs/reports/R609-1.html.

104 Ware, *Security Controls for Computer Systems*, vi.

105 Fred Kaplan, "*WarGames* and Cybersecurity's Debt to a Hollywood Hack," *New York Times*, February 19, 2016, https://www.nytimes.com/2016/02/21/movies/wargames-and-cybersecuritys-debt-to-a-hollywood-hack.html.

106 "Films Viewed by President and Mrs. Reagan," Ronald Reagan Presidential Library & Museum, https://www.reaganlibrary.gov/sreference/films-viewed-by-president-and-mrs-reagan.

107 National Security Decision Directive Number 145, "National Policy on Telecommunications and Automated Information Systems Security" (The White House, September 17, 1984), https://www.reaganlibrary.gov/sites/default/files/archives/reference/scanned-nsdds/nsdd145.pdf.

108 *Critical Foundations: Protecting America's Infrastructures: The Report of the President's Commission on Critical Infrastructure Protection* (October 1997), https://www.hsdl.org/?view&did=986.

109 "U.S. Cyber Command History," United States Cyber Command, accessed November 6, 2019, https://www.cybercom.mil/About/History/; "About CISA," Cyber Security and Infrastructure Agency, https://www.cisa.gov/about-cisa.

110 Computer Fraud and Abuse Act of 1986, 18 U.S. Code § 1030 (1986); Gramm-Leach-Bliley Act of 1999, 15 U.S. Code § 6801 (1999); Federal Information Security Management Act of 2002, Pub. L. No. 107-347 (2002); Cybersecurity and Information Sharing Act of 2015, Pub L. No. 114-113 (2015).

111 "Cyberspace Policy Review: Assuring a Trusted and Resilient Information and Communications Infrastructure" ([The White House, November 2009]), https://fas.org/irp/eprint/cyber-review.pdf; "The National Strategy to Secure Cyberspace" (The White House, February 2003), https://www.energy.gov/sites/prod/files/National%20Strategy%20to%20Secure%20Cyberspace.pdf.

112 See Joseph S. Nye Jr., "Deterrence and Dissuasion in Cyberspace," International Security 42, no. 3 (Winter 2016): 44–71, https://www.mitpressjournals.org/doi/pdf/10.1162/ISEC_a_00266.

113 The College of Information and Cyberspace at the National Defense University hosted the event.

114 On the concept of stress testing, see Nassim N. Taleb, Elie Canetti, Tidiane Kinda, Elena Loukoianova and Christian Schmieder, "A New Heuristic Measure of Fragility and Tail Risks: Application to Stress Testing" (IMF Working Paper, International Monetary Fund, 2012), https://www.imf.org/external/pubs/ft/wp/2012/wp12216.pdf.

STRATEGIC APPROACH: LAYERED CYBER DETERRENCE

115 "Critical Infrastructure Protection, Information Sharing and Cyber Security," U.S. Chamber of Commerce, accessed January 23, 2020, https://www.uschamber.com/issue-brief/critical-infrastructure-protection-information-sharing-and-cyber-security.

116 Anne-Marie Slaughter, *The Chessboard and the Web: Strategies of Connection in a Networked World* (New Haven: Yale University Press, 2017); Zeev Maoz, *Networks of Nations: The Evolution, Structure, and Impact of International Networks, 1816–2001*, Structural Analysis in the Social Sciences 32 (Cambridge: Cambridge University Press, 2010); Charles Cleveland et al., *Military Strategy in the 21st Century: People, Connectivity and Competition* (New York: Cambria Press, 2018).

117 Emily Goldman and Michael Warner, "History of Persistent Engagement and Defend Forward" (Minutes of U.S. Cyberspace Solarium Commission meeting, September 23, 2019); Michael Fischerkeller and Richard Harknett, "Persistent Engagement, Agreed Competition, Cyberspace Interaction Dynamics, and Escalation" (Institute for Defense Analyses, May 2018), https://www.ida.org/-/media/feature/publications/p/pe/persistent-engagement-agreed-competition-cyberspace-interaction-dynamics-and-escalation/d-9076.ashx; Michael Fischerkeller and Richard Harknett, "What Is Agreed Competition in Cyberspace?," *Lawfare*, February 19, 2019, https://www.lawfareblog.com/what-agreed-competition-cyberspace; Michael Fischerkeller and Richard Harknett, "Persistent Engagement and Tacit Bargaining: A Path toward Constructing Norms in Cyberspace," *Lawfare*, November 9, 2018, https://www.lawfareblog.com/persistent-engagement-and-tacit-bargaining-path-toward-constructing-norms-cyberspace.

118 Persistent engagement is how U.S. Cyber Command implements defend forward. It is based on the notion of being in "constant contact" with adversaries. It is defined by enabling partners across agencies, as well as in the private sector and international partners, and by acting by defending forward outside of DoD networks. *United States Special Operations Command and United States Cyber Command: Hearing before the Senate Armed Services Committee*, 116th Congress, 4, 6 (February 14, 2019) (statement of General Paul M. Nakasone, Commander United States Cyber Command); William T. Eliason, "An Interview with Paul M. Nakasone," *Joint Force Quarterly* 92 (1st Quarter 2019): 6–7.

119 Continuity of the Economy is an effort to ensure that the critical data and technology would be available, with priority for critical functions across corporations and industry sectors, to get the economy back up and running after a catastrophic event.

120 U.S. Department of Defense, "Summary: Department of Defense Cyber Strategy" (2018), 1, https://media.defense.gov/2018/Sep/18/2002041658/-1/-1/1/CYBER_STRATEGY_SUMMARY_FINAL.PDF.

121 Early cyber deterrence literature focused more on within-domain dynamics: see Robert Jervis, "Some Thoughts on Deterrence in the Cyber Era," *Journal of Information Warfare* 15, no. 2 (2016): 66–73; Nye, "Deterrence and Dissuasion in Cyberspace," 44–71; Martin Libicki, *Cyberspace in Peace and War* (Annapolis, MD: Naval Institute Press, 2016); Aaron Brantly, "The Cyber Deterrence Problem," in *CyCon X: Maximising Effects*, ed. T. Minárik, R. Jakschis, and L. Lindström, 10th International Conference on Cyber Conflict (CyCon) (Tallinn: NATO CCD COE Publications, 2018), 31–54; and Thomas Rid, *Cyber War Will Not Take Place* (London: Hurst, 2013). More recent literature focuses on coercion broadly defined and on cross-domain dynamics. For examples, see Erica Borghard and Shawn Lonergan, "The Logic of Coercion in Cyberspace," *Security Studies* 26, no. 3 (2017): 452–81; Brandon Valeriano, Benjamin Jensen, and Ryan Maness, *Cyber Strategy: The Evolving Character of Power and Coercion* (New York: Oxford University Press, 2018); and Erik Gartzke and Jon R. Lindsay, eds., *Cross-Domain Deterrence: Strategy in an Era of Complexity* (New York: Oxford University Press, 2019).

122 Alexander George and Richard Smoke, *Deterrence in American Foreign Policy: Theory and Practice* (New York: Columbia University Press, 1974).

123 Lawrence Freedman, *Deterrence* (Cambridge: Polity, 2004), 26.

124 Nye, "Deterrence and Dissuasion in Cyberspace," 45. For additional definitions of deterrence, see Glenn H. Snyder, *Deterrence and Defense* (Princeton, NJ: Princeton University Press, 1961); Robert J. Art, "To What Ends Military Power?," *International Security* 4, no. 4 (1980): 3–35, at 6; Robert Jervis, "Deterrence Theory Revisited," *World Politics* 31, no. 2 (1979): 289–324; Thomas C. Schelling, *The Strategy of*

Conflict (Cambridge, MA: Harvard University Press, 1980); Thomas C. Schelling, *Arms and Influence* (New Haven: Yale University Press, 1966).

125 It is important to note that the notion of deterrence by punishment existed before the nuclear age. See George H. Quester, *Deterrence before Hiroshima: The Airpower Background of Modern Strategy* (1966; reprint, Piscataway, NJ: Transaction Books, 1986).

126 For an overview of these debates on the viability of cyber operations as a form of cost imposition, see Valeriano, Jensen, and Maness, *Cyber Strategy*, and Borghard and Lonergan, "The Logic of Coercion."

127 Snyder, *Deterrence and Defense*, 14–15. Also see Daniel Byman and Matthew Waxman, *The Dynamics of Coercion: American Foreign Policy and the Limits of Military Might* (Cambridge: Cambridge University Press, 2002), and Robert Pape, *Bombing to Win: Air Power and Coercion in War* (Ithaca, NY: Cornell University Press, 1996).

128 John J. Mearsheimer, *Conventional Deterrence* (Ithaca, NY: Cornell University Press, 1985).

129 Nye, "Deterrence and Dissuasion in Cyberspace," 55.

130 Nye, "Deterrence and Dissuasion in Cyberspace," 58.

131 But see Farrell and Newman for how economic interdependence can become weaponized and support a coercion strategy: Henry Farrell and Abraham Newman, "Domestic Institutions beyond the Nation-State: Charting the New Interdependence Approach," *World Politics* 66, no. 2 (2014): 331–63.

132 Nye, "Deterrence and Dissuasion in Cyberspace," 60. See Tannenwald on the nuclear taboo or Price on the chemical weapons taboo: Nina Tannenwald, *The Nuclear Taboo: The United States and the Non-Use of Nuclear Weapons Since 1945* (Cambridge: Cambridge University Press, 2007); Richard Price, *The Chemical Weapons Taboo* (Ithaca, NY: Cornell University Press, 2018). Also refer to Tannenwald's more recent work on the strength of the nuclear taboo: Nina Tannenwald, "How Strong Is the Nuclear Taboo Today?," *Washington Quarterly* 41, no. 3 (2018): 89–109.

133 Martin Libicki, *Cyberdeterrence and Cyberwar* (Santa Monica, CA: RAND, 2009), 41–42; Jon Lindsay, "Tipping the Scales: The Attribution Problem and the Feasibility of Deterrence against Cyberattack," *Journal of Cybersecurity* 1, no. 1 (2015): 53–67; Nye, "Deterrence and Dissuasion in Cyberspace," 49–52.

134 Schelling, *Arms and Influence*.

135 Robert Jervis, *The Logic of Images in International Relations* (New York: Columbia University Press, 1970), 18.

136 Borghard and Lonergan, "The Logic of Coercion"; Valeriano, Jensen, and Maness, *Cyber Strategy*; Eliason, "An Interview with Paul M. Nakasone," 4.

137 Nye, "Deterrence and Dissuasion in Cyberspace," 49–50.

138 Brantly, "The Cyber Deterrence Problem"; Borghard and Lonergan, "The Logic of Coercion."

139 Libicki, *Cyberdeterrence and Cyberwar*, 56.

140 Jacquelyn Schneider, "Deterrence in and through Cyberspace," in Gartzke and Lindsay, *Cross-Domain Deterrence*, 95–120.

141 The White House, "National Security Strategy of the United States of America" (December 2017), 2, https://www.whitehouse.gov/wp-content/uploads/2017/12/NSS-Final-12-18-2017-0905.pdf.

142 U.S. Department of Defense, "Summary of the 2018 National Defense Strategy of the United States of America: Sharpening the American Military's Competitive Edge" (January 2018), https://dod.defense.gov/Portals/1/Documents/pubs/2018-National-Defense-Strategy-Summary.pdf.

143 Daniel R. Coats, "Worldwide Threat Assessment of the US Intelligence Community" (Office of the Director of National Intelligence, February 2018), https://www.dni.gov/files/documents/Newsroom/Testimonies/2018-ATA---Unclassified-SSCI.pdf.

144 U.S. Cyber Command, "Achieve and Maintain Cyberspace Superiority: Command Vision for US Cyber Command" (March 23, 2018), https://nsarchive2.gwu.edu//dc.html?doc=4421219-United-States-Cyber-Command-Achieve-and-Maintain; DoD, "Summary: Department of Defense Cyber Strategy" (2018).

145 Michael N. Schmitt, "'Virtual' Disenfranchisement: Cyber Election Meddling in the Grey Zones of International Law," *Chicago Journal of International Law* 19 (2018): 30–67, available at https://ssrn.com/abstract=3180631.

146 While the term "gray zone" is generally associated with conflict, it also applies to the space between the "black and white" of traditional legal frameworks, both international and domestic. See Gary P. Corn, "Cyber National Security: Navigating Gray-Zone Challenges in and through Cyberspace," in *Complex Battlespaces: The Law of Armed Conflict and the Dynamics of Modern Warfare*, ed. Winston S. Williams and Christopher M. Ford (New York: Oxford University Press, 2018), 345–428.

147 Michael P. Fischerkeller and Richard J. Harknett, "Persistent Engagement, Agreed Competition, Cyberspace Interaction Dynamics, and Escalation" (Institute for Defense Analyses, May 2018), https://www.ida.org/-/media/feature/publications/p/pe/persistent-engagement-agreed-competition-cyberspace-interaction-dynamics-and-escalation/d-9076.ashx.

148 DoD, "Summary: Department of Defense Cyber Strategy" (2018), 1.

149 As defined in Office of the Chairman of the Joint Chiefs of Staff, *Cyberspace Operations*, Joint Publication 3-12 (June 8, 2018), "The term 'blue cyberspace' denotes areas in cyberspace protected by the US, its mission partners, and other areas DOD may be ordered to protect," while "'red cyberspace' refers to those portions of cyberspace owned or controlled by an adversary or enemy." Finally, "all cyberspace that does not meet the description of either 'blue' or 'red' is referred to as 'gray' cyberspace" (I-4, I-5). Prior to the 2018 strategy, defending its networks had been DoD's primary focus; see U.S. Department of Defense, "Department of Defense Cyber Strategy" (April 2015), https://archive.defense.gov/home/features/2015/0415_cyber-strategy/final_2015_dod_cyber_strategy_for_web.pdf.

150 DoD, "Summary: Department of Defense Cyber Strategy" (2018), 2.

151 DoD, "Summary: Department of Defense Cyber Strategy" (2018), 2. Cyber Command's "Command Vision" provides a similar explanation: "Defending forward as close as possible to the origin of adversary activity extends our reach to expose adversaries' weaknesses, learn their intentions and capabilities, and counter attacks close to their origins" (6).

152 John S. McCain National Defense Authorization Act for Fiscal Year 2019, Pub. L. No. 115-232 (hereafter FY2019 NDAA), 132 Stat. 1636 (2018). Key changes in the FY2019 NDAA include Section 1632, which defines cyber operations as "traditional military activity," and Section 1642, which pre-delegates authority to U.S. Cyber Command to take proportional action in response to active, systematic, and ongoing campaigns by Russian, Chinese, Iranian, and North Korean cyberattacks, as determined by the National Command Authority, and defines these responses as constituting traditional military activities.

153 For new authorities outlined in NSPM-13, see *Hearing to Conduct a Confirmation Hearing on the Expected Nomination of: Honorable Mark T. Esper to Be Secretary of Defense*, 116th Cong. 37–38 (2019) (testimony of the Honorable Mark T. Esper), https://www.armed-services.senate.gov/imo/media/doc/19-59_07-16-19.pdf.

154 Ellen Nakashima, "NSA and Cyber Command to Coordinate Actions to Counter Russian Election Interference in 2018 Amid Absence of White House Guidance," *Washington Post*, July 17, 2018, https://www.washingtonpost.com/world/national-security/nsa-and-cyber-command-to-coordinate-actions-to-counter-russian-election-interference-in-2018-amid-absence-of-white-house-guidance/2018/07/17/baac95b2-8900-11e8-85ae-511bc1146b0b_story.html.

155 Statement of General Nakasone, *Hearing before the Senate Armed Services Committee*, 4.

156 Shannon Vavra, "NSA's Russian Cyberthreat Task Force Is Now Permanent," *CyberScoop*, April 2019, https://www.cyberscoop.com/nsa-russia-small-group-cyber-command/.

157 FY2019 NDAA, § 1642.

REFORM THE U.S. GOVERNMENT'S STRUCTURE AND ORGANIZATION FOR CYBERSPACE

158 Frederick M. Kaiser, *Legislative History of the Senate Select Committee on Intelligence* (Washington, DC: Congressional Research Service, August 16, 1978), 2, https://fas.org/sgp/crs/intel/ssci-leghist.pdf.

159 "Technology Assessment and Congress," Office of Technology Assessment Archive: Provided by the Federation of American Scientists, 2018, https://ota.fas.org/technology_assessment_and_congress/. Princeton University maintains an Office of Technology Assessment archive that captures and expands upon much of OTA's original work. See "The OTA Legacy," Princeton University, https://www.princeton.edu/~ota/.

160 The Office of Science and Technology Policy had 58 staff members as of April 2019. The Office of the United States Trade Representative has a staff of over 200 employees. In the 2017 budget, the White House requested 65 employees for the Office of National Drug Control Policy. John F. Sargent Jr. and Dana A. Shea, *Office of Science and Technology Policy (OSTP): History and Overview*, CRS Report No. R43935 (Washington, DC: Congressional Research Service, updated October 8, 2019), https://fas.org/sgp/crs/misc/R43935.pdf; "About Us," Office of the United States Trade Representative, https://ustr.gov/about-us; Robert O'Harrow Jr., "Meet the 24-Year-Old Trump Campaign Worker Appointed to Help Lead the Government's Drug Policy Office," *Washington Post*, January 14, 2018, https://www.washingtonpost.com/investigations/meet-the-24-years-old-trump-campaign-worker-appointed-to-help-lead-the-governments-drug-policy-office/2018/01/13/abdada34-f64e-11e7-91af-31ac729add94_story.html.

161 "NTSC Supports Bipartisan Legislation to Establish the Cybersecurity Advisory Committee," National Technology Security Coalition, March 28, 2019, https://www.ntsc.org/about-ntsc/press-releases/ntsc-supports-bipartisan-legislation-to-establish-the-cybersecurity-advisory-committee.html.

162 "Cybersecurity Supply/Demand Heat Map," CyberSeek, Burning Glass, CompTIA, and the National Initiative for Cybersecurity Education, accessed February 18, 2020, https://www.cyberseek.org/heatmap.html.

163 Kevin Pelphrey, "Autistic People Can Solve Our Cybersecurity Crisis," *Wired*, November 25, 2016, https://www.wired.com/2016/11/autistic-people-can-solve-cybersecurity-crisis/.

164 Exec. Order No. 13870, "America's Cybersecurity Workforce," 84 Fed. Reg. 20523 (May 2, 2019), https://www.federalregister.gov/documents/2019/05/09/2019-09750/americas-cybersecurity-workforce; Cybersecurity Skills Integration Act of 2019, H.R.1592, 116th Cong. (2019), https://www.congress.gov/bill/116t%C3%A5h-congress/house-bill/1592.

165 "Cybersecurity Supply/Demand Heat Map."

166 "Five Veterans Graduate from Cybersecurity Apprenticeship; 10 Vets to Join Program," North Carolina Department of Information Technology, November 15, 2018, https://it.nc.gov/blog/2018/11/15/five-veterans-graduate-cybersecurity-apprenticeship-10-vets-join-program.

167 "11 Federal Agencies Help Start Cybersecurity Talent Initiative," *FedScoop*, April 9, 2019, https://www.fedscoop.com/federal-cybersecurity-talent-initiative/.

STRENGTHEN NORMS AND NON-MILITARY TOOLS

168 Peter J. Katzenstein, "Introduction: Alternative Perspectives on National Security," in *The Culture of National Security: Norms and Identity in World Politics*, ed. Katzenstein (New York: Columbia University Press, 1996), 5. Current widely accepted norms for responsible state behavior in cyberspace are outlined in the 2015 report of the United Nations Group of Governmental Experts on Developments in the Field of Information and Telecommunications in the Context of International Security (UN GGE). See General Assembly Resolution 70/174, "Group of Governmental Experts on Developments in the Field of Information and Telecommunications in the Context of International Security," A/RES/70/174 (July 22, 2015), https://undocs.org/A/70/174.

169 Martha Finnemore and Duncan Hollis, "Construction Norms for Global Cybersecurity," *American Society of International Law* 110, no. 3 (July 2016): 447, https://jstor.org/stable/10.5305/amerjintelaw.110.3.0425.

170 General Assembly Resolution 73/27, "Developments in the Field of Information and Telecommunications in the Context of International Security," A/RES/73/27 (December 11, 2018), https://undocs.org/A/RES/73/27.

171 For example, 27 countries signed the Joint Statement on Advancing Responsible State Behavior in Cyberspace, agreeing that "[t]here must be consequences for bad behavior in cyberspace." See "Joint Statement on Advancing Responsible State Behavior in Cyberspace," U.S. Department of State, September 23, 2019, https://www.state.gov/joint-statement-on-advancing-responsible-state-behavior-in-cyberspace/.

172 Keith Alexander and Jamil Jaffer, "UN's Cybercrime 'Law' Helps Dictators and Criminals, Not Their Victims," *The Hill*, November 26, 2019, https://thehill.com/opinion/cybersecurity/471897-uns-cybercrime-law-helps-dictators-and-criminals-not-their-victims; Allison Peters, "Russia and China Are Trying to Set the U.N.'s Rules on Cybercrime," *Foreign Policy*, September 16, 2019, https://foreignpolicy.com/2019/09/16/russia-and-china-are-trying-to-set-the-u-n-s-rules-on-cybercrime/.

173 Ellen Nakashima, "U.N. Votes to Advance Russian-Led Resolution on a Cybercrime Treaty," *Washington Post*, November 19, 2019, https://washingtonpost.com/national-security/un-votes-to-advance-russian-led-resolution-on-a-cybercrime-treaty/2019/11/19/fb6a633e-0b06-11ea-97ac-a7ccc8dd1ebc_story.html.

174 "In the UN, China Uses Threats and Cajolery to Promote Its Worldview," *The Economist*, December 7, 2019, https://www.economist.com/china/2019/12/07/in-the-un-china-uses-threats-and-cajolery-to-promote-its-worldview.

175 While exact numbers are rare, research published in 2015 estimated the budget for Chinese "external propaganda" at $10 billion annually, compared to $666 million that the U.S. State Department spent on public diplomacy in FY2014. See David Shambaugh, "China's Soft-Power Push: The Search for Respect," *Foreign Affairs* 94, no. 4 (July/August 2015), https://www.foreignaffairs.com/articles/china/2015-06-16/china-s-soft-power-push.

176 Bonnie Bley, "The New Geography of Global Diplomacy: China Advances as the United States Retreats," *Foreign Affairs*, November 27, 2019, https://www.foreignaffairs.com/articles/china/2019-11-27/new-geography-global-diplomacy.

177 Garrett Hinck, "Private-Sector Initiatives for Cyber Norms: A Summary," *Lawfare*, June 25, 2018, https://www.lawfareblog.com/private-sector-cyber-norm-initiatives-summary.

178 "Joint Statement on Advancing Responsible State Behavior in Cyberspace."

179 General Assembly Resolution 73/27, "Developments in the Field of Information and Telecommunications."

180 Federal Bureau of Investigation, interviewed by the U.S. Cyberspace Solarium Commission, October 2, 2019.

181 "Cyber-attacks: Council Is Now Able to Impose Sanctions," European Council: Council of the European Union online, May 17, 2019, https://www.consilium.europa.eu/en/press/press-releases/2019/05/17/cyber-attacks-council-is-now-able-to-impose-sanctions/.

182 Jason Healey, John C. Mallery, Klara Tothova Jordan, and Nathaniel V. Youd, "Confidence-Building Measures in Cyberspace: A Multistakeholder Approach for Stability and Security," Atlantic Council, November 5, 2014, https://www.atlanticcouncil.org/in-depth-research-reports/report/confidence-building-measures-in-cyberspace-a-multistakeholder-approach-for-stability-and-security/.

183 General Assembly Resolution 70/174, "Group of Governmental Experts on Developments in the Field of Information and Telecommunications"; "Decision No. 1202: OSCE Confidence-Building Measures to Reduce the Risks of Conflict Stemming from the Use of Information and Communications Technologies," Organization for Security and Cooperation in Europe Permanent Council, March 10, 2016, available at https://www.osce.org/pc/227281?.

PROMOTE NATIONAL RESILIENCE

184 Richard Clarke and Robert Knake, *The Fifth Domain: Defending Our Country, Our Companies, and Ourselves in the Age of Cyber Threats* (New York: Penguin Random House, 2019).

185 *Cyber Threats to Our Nation's Critical Infrastructure: Hearing before the Senate Subcommittee on Crime and Terrorism, Committee on the Judiciary*, 115th Cong. (2018) (statement of Sujit Raman, Associate Deputy Attorney General, Department of Justice), https://www.judiciary.senate.gov/download/08-21-18-raman-testimony.

186 The 2010 *DHS Risk Lexicon* defines risk as the "potential for an unwanted outcome resulting from an incident, event, or occurrence, as determined by its likelihood and the associated consequences." It also offers an extended definition: the "potential for an adverse outcome assessed as a function of threats, vulnerabilities, and consequences associated with an incident, event, or occurrence." Risk Steering

Committee, *DHS Risk Lexicon: 2010 Edition* (U.S. Department of Homeland Security, September 2010), 27, https://www.dhs.gov/xlibrary/assets/dhs-risk-lexicon-2010.pdf.

187 Some sector-specific agencies—and their responsibilities and authorities—have been codified in law, such as the Department of Energy's in the Fixing America's Surface Transportation Act of 2015, Pub. L. No. 114-94, 129 Stat. 1312 (2015), https://www.congress.gov/114/plaws/publ94/PLAW-114publ94.pdf.

188 "DHS Announces Funding Opportunity for Fiscal Year 2019 Preparedness Grants," U.S. Department of Homeland Security, April 12, 2019, https://www.dhs.gov/news/2019/04/12/dhs-announces-funding-opportunity-fiscal-year-2019-preparedness-grants.

189 See "Continuity of Operations" (Federal Emergency Management Agency, accessed October 14, 2019), https://www.fema.gov/pdf/about/org/ncp/coop_brochure.pdf, and "National Security Presidential Directive/NSPD – 51, Homeland Security Presidential Directive/HSPD – 20," Federal Emergency Management Agency, May 4, 2007, https://www.fema.gov/txt/about/org/ncp/nspd_51.txt.

190 Christopher Bailey, "Networking Emergency Response: Empowering FEMA in the Age of Convergence and Cyber Critical Infrastructure," *Nebraska Law Review* 96, no. 2 (2017): 509–43, https://digitalcommons.unl.edu/cgi/viewcontent.cgi?article=3123&context=nlr.

191 For cyber risk posed by malign actors to water infrastructure that is known by water utility companies, see Judith H. Germano, "Cybersecurity Risk & Responsibility in the Water Sector" (American Water Works Association, 2019), 7–9, https://www.awwa.org/Portals/0/AWWA/Government/AWWACybersecurityRiskandResponsibility.pdf?ver=2018-12-05-123319-013. For current network defense limitations of water utilities, see Robert M. Clark, Srinivas Panguluri, Trent D. Nelson, and Richard P. Wyman, "Protecting drinking water utilities from cyberthreats" (Idaho National Labs, February 2, 2017), 13–15, https://www.osti.gov/servlets/purl/1372266.

192 Blake Sobczak, "Hackers Force Water Utilities to Sink or Swim," E&E News, March 28, 2019, https://www.eenews.net/stories/1060131769.

193 Clark, Srinivas, Nelson, and Wyman, "Protecting Drinking Water Utilities from Cyberthreats," 13–15.

194 For attempted breaches by Russia: "Alert (TA18-074A): Russian Government Cyber Activity Targeting Energy and Other Critical Infrastructure Sectors," U.S. Department of Homeland Security, Cybersecurity and Infrastructure Security Agency, March 15, 2018, https://www.us-cert.gov/ncas/alerts/TA18-074A. For attempted breaches by others: Germano, "Cybersecurity Risk & Responsibility in the Water Sector," 7–9.

195 See "Homeland Security Presidential Directive 7: Critical Infrastructure Identification, Prioritization, and Protection," U.S. Department of Homeland Security, Cybersecurity and Infrastructure Security Agency, December 17, 2003, https://www.cisa.gov/homeland-security-presidential-directive-7.

196 U.S. Department of Homeland Security, "National Cyber Incident Response Plan" (December 2016), https://www.us-cert.gov/sites/default/files/ncirp/National_Cyber_Incident_Response_Plan.pdf.

197 DHS, "National Cyber Incident Response Plan."

198 A primary lesson learned from the ransomware attack that impacted Colorado's Department of Transportation was the need to exercise preestablished response plans. "CDOT Cyber Incident: After-Action Report" (Colorado Division of Homeland Security and Emergency Management, July 17, 2018), available at https://www.colorado.gov/pacific/dhsem/news/after-action-report-released-cdot-cyber-incident.

199 "GridEx," North American Electric Reliability Corporation, accessed October 16, 2019, https://www.nerc.com/pa/CI/CIPOutreach/Pages/GridEx.aspx.

200 Financial Services Sector Coordinating Council, "FSSCC Cybersecurity Recommendations for Administration and Congress 2017" (January 18, 2017), https://fsscc.org/files/galleries/FSSCC_Cybersecurity_Recommendations_for_Administration_and_Congress_2017.pdf.

201 "Cyber Storm: Securing Cyber Space," U.S. Department of Homeland Security, accessed October 16, 2019, https://www.dhs.gov/cisa/cyber-storm-securing-cyber-space.

202 Examples of states relying on National Guard units to deal with cybersecurity incidents include Colorado, Louisiana, and Texas, where the governors declared state of emergencies to activate their National Guard.

203 Information gleaned from interviews with National Guard units and from Monica M. Ruiz and David Forscey, "The Hybrid Benefits of the National Guard," *Lawfare*, July 23, 2019, https://www.lawfareblog.com/hybrid-benefits-national-guard.

204 One Guardsman told us that in the midst of responding to a cyber incident, lawyers halted his unit's activities until all members could sign memorandums of understanding (MOUs) with the affected entities to clarify liability exemptions.

205 Daniel R. Coats, "Statement for the Record: Worldwide Threat Assessment of the US Intelligence Community," Office of the Director of National Intelligence, January 29, 2019, https://www.odni.gov/files/ODNI/documents/2019-ATA-SFR---SSCI.pdf; David E. Sanger, "'Chaos Is the Point': Russian Hackers and Trolls Grow Stealthier in 2020," *New York Times*, January 10, 2020, https://www.nytimes.com/2020/01/10/us/politics/russia-hacking-disinformation-election.html.

206 Robby Mook, Matt Rhoades, and Eric Rosenbach, "Cybersecurity Campaign Playbook," Belfer Center for Science and International Affairs, Harvard Kennedy School, November 2017, https://www.belfercenter.org/CyberPlaybook#vulnerable; Nicole Perlroth and David Sanger, "Iranian Hackers Target Trump Campaign as Threats to 2020 Mount," *New York Times*, October 4, 2019, https://www.nytimes.com/2019/10/04/technology/iranian-campaign-hackers-microsoft.html.

207 Claire Allbright, "A Russian Facebook Page Organized a Protest in Texas: A Different Russian Page Launched the Counterprotest," *Texas Tribune*, November 1, 2017, https://www.texastribune.org/2017/11/01/russian-facebook-page-organized-protest-texas-different-russian-page-l/.

208 Allbright, "A Russian Facebook Page Organized a Protest in Texas."

209 "Exposing Russia's Effort to Sow Discord Online: The Internet Research Agency and Advertisements," U.S. House of Representatives Permanent Select Committee on Intelligence, accessed December 11, 2019, https://intelligence.house.gov/social-media-content/.

210 Natasha Singer, "'Weaponized Ad Technology': Facebook's Moneymaker Gets a Critical Eye," *New York Times*, August 16, 2018, https://www.nytimes.com/2018/08/16/technology/facebook-microtargeting-advertising.html.

211 "How Social Media Companies Are Failing to Combat Inauthentic Behaviour Online | StratCom," accessed December 11, 2019, https://www.stratcomcoe.org/how-social-media-companies-are-failing-combat-inauthentic-behaviour-online.

212 Rush Doshi, "China Steps Up Its Information War in Taiwan," *Foreign Affairs*, January 9, 2019, https://www.foreignaffairs.com/articles/china/2020-01-09/china-steps-its-information-war-taiwan; Emily Feng, "Taiwan Gets Tough on Disinformation Suspected from China Ahead of Elections," National Public Radio, December 6, 2019, https://www.npr.org/2019/12/06/784191852/taiwan-gets-tough-on-disinformation-suspected-from-china-ahead-of-elections; Harry Krejsa, "Under Pressure: The Growing Reach of Chinese Influence Campaigns in Democratic Societies" (Center for a New American Security, April 27, 2018), available at https://www.cnas.org/publications/reports/under-pressure.

213 Herbert Lin, Alex Stamos, Nate Persily, and Andrew Grotto, "Increasing the Security of the U.S. Election Infrastructure," in *Securing American Elections: Prescriptions for Enhancing the Integrity and Independence of the 2020 U.S. Presidential Election and Beyond*, ed. Michael McFaul (Stanford: Stanford Cyber Policy Center, Freeman Spogli Institute, June 6, 2019), 17–26, available at https://fsi.stanford.edu/news/securing-american-elections-report-offers-policy-road-map.

214 Verizon, *2019 Data Breach Investigations Report* (May 2019), 5, https://enterprise.verizon.com/resources/reports/2019-data-breach-investigations-report.pdf.

215 Joseph S. Nye, "Protecting Democracy in an Era of Cyber Information War" (Belfer Center for Science and International Affairs, Harvard Kennedy School, February 2019), 14, https://www.belfercenter.org/sites/default/files/files/publication/ProtectingDemocracy.pdf.

216 Pete Williams, "FBI Chief Wray: Russia Works '365 Days a Year' to Undermine American Democracy," NBC News, April 26, 2019, https://www.nbcnews.com/politics/national-security/fbi-chief-wray-russia-works-365-days-year-undermine-american-n999086.

217 Indictment, *United States v. Viktor Borisovich Netyksho, et al.*, No. 1:18-cr-00215-ABJ (D. D.C. July 13, 2018), https://www.justice.gov/file/1080281/download; Indictment, *United States v. Internet Research Agency LLC, et al.*, No. 1:18-cr-00032-DLF (D. D.C. Feb. 16, 2018), https://www.justice.gov/file/1035477/download.

218 Suzanne Spaulding, Devi Nair, and Arthur Nelson, "Beyond the Ballot: How the Kremlin Works to Undermine the U.S. Justice System" (Center for Strategic and International Studies, May 2019), 4, https://csis-prod.s3.amazonaws.com/s3fs-public/publication/190430_RussiaUSJusticeSystem_v3_WEB_FULL.pdf.

219 "Exposing Russia's Effort to Sow Discord Online."

220 Kurt Thomas and Angelika Moscicki, "New Research: How Effective Is Basic Account Hygiene at Preventing Hacking," Google Security Blog, May 17, 2019, https://security.googleblog.com/2019/05/new-research-how-effective-is-basic.html.

RESHAPE THE CYBER ECOSYSTEM TOWARDS GREATER SECURITY

221 The early markets for internet and connected technologies rewarded first movers and did not punish insecurity in products, giving rise to a deeply ingrained culture of prioritizing speed to market over security—a misalignment of market incentives that persists today. See, for example, Craig Timberg, "A Flaw in the Design: The Internet's Founders Saw Its Promise But Didn't Foresee Users Attacking One Another," *Washington Post*, May 30, 2015, https://www.washingtonpost.com/sf/business/2015/05/30/net-of-insecurity-part-1/?utm_term=.55c95fc02ab8, and Commission on Enhancing National Cybersecurity, *Report on Securing and Growing the Digital Economy* (December 1, 2016), 7, 25–26, https://www.nist.gov/system/files/documents/2016/12/02/cybersecurity-commission-report-final-post.pdf.

222 "Implementing a certification and labeling program that follows a consensus security capabilities baseline represents a single government action that can simultaneously build awareness about secure products, foster innovation, and improve security throughout the internet ecosystem, without the need for direct regulation." Mark Peterson, "Creating a Cybersecurity 'Energy Star,'" *Public Knowledge*, July 20, 2018, https://www.publicknowledge.org/blog/creating-a-cybersecurity-energy-star/.

223 Several nongovernmental initiatives, such as Digital Standard and the Cyber Independent Testing Laboratory, are aimed at testing and providing security information for consumer IT and IoT devices. NIST, under Section 401 of the Cybersecurity Enhancement Act of 2014, is tasked with coordinating the development and dissemination of standards and best practices for cybersecurity.

224 Certifications are review processes that certify that a product meets the standards to which it is tested; labels are clear, visual, and easy to understand symbols that convey specific information about a product's attributes, characteristics, functionality, components, or other features.

225 Allan Friedman, "Moving toward a More Transparent Software Supply Chain," U.S. Department of Commerce, National Telecommunications and Information Administration, September 30, 2019, https://www.ntia.doc.gov/blog/2019/moving-toward-more-transparent-software-supply-chain.

226 U.S. Department of Commerce, NTIA [National Telecommunications and Information Administration] Standards and Formats Working Group, "Draft White Paper" [on Software Bill of Materials Standards] (June 25, 2019), https://www.ntia.doc.gov/files/ntia/publications/ntia_sbom_formats_draft_whitepaper_06.25.pdf.

227 "Secure by Default," U.K. National Cyber Security Centre, March 7, 2018, https://www.ncsc.gov.uk/information/secure-default.

228 The President's National Infrastructure Advisory Council made a similar recommendation to test the security of critical technologies. President's National Infrastructure Advisory Council, "Transforming the U.S. Cyber Threat Partnership" (December 12, 2019), 11, https://www.cisa.gov/sites/default/files/publications/NIAC-Working-Group-Report-DRAFT-508.pdf.

229 Open-source software forms the basis for most software written and deployed today. One survey found that 96 percent of applications contain open-source components (Zeljka Zorz, "The Percentage of Open Source Code in Proprietary Apps Is Rising," Help Net Security, May 22, 2018, https://www.helpnetsecurity.com/2018/05/22/open-source-code-security-risk/). When vulnerabilities are found in open-source code, many of the projects that rely on that code have neither mechanisms for fixing those vulnerabilities nor mechanisms for notifying users of the code about the patch.

230 The National Institute of Standards and Technology at the Department of Commerce is currently the governmental entity tasked with identifying, setting, and harmonizing security standards and best practices. "Cybersecurity," National Institute of Standards and Technology, updated December 2019, https://www.nist.gov/topics/cybersecurity.

231 Trey Herr, "Countering the Proliferation of Malware: Targeting the Vulnerability Lifecycle" (Belfer Center for Science and International Affairs, Harvard Kennedy School, June 2017), https://www.belfercenter.org/sites/default/files/files/publication/CounteringProliferationofMalware.pdf.

232 Frank Li and Vern Paxson, "A Large-Scale Empirical Study of Security Patches" (University of California, Berkeley, and International Computer Science Institute, 2017), https://www.icir.org/vern/papers/patch-study.ccs17.pdf.

233 Karen Mercedes Goertzel, "Legal Liability for Bad Software," CrossTalk, 2016, https://www.researchgate.net/publication/310674753_Legal_liability_for_bad_software.

234 For example, as long as a vendor or assembler is providing usability updates and bug fixes for a given product or service, it must also provide security updates.

235 See "The National Vulnerability Database," National Institute of Standards and Technology, updated December 2019, https://nvd.nist.gov/; "Common Vulnerabilities and Exposures," MITRE, updated December 17, 2019, https://cve.mitre.org/.

236 See NTIA Safety Working Group, "Coordinated Vulnerability Disclosure 'Early Stage' Template and Discussion" (November 14, 2016), https://www.ntia.doc.gov/files/ntia/publications/safetywg_draft_11-04-16_clean.pdf, and Allen D. Householder, Garret Wassermann, Art Manion, and Chris King, *The CERT® Guide to Coordinated Vulnerability Disclosure* (Carnegie Mellon University, Software Engineering Institute, August 2017), https://resources.sei.cmu.edu/asset_files/SpecialReport/2017_003_001_503340.pdf.

237 Verizon, *2015 Data Breach Investigations Report* (April 15, 2015), 15, https://cybersecurity.idaho.gov/wp-content/uploads/sites/87/2019/04/data-breach-investigation-report_2015.pdf.

238 The required information on cyber incidents could include the type of incident, method of compromise, bill of materials of affected systems, vulnerability or vulnerabilities revealed by the incident (if applicable), and the consequences of the incident.

239 "Cyber incidents" should be defined to include events that result in a significant loss of data, system availability, or control of systems; impact a large number of victims; indicate unauthorized access to, or malicious software present on, critical information technology systems; affect critical infrastructure or core government functions; or threaten national security, economic security, or public health and safety.

240 National Association of Insurance Commissioners, "State Insurance Regulation: History, Purpose and Structure" (accessed September 10, 2019), 3, https://www.naic.org/documents/consumer_state_reg_brief.pdf.

241 Sasha Romanosky, Lillian Ablon, Andreas Kuehn, and Therese Jones, "Content Analysis of Cyber Insurance Policies: How Do Carriers Price Cyber Risk?," *Journal of Cybersecurity* 5, no. 1 (2019): 13, https://academic.oup.com/cybersecurity/article/5/1/tyz002/5366419.

242 U.S. Department of Homeland Security, Cyber Incident Data and Analysis Working Group, "Overcoming Perceived Obstacles to Sharing into a Cyber Incident Data Repository" (December 2015), https://www.cisa.gov/sites/default/files/publications/Overcoming%20Perceived%20Obstacles%20White%20Paper_1.pdf.

243 Further Consolidated Appropriations Act, 2020, Pub. L. No. 116-94 (2019), https://www.congress.gov/bill/116th-congress/house-bill/1865/text.

244 "Cybersecurity Insurance," Department of Homeland Security, February 17, 2016, https://www.dhs.gov/cybersecurity-insurance.

245 "Estimated Value of Cyber Insurance Premiums Written Worldwide from 2014 to 2020," Statista, August 9, 2019, https://www.statista.com/statistics/533314/estimated-cyber-insurance-premiums/.

246 "Global Commercial Insurance Market to Grow $170B in P/C Premium by 2021: Aon Inpoint," *Insurance Journal*, June 18, 2018, https://www.insurancejournal.com/magazines/mag-features/2018/06/18/492041.htm.

247 Nour Aburish, Annie Fixler, and Michael Hsieh, "The Role of Cyber Insurance in Securing the Private Sector," Foundation for Defense of Democracies, September 13, 2019, https://www.fdd.org/analysis/2019/09/11/cyber-insurance/#easy-footnote-bottom-9-98098.

248 For example, federal acquisition regulations place requirements on vendors. "Federal Agencies and Their Procurement Regulation Websites," Acquisition.gov, updated December 30, 2019, https://www.acquisition.gov/content/supplemental-regulations.

249 The Binding Operational Directives (BODs) identify requirements for federal agencies in the executive branch. Each BOD prescribes a set of actions that agency chief information security officers or their equivalents must take to manage their enterprise networks.

250 Donna Dodson, Murgiah Soppaya, and Karen Scarfone, "Mitigating the Risk of Software Vulnerabilities by Adopting a Secure Software Development Framework" (National Institute of Standards and Technology, 2019), https://csrc.nist.gov/CSRC/media/Publications/white-paper/2019/06/07/mitigating-risk-of-software-vulnerabilities-with-ssdf/draft/documents/ssdf-for-mitigating-risk-of-software-vulns-draft.pdf.

251 International Organization for Standardization, "ISO/IEC 27001 Information Security Management" International Organization for Standardization, https://www.iso.org/isoiec-27001-information-security.html

252 "NTIA Software Component Transparency," National Telecommunications and Information Administration, September 5, 2019, https://www.ntia.doc.gov/SoftwareTransparency.

253 Sarbanes-Oxley Act of 2002, Pub. L. No. 107-204, 116 Stat. 745 (2002), https://www.congress.gov/107/plaws/publ204/PLAW-107publ204.pdf.

254 Securities and Exchange Commission, "Commission Statement and Guidance on Public Company Cybersecurity Disclosures" (February 26, 2018), https://www.sec.gov/rules/interp/2018/33-10459.pdf.

255 The desired metric (in minutes) for the detection, investigation, and remediation of cyber breaches is 1-10-60. For more information, see Robert Lemos, "Most Companies Lag Behind '1-10-60' Benchmark for Breach Response," Dark Reading, November 19, 2019, https://www.darkreading.com/threat-intelligence/most-companies-lag-behind-1-10-60-benchmark-for-breach-response/d/d-id/1336401.

256 Cloud-based services deliver computing services over the internet ("the cloud") through a third-party provider rather than through capital investment in building and maintaining data centers. According to NIST, "Cloud computing is a model for enabling convenient, on-demand network access to a shared pool of configurable computing resources (e.g., networks, servers, storage, applications, and services) that can be rapidly provisioned and released with minimal management effort or service provider interaction"; "NIST Cloud Computing Program – NCCP," NIST, updated July 9, 2019, https://www.nist.gov/programs-projects/nist-cloud-computing-program-nccp. For more information, see Navdeep Aggarwal, Parshant Tyagi, Bhanu P. Dubey, and Emmanuel S. Pilli, "Cloud Computing: Data Storage Security Analysis and Its Challenges," *International Journal of Computer Applications* 70, no. 24 (May 2013): 33–37, https://pdfs.semanticscholar.org/4c74/46c1b97ff8947166e02cf3f465022a4d13c3.pdf; "What Is Cloud Computing? A Beginner's Guide," Microsoft Azure, 2020, https://azure.microsoft.com/en-us/overview/what-is-cloud-computing/; and "What Is Cloud Computing?," Google Cloud, accessed February 3, 2020, https://cloud.google.com/what-is-cloud-computing/.

257 For example, cloud computing strengthens data backup and lessens the impact of disaster recovery because data is stored independently on the third-party provider's data center.

258 "What Is Cloud Computing," Microsoft Azure.

259 Palo Alto Networks, "Cloud Threat Report: Putting the Sec in DevOps," Palo Alto Networks, 2020, https://start.paloaltonetworks.com/unit-42-cloud-threat-report?CampaignId=7010g000001J2yiAAC&referer=null&utm_medium=direct-mail&utm_source=Unit+42+Cloud+Threat+Risk+Report%3A+Cloudy+with+a+Chance+of+Entropy.

260 "69% of Enterprises Will Have Multi-cloud/Hybrid IT Environments by 2019, But Greater Choice Brings Excessive Complexity" (451 Research, November 27, 2017), https://451research.com/images/Marketing/press_releases/Pre_Re-Invent_2018_press_release_final_11_22.pdf.

261 The ransomware that impacted 23 Texas entities was transmitted through a compromised managed service provider that was used by those entities. Benjamin Freed, "How Texas Used Its Disaster Playbook after a Huge Ransomware Attack," State Scoop, October 15, 2019, https://statescoop.com/texas-ransomware-emergency-declaration-nascio-19/.

262 "Towards a More Secure and Trusted Cloud in Europe," European Commission, December 9, 2019, https://ec.europa.eu/digital-single-market/en/news/towards-more-secure-and-trusted-cloud-europe.

263 See, for example, Dothang Truong, "How Cloud Computing Enhances Competitive Advantages: A Research Model for Small Businesses," *Business Review* 12, no. 1 (2010): 59–65, https://www.researchgate.net/profile/Dothang_Truong/publication/273447113_How_cloud_computing_enhances_competitive_advantages_A_research_model_for_small_businesses/links/554286940cf23ff716835f5e.pdf.

264 Timberg, "A Flaw in the Design."

265 The President's National Infrastructure Advisory Council made a similar recommendation to encourage broader implementation of security measures. President's National Infrastructure Advisory Council, "Transforming the U.S. Cyber Threat Partnership," 10.

266 Jason Healey and Robert Knake, "Zero Botnets," *Council on Foreign Relations* (2018), https://www.cfr.org/sites/default/files/report_pdf/CSR83_HealeyKnake_Botnets_0.pdf.

267 Joy Ma and Tim Matthews, "The Underground Bot Economy: How Bots Impact the Global Economy," *Imperva Incapsula*, 2016, http://incapsula.com/blog/how-bots-impact-global-economy.html.

268 International Cybercrime Prevention Act of 2018, S. 3288, 115th Cong. (2018), https://www.congress.gov/bill/115th-congress/senate-bill/3288/text.

269 U.S. Department of Justice, *Report of the Attorney General's Cyber Digital Task Force* (Washington, DC: U.S. Department of Justice, July 2, 2018), 124, https://www.justice.gov/ag/page/file/1076696/download.

270 "Two International Cybercriminal Rings Dismantled and Eight Defendants Indicted for Causing Tens of Millions of Dollars in Losses in Digital Advertising Fraud," press release, United States Attorney's Office, Eastern District of New York, November 27, 2018, https://www.justice.gov/usao-edny/pr/two-international-cybercriminal-rings-dismantled-and-eight-defendants-indicted-causing.

271 "Two International Cybercriminal Rings Dismantled."

272 "About Us," National Cyber-Forensics and Training Alliance, accessed January 20, 2020, https://www.ncfta.net/home-2/about-us/.

273 "Two International Cybercriminal Rings Dismantled."

274 Jared T. Brown and Moshe Schwartz, "The Defense Production Act of 1950: History, Authorities, and Considerations for Congress" (Congressional Research Service, updated November 20, 2018), https://fas.org/sgp/crs/natsec/R43767.pdf.

275 The Office of the Director of National Intelligence noted this vulnerability and made addressing it a strategic objective in "National Counterintelligence Strategy of the United States of America, 2020–2022" (February 2020), 7, https://www.dni.gov/files/NCSC/documents/features/20200205-National_CI_Strategy_2020_2022.pdf.

276 National Defense Authorization Act for Fiscal Year 2020, Pub. L. No. 116-92 (2019), https://www.congress.gov/bill/116th-congress/senate-bill/1790/text.

277 "Information and Communications Technology Supply Chain Risk Management Task Force," Department of Homeland Security, accessed January 10, 2020, https://www.cisa.gov/information-and-communications-technology-ict-supply-chain-risk-management-scrm-task-force.

278 This aggregated information relating to supply chains would include classified and unclassified information, threat information, and proprietary and sensitive information (e.g., software transparency and software bill of materials).

279 In the 2020 National Defense Authorization Act, Congress created a Supply Chain and Counterintelligence Risk Management Task Force to "standardize information sharing between the intelligence community and the acquisition community of the United States Government with respect to the supply chain and counterintelligence risks" (§ 6306(b)).

280 Robert D. Hof, "Lessons from Sematech," *MIT Technology Review*, July 25, 2011, https://www.technologyreview.com/s/424786/lessons-from-sematech/.

281 Altaf H. (Tof) Carim, William T. (Tim) Polk, and Erin Szulman, "Realizing the Potential of Quantum Information Science and Advancing High-Performance Computing," The White House, July 26, 2016, https://obamawhitehouse.archives.gov/blog/2016/07/26/realizing-potential-quantum-information-science-and-advancing-high-performance.

282 National Security Commission on Artificial Intelligence, *Interim Report* (November 2019), 25, https://www.nationaldefensemagazine.org/-/media/sites/magazine/03_linkedfiles/nscai-interim-report-for-congress.ashx?la=en.

283 Russell T. Vought and Kelvin K. Droegemeier, "Fiscal Year 2021 Administration Research and Development Budget Priorities" (Executive Office of the President, August 30, 2019), https://www.whitehouse.gov/wp-content/uploads/2019/08/FY-21-RD-Budget-Priorities.pdf.

284 National Security Telecommunications Advisory Committee (NSTAC), "NSTAC Report to the President on a Cybersecurity Moonshot" (November 14, 2018), ES-1, ES-2, https://www.dhs.gov/sites/default/files/publications/NSTAC_CyberMoonshotReport_508c.pdf.

285 NSTAC, "NSTAC Report to the President," 10.

286 "Most Profitable," *Fortune*, accessed September 30, 2019, https://fortune.com/fortune500/2019/search/; "Cyberstates," CompTIA, accessed October 2, 2019, https://www.cyberstates.org/.

287 The requirements of a data breach notification law are not to be confused with statistical data gathering associated with the cyber incident reporting discussed earlier in this section or those of the "National Cyber Incident Reporting Law" advocated in the following pillar (recommendation 5.2.2).

288 "2019 Security Breach Legislation," National Conference of State Legislatures, July 26, 2019, http://www.ncsl.org/research/telecommunications-and-information-technology/2019-security-breach-legislation.aspx.

289 Arne Holst, "Number of iPhone Users in the United States from 2012 to 2021," Statista, September 13, 2019, https://www.statista.com/statistics/232790/forecast-of-apple-users-in-the-us/; J. Clement, "Number of Daily Active WhatsApp Status Users from 1st Quarter 2017 to 1st Quarter 2019," Statista, August 9, 2019, https://www.statista.com/statistics/730306/whatsapp-status-dau/.

290 David Kaye, "Report of the Special Rapporteur on the Promotion and Protection of the Right to Freedom of Opinion and Expression," UN Human Rights Council, A/HRC/29/32 (May 22, 2015), available at https://digitallibrary.un.org/record/798709?ln=en.

OPERATIONALIZE CYBERSECURITY COLLABORATION WITH THE PRIVATE SECTOR

291 "Exec. Order No. 13636: Improving Critical Infrastructure Cybersecurity," 78 Fed. Reg. 11739, 11740 (Feb. 12, 2013), https://www.federalregister.gov/documents/2013/02/19/2013-03915/improving-critical-infrastructure-cybersecurity.

292 The U.S. government recognizes critical entities through a process designated under Section 9 of Executive Order 13636, but this designation neither affords the U.S. government new responsibilities, authorities, resources, or funding to assist these entities nor establishes requirements for such entities in light of their criticality to U.S. national security, economic security, and public health and safety.

293 The President's National Infrastructure Advisory Council detailed a similar recommendation to make cyber intelligence more actionable. President's National Infrastructure Advisory Council, "Transforming the U.S. Cyber Threat Partnership" (December 12, 2019), 8, https://www.cisa.gov/sites/default/files/publications/NIAC-Working-Group-Report-DRAFT-508.pdf.

294 Examples of current voluntary network monitoring and threat detection programs include the Department of Energy's Cybersecurity Risk Information Sharing Program, Cyber Analytics Tools and Techniques Pilot, the Department of Homeland Security's CyberSentry, and law enforcement consent and monitoring programs.

295 Working with the DoD Chief Information Officer and NSA, U.S. Cyber Command developed the Pathfinder initiative alongside DHS, sector-specific agencies, and select critical infrastructure partners to share threat information, conduct collaborative analysis of vulnerabilities and threats, and mitigate those risks. U.S. Cyber Command's efforts in this field occur at the request of and in collaboration with federal government partners, particularly DHS and the FBI.

296 "U.S. Department of Energy, U.S. Department of Homeland Security, and U.S. Department of Defense Announce Pathfinder Initiative to Protect U.S. Energy Critical Infrastructure," U.S. Department of Energy, February 2020, https://www.energy.gov/articles/us-department-energy-us-department-homeland-security-and-us-department-defense-announce.

PRESERVE AND EMPLOY THE MILITARY INSTRUMENTS OF POWER

297 Defend forward, as the Commission defines it, entails proactively observing, pursuing, and countering adversary operations and imposing costs in day-to-day competition to disrupt and defeat ongoing malicious adversary cyber campaigns, deter future campaigns, and reinforce favorable international norms of behavior, using all of the instruments of national power. This is a reimagining and expansion of the defend forward concept as initially conceived of in the 2018 DoD Cyber Strategy, which focuses solely on the military

instrument. U.S. Department of Defense, "Summary: Department of Defense Cyber Strategy" (2018), https://media.defense.gov/2018/Sep/18/2002041658/-1/-1/1/CYBER_STRATEGY_SUMMARY_FINAL.PDF.

298 *United States Special Operations Command and United States Cyber Command: Hearing before the Senate Armed Services Committee*, 116th Congress, 4 (February 14, 2019) (statement of General Paul M. Nakasone, Commander United States Cyber Command).

299 William T. Eliason, "An Interview with Paul M. Nakasone," *Joint Forces Quarterly* 92 (1st Quarter 2019): 6–7.

300 DoD, "Summary: Department of Defense Cyber Strategy" (2018), 1.

301 U.S. Department of Defense Directive 5100.03, "Support of the Headquarters of Combatant and Subordinate Unified Commands" (February 9, 2011; incorporating Change 1, September 7, 2017), https://www.esd.whs.mil/Portals/54/Documents/DD/issuances/dodd/510003p.pdf.

302 "U.S. Cyber Command Shares 11 New Malware Samples," *CISA*, September 8, 2019, https://www.us-cert.gov/ncas/current-activity/2019/09/08/us-cyber-command-shares-11-new-malware-samples; "@CYBERCOM_Malware_Alert," VirusTotal, accessed February 12, 2020, https://www.virustotal.com/en/user/CYBERCOM_Malware_Alert/.

303 As defined in Office of the Chairman of the Joint Chiefs of Staff, *Cyberspace Operations*, Joint Publication 3-12 (June 8, 2018), "The term 'blue cyberspace' denotes areas in cyberspace protected by the US, its mission partners, and other areas DOD may be ordered to protect," while "'red cyberspace' refers to those portions of cyberspace owned or controlled by an adversary or enemy." Finally, "all cyberspace that does not meet the description of either 'blue' or 'red' is referred to as 'gray' cyberspace" (I-4, I-5). These are distinctly U.S. terms of reference; as part of an effective defend forward strategy in the future, the United States must come to a shared understanding of blue, gray, and red space with allied and partner countries.

304 As DoD begins to use and incorporate emerging technology, such as artificial intelligence (AI), into its weapon platforms and systems, cybersecurity will also need to be incorporated into the early stages of the acquisition process.

305 "Weapon Systems Cybersecurity: DOD Just Beginning to Grapple with Scale of Vulnerabilities," GAO-19-128 (U.S. Government Accountability Office, October 2018), 28, https://www.gao.gov/assets/700/694913.pdf.

306 This recommendation applies to the DIB, defined as "[t]he Department of Defense, government, and private sector worldwide industrial complex with capabilities to perform research and development and design, produce, and maintain military weapon systems, subsystems, components, or parts to meet military requirements." This recommendation does not include entities such as Defense Critical Infrastructure (DCI), defined as "Department of Defense and non-Department of Defense networked assets and facilities essential to project, support, and sustain military forces and operations worldwide." Office of the Chairman of the Joint Chiefs of Staff, *DOD Dictionary of Military and Associated Terms* (January 2020), 59, https://www.jcs.mil/Portals/36/Documents/Doctrine/pubs/dictionary.pdf.

307 "Strengthening the Front Line: NSA Launches New Cybersecurity Directorate," National Security Agency/Central Security Service, October 1, 2019, https://www.nsa.gov/News-Features/News-Stories/Article-View/Article/1973871/strengthening-the-front-line-nsa-launches-new-cybersecurity-directorate/.

308 Frank Arute et al., "Quantum Supremacy Using a Programmable Superconducting Processor," *Nature* 574 (October 24, 2019): 505, https://www.nature.com/articles/s41586-019-1666-5.pdf.

309 Lamont Wood, "The Clock Is Ticking for Encryption," Computerworld, March 21, 2011, https://www.computerworld.com/article/2550008/the-clock-is-ticking-for-encryption.html.

310 Elsa B. Kania and John K. Costello, "Quantum Hegemony? China's Ambitions and the Challenge to U.S. Innovation Leadership" (Center for a New American Security, September 2018), available at https://www.cnas.org/publications/reports/quantum-hegemony.

www.ingramcontent.com/pod-product-compliance
Lightning Source LLC
LaVergne TN
LVHW060141070326
832902LV00018B/2894